STUDY GUIDE

Douglas A. Johnson
West Michigan University

PSYCHOLOGY
TENTH EDITION

Carole Wade

Dominican University of California

Carol Tavris

Prentice Hall

Boston   Columbus   Indianapolis   New York   San Francisco   Upper Saddle River
Amsterdam   Cape Town   Dubai   London   Madrid   Milan   Munich   Paris   Montreal   Toronto
Delhi   Mexico City   Sao Paulo   Sydney   Hong Kong   Seoul   Singapore   Taipei   Tokyo

Prentice Hall
is an imprint of

10 9 8 7 6 5 4 3 2 1

ISBN 10: 0-205-77722-8
ISBN 13: 978-0-205-77722-8

TABLE OF CONTENTS

THE BEST WAY TO USE THIS STUDY GUIDE   iv

CHAPTERS

ANSWER KEYS

THE BEST WAY TO USE THIS STUDY GUIDE

This Study Guide has been developed utilizing psychological research findings in the areas of learning and memory. Students should be ACTIVELY engaged with the material.

LEARNING OBJECTIVES Learning objectives begin each chapter. Students should read the Learning Objectives before they begin reading the chapter. Students can also formulate additional questions on a separate sheet of paper by using headings, key terms, and concepts.

CHAPTER SUMMARIES Following the learning objectives, each chapter has a chapter summary. It provides a general overview of the chapter.

PREVIEW OUTLINES Each section of the chapter is presented in a general outline format, which students are intended to examine before they read the chapter. Students should preview or survey a section of text before they read it. It is also highly recommended that students attempt to summarize the chapter in outline form after they read it.

TABLES Many chapters have tables that help students organize, categorize, and form associations to the information. The completed table will be a great study aid, but the act of completing the table is just as important; it is another way to make the information meaningful.

THREE PRACTICE TESTS Each chapter has three practice tests that represent different testing methods. Practice Test 1 is a multiple-choice test. Practice Test 2 is a fill-in-the-blank test and requires students to recall (rather than just recognize) information. Practice Test 3 requires students to apply, analyze, and synthesize information in essay or short-answer responses.

CONCEPT MAP The concept maps are designed for students to visually overview the chapters. There are many different possible concept maps—try making one of your own!

ANSWER KEYS Answer keys for all practice tests are presented at the end of the Study Guide. They were separated from the chapters to encourage students to try to answer the questions *before* looking at the key. **Each answer in the key references the relevant learning objective.**

HOW TO STUDY

TIRED?

∞ of reading a chapter and not remembering any of the contents five minutes later?

∞ of fighting against drooping eyelids and losing?

∞ of thinking you've studied enough only to find that you can't remember anything that's on the test?

∞ of studying definitions and terms only to find that the test questions don't ask for definitions and terms; instead, they ask for examples that you never saw in the text?

∞ of test scores that don't reflect what you know?

It would be nice to be able to say, "Guaranteed, 100%! Follow these simple guidelines and you, too, can get an A! Simple! Easy! Money-back guarantee! Teachers and parents will love you, and it will change your life!!" Of course, I cannot make those claims, but I can say the following: "You **CAN** change the above behaviors **IF** you read **AND** attempt to use the techniques that are described in this section of the Study Guide." Changing your study habits is like going on a diet. First, you must know the details of the diet: How does it propose to help you eat healthier? However, knowing how the diet works and what you are supposed to eat will NOT cause you to develop healthier eating habits. You must implement the diet. In other words, to receive the benefits, you must do it! It is not enough to know what you are supposed to do...you must actually do it! It is the same thing with changing your study habits. It is not enough to know the changes you need to make...you must make the changes!

STEP 1: DIAGNOSING THE PROBLEM

Some students have developed study skills that work well for them, and they do not wish to change their habits. Some students have many study skills with which they are generally satisfied, but they have one or two areas that need improvement. Other students have difficulty with a number of their study skills. Below is a list of some study skills. Review this list and try to identify whether you are satisfied or dissatisfied with each of these abilities. The preface to this Study Guide focuses on study skills and how to use this manual. As you read the preface, focus on the areas in which you need improvement. If this chapter does not cover that particular area, identify and **USE** the resources that are available on your campus to get assistance. **DON'T** ignore study problems. It is unlikely that they will just disappear on their own or that they will improve simply by your trying to do more of what you are already doing!

Check all of the following areas that are problems for you:

Reading the Text _____
    Comprehending the material _____
    Concentrating while reading _____
    Identifying what is important _____
    Recalling what you have read _____
    Being distracted easily _____
Time Management _____
    Not planning your time _____
    Not having enough time to study _____
    Not using the time you have allotted to study _____
    Underestimating the time you need to study _____
    Difficulty saying no to other plans _____
    Not sticking to your study schedule _____
Getting the Most out of Class _____
    Trouble paying attention in class _____
    Not going to classes _____
    Not understanding what is important _____
Taking Notes _____
    Your notes aren't helpful _____
    Your notes are disorganized _____
Taking Tests _____
    Trouble recalling information _____
    Test anxiety _____
    Trouble on multiple choice questions _____
    Trouble on fill-in-the-blank questions _____
    Trouble on essay questions _____
    Trouble predicting what will be on the test _____
    Trouble going from definitions to examples _____

Identifying your problem areas should help you to focus on the skills that you most need in order to improve. Think about your problem areas as you read the preface and apply the information to your particular situation.

ON BEING A LEARNER or DON'T STOP BEFORE YOU BEGIN!

What was the last new skill you tried to learn? Were you learning to play basketball, softball, tennis, or the guitar? Or were you learning a new language? Whatever you were learning to do, it is very likely that you were not very good at it at first. In fact, you were probably bad at it! <u>That is how it is supposed to be!</u> Your ability to do something well depends on gaining experience with that activity; the more you do it, the better you become at the task. This means that it is necessary to go beyond the beginning period of learning when the new skill is difficult and awkward and you are not very good at it. This can be frustrating for students who often think they already should know how to study, and if they have to learn new study skills, they should be learned quickly and easily. During the early stages of learning a new skill, a person may be tempted to say, "This isn't working," or "This will never work," or "These techniques feel so artificial." **RESIST** those thoughts. Learning these skills may be difficult at first, but no more difficult than continuing to use skills that you already know **DO NOT WORK!** If you want to change any long-standing behavior, you will have to tolerate the early phases of learning when the new behaviors won't yet feel like "your own." In college, graduate school, and employment, you will find that persistence pays. So, **RESIST** returning to your old habits and **PERSIST** with learning the new habits. Don't stop before you begin...give it some time.

MASTERING YOUR MEMORY (OR AT LEAST GETTING THE UPPER HAND!)

A great deal of the information contained in most study skills manuals and courses is based on what is known about how human memory works. Experimental psychologists study memory and how it works; therefore, it is appropriate in this course for you to understand the findings of scientific research on memory and how they apply to **YOU**. Ignore these findings at your peril! This section will present a few general findings about memory that are particularly relevant to your studying. This information comes directly from Chapter 10, which will discuss memory in more detail. Information about memory has applicability not only to your psychology class, but to all your classes.

KEEPING INFORMATION IN SHORT-TERM MEMORY The three-box model of memory suggests there are three types of memory: sensory memory, short-term memory (STM), and long-term memory (LTM). Sensory memory is a very brief type of memory that lasts less than a second. Sensory memory is important because if information does not get noticed in sensory memory, it cannot be transferred into either short-term or long-term memory. The limits of short-term memory are known. Short-term memory can hold seven (plus or minus two) pieces of information for about 30 seconds or less. A person can extend the amount of time information is held in STM by repeating it over and over (this is called maintenance rehearsal); however, once you stop repeating the information, it is quickly lost. Think of times that you have called information to get the number of the nearest pizza place. You repeat the number over and over and hope your roommate does not come along and ask to borrow your comb, because if your repetition is interrupted, you will forget the number. Many professors believe that most students study in ways that get information into short-term memory, but not in ways that get it into long-term memory.

GETTING INFORMATION INTO LONG-TERM MEMORY Long-term memory can hold an infinite amount of information for an unlimited amount of time. **THAT'S** where you want to store all the information you are studying!! The important question is how to transfer information from short-term memory into long-term memory. The transfer of memory from STM into LTM relies upon the use of elaborative rehearsal. Elaborative rehearsal involves more than the simple repetition of information required by short-term memory; it requires that you make the information meaningful. Making information meaningful requires more than saying "This has deep meaning to me."

Meaningfulness can be accomplished by interacting with the material in any **ACTIVE** way. Some examples of ways to make information meaningful include putting it into a story, putting it into a rhyme (i.e., "30 days has September"), forming visual images of the information, forming associations with people or things already familiar to you, or associating information to other pieces of information, organizing it into categories, putting it into your own words, explaining it to someone else--almost anything that you do with the information that is **ACTIVE**. Being **ACTIVE** with the information and aiming for **UNDERSTANDING** and not simple repetition of the material are the keys. Almost anything you do with the material that is active will help move it into long-term memory. Passively reading the material will not help the information transfer into long-term memory, but that is the technique most students use.

CRITICAL THINKING AND LONG-TERM MEMORY Critical thinking is emphasized throughout this textbook. Every chapter includes information on how to approach topics critically. Critical thinking requires organizing, analyzing, and evaluating information. This may sound suspiciously like elaborative rehearsal. Critical thinking is important for many reasons. In the context of study skills, critical thinking is important because it involves the same processes that promote the transfer of information into long-term memory.

GETTING MORE INFORMATION INTO SHORT-TERM AND LONG-TERM MEMORY One last piece of information about memory has to do with expanding the amount of information contained in short-term memory. To get information into LTM, it must pass through STM, and we know that STM holds only about seven (plus or minus two) units of information. That does not seem like a practical system, since most textbook chapters seem to contain hundreds of pieces of new information in each chapter! Short-term memory holds **units** or chunks of information, and a strategy to increase the amount of information being held in STM is to include more information in each chunk. For example, you can change 26 separate pieces of information (which far exceeds the capacity of STM) into one piece of information (well within the capacity of STM) by chunking! Whenever you use the word "alphabet" to refer to 26 separate letters, you are chunking. If you organize the information you are studying into categories, or chunks, you will improve your chances of getting more information into LTM in two ways: 1) you will increase the information contained in the units getting into STM, and 2) you will be making the information meaningful by the act of organizing it into the chunks! You can't lose! Making outlines is a good way to chunk information. Outlines naturally organize information into categories (chunks) and subcategories. This study guide presents the information in ways that help you to organize information into chunks, which also helps make the information meaningful.

STUDYING WITH THE SQ3R OR STAYING AWAKE, STAYING ACTIVE, AND OPENING THE DOOR TO LONG-TERM MEMORY

The SQ3R method was developed by Francis Robinson, a psychology professor at Ohio State University. It is a method of reading assignments that implements many techniques that promote the transfer of information into long-term memory. The letters "SQ3R" stand for <u>survey, question, read, receive, review</u>.

SURVEY Before you read a chapter or reading assignment, it is important to survey what is in the chapter and how the information is organized. You can do this by simply looking over the headings or the chapter outlines at the beginning of each chapter. This Study Guide also provides more detailed preview outlines for this purpose. It is important that you survey the information before you read, because surveying turns what otherwise would seem like hundreds of independent facts (which far exceeds the capacity of STM) into a much smaller number (probably five to nine – textbook authors know how memory works) of main topics identified in separate headings. Once you have seen the main headings, you have an organizational structure to begin your reading. This helps you organize the information when you begin reading (remember that organizing is one way to make information meaningful, which transfers it into LTM). Surveying a chapter in the text is like going on a trip. Before you arrive at a city you do not know, it is very helpful to look at a map. You quickly can see the location of the airport, your hotel, downtown, the river, and the three important sites you want to see. This orients you to your journey. If you do not look at a map before your arrival, you are wandering around without knowing where you are going. You do not want to wander around a 40-page chapter that contains a great deal of information without knowing where you are going.

QUESTION Assume you are taking a college entrance exam that contains a comprehension section. There are several paragraphs for you to read, and then you are to answer five questions about the reading. Would you read the questions before you read the paragraphs, or would you read the paragraphs and then begin to try to answer the questions? Most of you would read the questions first, so that as you read the paragraphs, you could keep the questions in mind and look for the answers while you read. The reasons for formulating questions before you read your text are: 1) to help you read with a purpose, and 2) to help you be more active while you read.

After you have surveyed the chapter, formulate questions by converting the headings, key terms, and definitions into questions. For example, "The Major Psychological Perspectives" is a subheading in Chapter 1. "What are the names and key concepts of the major psychological perspectives?" would be an example of changing that subheading into a question. This Study Guide has listed the relevant learning objectives for each. In addition, you should try to formulate additional questions and write them on a separate piece of paper. The intention is that you will write the answers to all these questions while you read the chapter. This helps you read with a purpose: your purpose is to answer the questions. This also helps you to be active while you read. You are being active by looking for the answers to the questions **AND** by writing down the answers as you find them. You will also have answers to all the learning objectives in writing when you go to study for quizzes and exams.

READ You are now ready to read. You have surveyed the chapter in order to know where you are going and how the chapter is organized. You have formulated your questions in order to know what you are looking for as you read. While reading, you will be organizing the information and answering the questions. These are both ways to increase the transfer of information into long-term memory. As you begin your reading, look at your first question. Open your textbook to the part of the chapter that applies to the question and read in order to answer that question.

RECITE   After you have surveyed the reading assignment to get the general idea of its content, have turned the first heading into a question, and have read that section to answer the question, you are now ready to recite. Reciting helps make information meaningful (did you ever notice that when you speak in class, you tend to remember the information you spoke or asked about?). Also, it is another way that you can be active (which also makes the information meaningful). Reciting requires that you put the information into your own words, and it is an excellent way to identify what you don't yet understand. There are a number of ways to recite.

Using the learning objectives and the questions that you have formulated, recite aloud the answers to the questions (without looking at the answers). You can say definitions or examples of key terms, terms that are listed in bold, or terms that are underlined as a vehicle for reciting information. You can recite responses to learning objectives. Explaining information to other people, either classmates or patient friends who are willing to help, is also a good way to recite the information. Explaining the information to others also allows you to identify areas that you do not understand well. Remember, your recitation of information should be in your own words and should attempt to give examples of the concepts you are describing. If you simply try to memorize definitions given in the text and recite these definitions, you are simply camouflaging maintenance rehearsal. Remember, getting information into long-term memory involves meaning--so make sure you understand the material and can make it "your own" to get it into long-term memory.

REVIEW   The final step in the SQ3R approach is to review the material again. Frequent reviews, even brief reviews, are among the important keys to learning. After at least one hour, review the material once more. This can be done by going over the main points of the chapter (with your book closed), going over the answers to the questions you have written (without looking at them), and reviewing key terms and concepts. Limit your reviews to about five minutes. Reviews can be used in other ways too. Begin each study session with a five-minute review. Before each class, review notes from the previous class for five minutes. At the end of every class, review your notes for five minutes.

SUMMARY   The SQ3R method incorporates the information that psychologists know about how people learn and remember. The key points to remember include: **BE ACTIVE, MAKE INFORMATION MEANINGFUL, INTERACT WITH THE INFORMATION, AIM FOR UNDERSTANDING NOT JUST REPETITION, THINK CRITICALLY.** All this can be achieved by writing, talking, thinking, making outlines, forming associations, developing questions and examples, and putting definitions in your own words. The SQ3R method suggests that these goals can be achieved if you:

1. Survey the information: Use headings and chapter summaries to orient yourself to the information you plan to read. Give the information an organizational structure.
2. Question: Turn the headings, terms, and concepts into questions.
3. Read: Read each section to answer the specific questions that you asked. Write your answers on a separate sheet of paper.
4. Recite: Close your book and rehearse the information contained in the section by answering the relevant questions or giving examples of key terms or concepts.
5. Review: After at least an hour-long break, close your book, turn over your notes, and list the main points of the chapter and the answers to your questions.

REMEMBER, this may feel awkward or cumbersome at first, **BUT** the more you use this method, the easier it will become.

WHEN AND WHERE TO STUDY

In many courses, several weeks can pass between tests. You might wonder whether it is better to study intensely the night before the test or to spread out your studying time. Memory research clearly suggests that "cramming" just doesn't work. You may know this from personal experience. Rather than studying for hours and hours just before the test, it is much more effective to study as you go along in the course.

In terms of when to study, the best time to study is immediately after class. **BEFORE** going to class, you should preview the material to be covered, form general questions, and read the text. Study the subject that was covered as soon after the lecture as possible. You will find it easier to master the material and will have an opportunity to test your understanding of the lecture if you study right away. The procedure of continuously studying fairly small chunks will also help you to avoid the nightmare of the infrequent studier--the sudden realization that you don't understand any of what you have been covering for the last few weeks. If you study for a short period after each lecture, you will not have to worry about this. You will also find that tomorrow's lecture will be easier to understand if you study today's material and master the essential points covered by your teacher. Most professors structure lectures so that each one builds on earlier lectures and readings. Studying as you go along will guarantee that you are well prepared to get the most out of each new lecture. It is also a good idea to set a specific time to study. Even if it is for a short time, you should study at a regular time every day.

In terms of where to study, many students indicate that they have difficulty concentrating. Upon further examination, it seems that many students study with their T.V. or CD player on at the same time and place their roommates are having a snack or are on the phone. Some general guidelines about where to study include:

1.   Limit the places that you study to one or two special locations. These could be the library, a desk, or a designated study area. They are special in the sense that they should be places where the only thing you do there is study. That means you should not study in places where you regularly do something else (such as the dining room table or bed).

2.   Make these places free from distractions. Distractions like the T.V., telephone, or friends can cause studying to be abandoned.

3.   Set a specific time to begin studying and then study in the same place every day. In that way, that place will become a cue to study and concentrate.

A NOTE ON FLASHCARDS

Many students try to develop flashcards as a way of reviewing material. I consider this an excellent technique to supplement this Study Guide, but only if you use do the cards correctly. One of the more effective methods available is the SAFMEDS technique, as developed by Ogden Lindsley. This method adheres to the following rules:

S – Say: When rehearsing your study cards, actually say your answer out loud before looking at the card's answer (note: the answer should be on the side of the card opposite the question). It is far too easy to trick yourself into thinking you would have said the answer while you have the answer directly in front of you (you'll learn more about this when studying hindsight bias later). Commit to a response before looking at the feedback. This rule applies to this study guide practice tests and the answer key in the back as well.

A – All: Review your entire deck of study cards.

F – Fast: When practicing your cards, work through them quickly. Knowledge tends to stick better when your practice answer are fast and accurate, not just accurate alone. Don't stop studying just because you got all the answers right. Keep going until you can get all the answers right instantaneously.

M – Minute: Time yourself for a one minute period and see how many cards you get right and wrong. Write this information down so you can see it you're on the right track or need to adjust your study techniques.

E – Every

D – Day: Conduct the one minute timings every single day. This will allow you to see small gains in performance that will make the learning experience more rewarding.

S – Shuffle: Shuffle your study cards between every use. You do not want to become dependent upon order in which you studied the material because your instructor may not have the test questions in the same order.

Also, remember to break the material into as small chunks as possible on these study cards. Learning works better in smaller bites!

OTHER SKILLS THAT INFLUENCE STUDYING

Many skills influence study habits. The diagnostic checklist at the beginning of this section identifies some of the skills that students must possess to study effectively. Skills that affect studying include the following: time management, note taking, test-preparation, test taking, stress management, using the library, dealing with professors, and classroom participation. All of these abilities are important. In fact, they are so important that entire books have been devoted to helping students develop these skills. Many colleges and universities offer various types of academic assistance, from courses on study skills to individual counseling on study skills. One of the survival skills necessary for college students is to be aware of the services offered by your institution and to make use of them as needed. If you have identified problem areas that influence your performance, you have several choices: find a book on study skills in your library, look for courses at your school that deal with study skills, or identify other campus resources that are available to assist you in developing these abilities.

ACKNOWLEDGEMENTS

I would like to thank Jane Cirillo and others who have contributed to previous versions of this Study Guide. I have revised and updated it for the current edition of Wade and Tavris' *Psychology* textbook. The format of this Study Guide is user-friendly, challenging, and practical. It presents students with a variety of assessment techniques and tries to take advantage of what psychologists know about learning and memory. We hope that you find it to be a useful resource in your studies.

Douglas A. Johnson

CHAPTER 1

What Is Psychology?

LEARNING OBJECTIVES

Psychology, Pseudoscience, and Popular Opinion
1.1 - How "psychobabble" differs from serious psychology.
1.2 - What's wrong with psychologists' nonscientific competitors, such as astrologers and psychics.

Thinking Critically and Creatively about Psychology
1.3 - What it means to think critically.
1.4 - Why not all opinions are created equal.
1.5 - Eight guidelines for evaluating psychological claims.

Psychology's Past: From the Armchair to the Laboratory
1.6 - The lesson of phrenology for modern psychology.
1.7 - How and when psychology became a formal discipline.
1.8 - Three early schools of psychology.

Psychology's Present: Behavior, Body, Mind, and Culture
1.9 - The five major perspectives in psychology.
1.10 - Why the psychodynamic perspective is the "thumb on the hand of psychology."
1.11 - How humanism and feminism have influenced psychology.

What Psychologists Do
1.12 - Why you can't assume that all therapists are psychologists, or that all psychologists are therapists.
1.13 - The three major areas of psychologists' professional activities.
1.14 - The difference between a clinical psychologist and a psychiatrist.

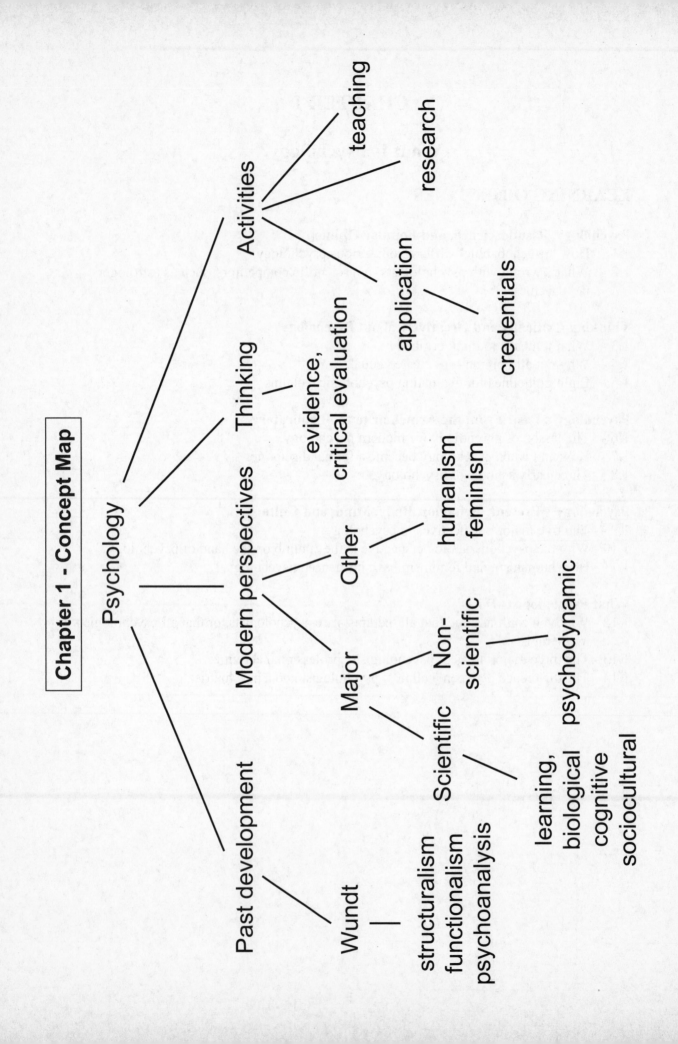

Chapter 1 - Concept Map

Psychology

- Past development
  - Wundt
    - structuralism
    - functionalism
    - psychoanalysis
- Modern perspectives
  - Major
    - Scientific
      - learning,
      - biological
      - cognitive
      - sociocultural
    - Non-scientific
      - psychodynamic
  - Other
    - humanism
    - feminism
- Thinking
  - evidence,
  - critical evaluation
- Activities
  - teaching
  - research
  - application
  - credentials

BRIEF CHAPTER SUMMARY

Chapter 1 defines psychology and traces the historical and disciplinary roots of the field to its current perspectives, specializations, and professional activities. Critical thinking guidelines are described, and students are encouraged to understand and apply these concepts as they read the text. The complexity of human behavior requires that psychology students resist simplistic thinking and reject overly simple answers. Five current perspectives and two important movements are identified. The current perspectives include the biological perspective, learning perspective, cognitive perspective, psychodynamic perspective, and sociocultural perspective. The two important movements are the humanist and feminist movements. Each of these approaches reflects a different emphasis and approach to understanding human behavior. Students are encouraged to think about human behavior from each different perspective and use their critical thinking skills to compare and contrast these approaches. A review of the specialty areas within the field helps students appreciate that psychology includes vastly diverse topics and that psychologists are engaged in a wide variety of occupations. Examples of specializations include experimental psychology, educational psychology, developmental psychology, and industrial/organizational psychology. The practice of psychology, which helps people with mental health problems, is discussed along with a description of types of practitioners within the field of psychology (e.g., counseling psychologists, school psychologists) and those outside of it. Although psychologists have different orientations and different occupational activities, all of them share a fascination with the human mind and behavior. They also stress the importance of empirical evidence that is so critical to making psychology a science.

PREVIEW OUTLINE

Before you read the chapter, review the preview outline for each section of the text. After you have read the chapter, close this book and try to <u>recreate</u> the outlines on a blank piece of paper.

I.   **PSYCHOLOGY, PSEUDOSCIENCE, AND POPULAR OPINION**
      A.   **Psychology** – the discipline concerned with behavior and mental processes, and how they are affected by an organism's physical state, mental state, and the external environment
      B.   **Psychobabble** – pseudoscience covered by veneer of psychological language
          1. Psychology is based on research evidence, whereas popular opinion is not
          2. Psychobabble <u>confirms</u> existing beliefs and prejudices; psychology <u>challenges</u> them and deepens our understanding of accepted facts

II.   **THINKING CRITICALLY AND CREATIVELY ABOUT PSYCHOLOGY**
     A.   **Critical thinking** – ability and willingness to assess claims and make judgments on the basis of well-supported reasons and evidence rather than emotion and anecdote
     B.   **Eight critical-thinking guidelines**
          1.   Ask questions; be willing to wonder
          2.   Define your terms
          3.   Examine the evidence
          4.   Analyze assumptions and biases
          5.   Avoid emotional reasoning
          6.   Don't oversimplify
          7.   Consider other interpretations
          8.   Tolerate uncertainty

III.   **PSYCHOLOGY'S PAST: FROM THE ARMCHAIR TO THE LABORATORY**
     A.   **Early history** – Hippocrates, the Stoics, Locke
     B.   **The birth of modern psychology** – Wilhelm Wundt and his laboratory
     C.   **Three early psychologies**
          1.   Structuralism and E.B. Titchener
          2.   Functionalism, William James, and Charles Darwin
          3.   Psychoanalysis and Sigmund Freud

IV.   **PSYCHOLOGY'S PRESENT: BEHAVIOR, BODY, MIND, AND CULTURE**
     A.   **The major psychological perspectives**
          1.   The biological perspective examines how bodily events interact with the environment to produce behavior, feelings, and thoughts
          2.   The learning perspective examines how the environment and experience affect the actions of individuals (or animals)
          3.   The cognitive perspective emphasizes what goes on in people's heads; reasoning, remembering, understanding language, problem solving
          4.   The sociocultural perspective focuses on the social and cultural forces outside the individual that shape every aspect of behavior
          5.   The psychodynamic perspective deals with unconscious dynamics within the individual, such as inner forces, conflicts, or instinctual energy
     B.   **Other influential movements in psychology**
          1.   Humanistic psychology emphasizes free will, personal growth, resilience, and the achievement of human potential
          2.   Feminist psychology analyzes the influence of social inequities on gender relations and on the behavior of the two sexes

V. **WHAT PSYCHOLOGISTS DO**
    A.   **Overview of professional activities**
        1.   Teach and conduct research in colleges and universities
        2.   Provide health or mental health services (psychological practice)
        3.   Conduct research or apply its findings in nonacademic settings
    B.   **Psychological research**
        1.   Basic psychology – research that seeks knowledge for its own sake
        2.   Applied psychology – research concerned with practical uses of knowledge
        3.   Some major non clinical specialties in psychology: experimental psychologists, psychometric psychologists, developmental psychologists, industrial/organizational psychologists, educational psychologists
    C.   **Psychological practice**
        1.   Those who try to understand and improve physical and mental health
        2.   Practitioners of psychology work in mental or general hospitals, clinics, schools, counseling centers, and private practice
        3.   Types of practitioners: counseling psychologists, school psychologists, clinical psychologists; Degrees for practice: Ph.D., Ed.D., Psy.D.
        4.   Types of non clinical psychologist practitioners: psychotherapist (not legally regulated), psychoanalyst, psychiatrist, social worker, marriage and family counselors
    D.   **Psychology in the community**
        1.   The field is experiencing a knowledge explosion due to the rapid expansion of the field during the second half of the twentieth century
        2.   Today, psychologists contribute to and work in many fields

VI. **BIOLOGY, CULTURE, AND PSYCHOLOGY: BEYOND THE BORDERS**
    A.   **Variety in psychologists' activities, goals, and perspectives creates a mosaic**
    B.   **Though there is disagreement about emphasis, psychological scientists and scientist-clinicians agree on basic guidelines:**
        1.   Most believe in importance of gathering empirical evidence
        2.   Most avoid one-note explanations of behavior and either-or thinking
        3.   Most share a fascination with human behavior and mind

PERSPECTIVES TABLE
Complete this table, and then identify similarities and differences between perspectives.

PERSPECTIVE OR MOVEMENT	KEY FIGURES	KEY CONCEPTS AND TERMS	MAJOR INFLUENCES ON BEHAVIOR
BIOLOGICAL PERSPECTIVE			
LEARNING PERSPECTIVE			
COGNITIVE PERSPECTIVE			
SOCIOCULTURAL PERSPECTIVE			
PSYCHODYNAMIC PERSPECTIVE			
HUMANISTIC MOVEMENT			
FEMINIST MOVEMENT			

PRACTICE TEST 1 – Multiple Choice

1.   Psychology is defined as the:
     A.   scientific study of mental processes that are covered by a veneer of scientific-sounding language.
     B.   discipline concerned with behavior and mental processes and how they are affected by an organism's physical state, mental state, and the external environment.
     C.   study of behavior that confirms our existing beliefs and prejudices.
     D.   scientific study of groups and institutions in society.

2.   The main difference between psychological knowledge and popular opinion is that:
     A.   psychological knowledge is contained in text books; popular opinion is not.
     B.   psychological knowledge is based on research evidence; popular opinion is not.
     C.   findings based on psychological knowledge are often the opposite of popular opinion.
     D.   popular opinion is usually very obvious and psychological knowledge is rarely the expected result.

3.   One of the main problems with the claims put forward by astrologers and psychics is that:
     A.   they do not address major life problems that are relevant to people.
     B.   it often takes many years to verify the accuracy of the prediction.
     C.   such claims can only be made by fully licensed individuals.
     D.   they are often so vague that they become meaningless.

4.   The ability and willingness to assess claims and make objective judgments on the basis of well-supported reasons and evidence rather than emotion and anecdote defines:
     A.   critical thinking.
     B.   psychobabble.
     C.   common sense.
     D.   psychology.

5.   All of the following are essential elements of critical thinking EXCEPT:
     A.   all opinions are equally valid.
     B.   examine the evidence.
     C.   avoid emotional reasoning.
     D.   analyze assumptions and biases.

6.   _____ established the first psychology lab in 1879.
       A.   E.B. Titchener
       B.   William James
       C.   B.F. Skinner
       D.   Wilhelm Wundt

7.   An early school of psychology popularized by E.B. Titchener, attempted to
       analyze sensations, images, and feelings into their most basic elements. This
       school was called:
       A.   structuralism.
       B.   introspection.
       C.   functionalism.
       D.   behaviorism.

8.   An early school of psychological thought asked how an organism's behavior helps
       it to adapt to its environment. It was called:
       A.   structuralism.
       B.   introspection.
       C.   functionalism.
       D.   behaviorism.

9.   Titchener is to James as:
       A.   trained introspection is to Wundt.
       B.   functionalism is to structuralism.
       C.   trained introspection is to functionalism.
       D.   structuralism is to functionalism.

10.   Proponents of the _____ perspective believe that to understand the mind one
       must study bodily events, because all actions, feelings, and thoughts are
       associated with our physical bodies.
       A.   behavioral
       B.   psychodynamic
       C.   cognitive
       D.   biological

11.   Tom states that, "facilitated communication is an effective means of promoting
       genuine verbal dialogue from autistic individuals." Sophia claims that, "facilitated
       is an empty hoax that exploits desperate parents." Which of the following is true?
       A.   Both beliefs are opinions and therefore equal to one another.
       B.   Tom's belief is more valid because Sophia is being narrow-minded.
       C.   Neither belief is valid because they both need to tolerate uncertainty.
       D.   The more valid belief is whichever one is supported by the evidence.

12. "To understand a person's actions, we must concentrate on the environmental conditions—the rewards and punishers—that maintain or discourage specific behaviors rather than studying the mind or mental states." This reflects the position of the _____ perspective.
    A. learning
    B. psychodynamic
    C. cognitive
    D. biological

13. Mental processes and structures inside one's head (as opposed to the physical composition of the head), including how people reason, remember, understand language, and solve problems are some of the topics emphasized by the:
    A. sociocultural perspective.
    B. humanists.
    C. social-cognitive theory.
    D. cognitive perspective.

14. _____ theorists combine elements of behaviorism with research on thoughts, values, expectations, and intentions.
    A. Social-cognitive learning
    B. Psychodynamic
    C. Humanist-biological
    D. Biological

15. One of main reasons phrenology failed to produce useful outcomes was that:
    A. it did not use empirical methods.
    B. people eventually lost interest in personality traits.
    C. it was never applied to areas besides employment decisions.
    D. it could not explain counterevidence.

16. Psychodynamic psychology:
    A. studies issues that other approaches do not consider, such as fears and sexual functioning.
    B. is fundamentally different in how it examines and accepts evidence than the other approaches to psychology.
    C. uses the same methods as approaches to psychology in order to under human phenomenon.
    D. focuses on how the nervous system impacts thinking and problem solving across different cultural contexts.

17. "The answer to violence and cruelty doesn't reside in instincts, brain circuits, or personal dispositions, but in social, economic and cultural factors." This statement is consistent with the thinking of _____ psychologists.
   A. cognitive
   B. humanistic
   C. sociocultural
   D. psychodynamic

18. "Psychological distress is a result of inner forces, specifically unresolved unconscious conflicts from early childhood." This statement reflects the position of the _____ perspective.
   A. behavioral
   B. psychodynamic
   C. cognitive
   D. biological

19. The field of _____ was developed in reaction to Freudian pessimism and behaviorist "mindlessness," and is based on the idea that human beings have free will.
   A. feminist psychology
   B. social learning theory
   C. sociocultural psychology
   D. humanistic psychology

20. Which of the following might be one of the goals of feminist psychology?
   A. Encourage research on menstruation and motherhood.
   B. Identify biases in psychological research and psychotherapy.
   C. Make sure that both male and female subjects are used in research design.
   D. All of the above.

21. Which of the following best describes the difference between applied and basic research?
   A. Basic research examines the basic elements of sensations, images, and feelings, whereas applied research studies how these processes help a person adapt to the environment.
   B. Basic psychological research seeks knowledge for its own sake, whereas applied psychological research is concerned with the practical uses of knowledge.
   C. Applied research seeks knowledge for its own sake, whereas basic research is concerned with the practical uses of knowledge.
   D. Basic research is based on the psychoanalytic perspective, whereas applied research is based on the humanistic approach.

22. Caio sees an advertisement in the phone book for a psychotherapist. Given that this practitioner is called a "psychotherapist," Caio knows that the therapist:
    A. has a doctorate in psychology.
    B. has extensive training in psychometrics.
    C. will likely take a biological approach to therapy.
    D. may not have a degree or any training.

23. A developmental psychologist would:
    A. conduct a study on infant attachment behavior.
    B. conduct research on the role of arousal in the experience of emotions.
    C. develop a new test to measure personality.
    D. design and evaluate tests of mental abilities, aptitudes, interests, and personality.

24. A psychometric psychologist:
    A. studies how groups, institutions, and the social context influence individuals.
    B. studies how people change and grow over time physically, mentally, and socially.
    C. designs and evaluates tests of mental abilities, aptitudes, interests, and personality.
    D. studies behavior in the workplace.

25. Psychologists who help people deal with problems of everyday life, such as test anxiety, family or marital problems, or low job motivation, are called _____ psychologists.
    A. psychometric
    B. clinical
    C. counseling
    D. school

26. Which type of psychologist would be most likely to work with highly disturbed people?
    A. Clinical
    B. Experimental
    C. Counseling
    D. School

27. A psychotherapist:
    A. has specialized training at a psychoanalytic institute.
    B. is not required to have any training at all in most states.
    C. has a medical degree.
    D. is a psychologist.

11

28. Dr. Iriko believes that Jon's depression is biochemical and writes him a prescription for antidepressant drugs. She is most likely a:
   A. counseling psychologist.
   B. psychotherapist.
   C. psychiatrist.
   D. social worker.

29. Every week Anna has been visiting a mental health professional who has been helping her manage her anxiety more effectively. This professional has been using techniques from Freud's psychoanalytic approach to treat Anna, but is unable to prescribe medication. This professional could be any of the following except a:
   A. psychotherapist.
   B. clinical psychologist.
   C. psychiatrist.
   D. psychoanalyst.

PRACTICE TEST 2 – Short Answer

1. Psychology is defined as the discipline concerned with _behavior_ and how they are affected by an organism's physical state, mental state, and the external environment. [*mental process & behavior*]

2. Scientific psychology differs from popular psychology in that it is based on _empirical_ evidence.

3. _Critical thinking_ is the ability and willingness to assess claims and make objective judgments on the basis of well-supported reasons and evidence rather than emotion and anecdote.

4. Two of the eight guidelines for critical thinking are: _define your terms, avoid emotional reasoning_

5. Phrenology was one of the forerunners of psychology. Unfortunately, it came to many false conclusions because its methods were not _empirical_.

6. Wilhelm Wundt established the _1st lab 1879 Leipzig, Ger._

7. The early school of psychological thought founded by Titchener was called _Structuralism_.

8. According to psychoanalysis, distressful symptoms are due to _hidden conflict_

9. The _Psychodynamic_ perspective has its origins in Freud's theory of psychoanalysis.

10. The five major current psychological perspectives are: _Cognitive, psychodynamic biological, learning, sociocultural_

11. The _learning_ perspective is concerned with how the environment and experience affect a person's actions.

12. Unlike behaviorists and psychoanalysts, humanists believe that human beings have _free will_.

13. The _Cognitive_ emphasizes the mental processes and structures underlying how people reason, remember, understand language, solve problems, and form beliefs.

14. The sociocultural perspective focuses on _Social + cultural_.

15. The _Sociocultural_ is likely to study issues such as factors that make an individual violent and why certain cultures have higher rates of violence than other cultures.

16. Psychologists from the _feminist_ movement have noted that many research studies have used only men as subjects.

17. Viewpoints and opinions are considered less valid if they are not _backed by empirical evidence_.

18. _Occupational_ psychologists study behavior in the workplace, whereas _educational_ psychologists study principles that explain learning and look for ways to improve educational systems.

19. Three examples of practice specialties in psychology are _therapist_ , _analyst_ , and _psychiatrist_ .

20. The help of astrologers and psychics is often meaningless because _vague_.

21. To practice psychology, one must have a _license_ , and in almost all states, this requires a _doctorate_ degree.

22. People often confuse clinical psychology with three other terms: _____, _____, or _____.

23. _Psychiatrist_ have a medical degree and may prescribe medication, whereas _psychotherapist_ are not required to have any degree at all since the term is not legally regulated.

24. The psychodynamic perspective is connected to the rest of psychology because it often studies the same topics. However, it is also set apart from the other perspectives because it differs radically in _____.

25. _Evolutionary_ psychology focuses on how genetically influenced behavior that was adaptive during our ancestral past may be reflected in our present behaviors.

26. There are three broad areas of activity that psychologists engage in: _academics_ , _mental health_, and _non-academics_

14

PRACTICE TEST 3 – Essay

1. Several activities are described below. For each activity, indicate (a) whether it is an example of applied or basic psychology, (b) the area of specialization most likely to be involved, and (c) whether that area of specialization is a clinical or non clinical area. Explain the reasons for your answers.

      A.   Psychologist David Wechsler designed an intelligence test expressly for use with adults.

      B.   Researchers Hubel and Wiesel (1962, 1968) received a Nobel Prize for their work in the area of vision. They found that special cells in the brain are designed to visually code complex features of an object. Their research involved recording impulses from individual cells in the brains of cats and monkeys.

      C.   Swiss biologist Jean Piaget observed that children of different ages understand concepts and reason differently. Based on his observations, he developed a theory of cognitive development.

      D.   Several researchers have studied work motivation. They have been interested in the conditions that influence productivity and satisfaction in organizations.

      E.   In 1963, Stanley Milgram conducted a classic study on obedience to authority. In subsequent variations of the original study, Milgram and his colleagues investigated the conditions under which people might disobey.

      F.   Strupp conducted research in 1982 to examine the characteristics of effective psychotherapy. He found that the relationship between the therapist and client greatly affects the success of the therapy.

      G.   A national study of 3,000 children in fourth through tenth grades found that over this period of time girls' self-esteem plummeted (American Association of University Women, 1991). As a result of recommendations based on the findings of this and other research, changes in school systems have been suggested.

      H.   Several psychologists have studied the process of career development and use career development theories to assist college students in selecting their careers.

2. Harold is 17 years old and has been abusing alcohol and marijuana for the past year. He has been missing school and his academic performance is declining. Harold was formerly a B student and was involved in sports. He is now getting D's and F's and has dropped out of most extracurricular activities.   Answer the following questions: What influences would each of the five perspectives (learning, psychodynamic, biological, cognitive, and sociocultural) and two movements in psychology (humanist and feminist) identify as central to the development of Harold's drug problem?

3. Juanita is suffering from depression and she is interested in seeking professional help for her problem. Briefly describe the general types of treatment that would most likely be utilized by a psychologist, a psychiatrist, a psychoanalyst and a psychotherapist. Indicate the types of training they are likely to have had.

4. Suppose that your friend Zainab dreamed that she would meet a hero of hers and have a personal discussion with him. A few days later, it actually happens! Zainab is convinced that she is psychic—she has special, paranormal powers. Using the critical thinking concepts, explain this event differently than Zainab. What type of advice would you give her to help her think critically about this event?

CHAPTER 2

How Psychologists Do Research

LEARNING OBJECTIVES

What Makes Psychological Research Scientific?
2.1 - The characteristics of an ideal scientist.
2.2 - The nature of a scientific theory.
2.3 - The secret of a good scientific definition.
2.4 - The risk scientists take when testing their ideas.
2.5 - Why secrecy is a big "no-no" in science.

Descriptive Studies: Establishing the Facts
2.6 - How participants are selected for psychological studies, and why it matters.
2.7 - The methods psychologists use to describe behavior.
2.8 - The advantages and disadvantages of using descriptive research methods.

Correlational Studies: Looking For Relationships
2.9 -   What positive and negative correlations signify about the relationship between two variables.
2.10 - Why a correlation does not establish a causal relationship between two variables.

Experiments: Hunting For Causes
2.11 - Why psychologists rely so heavily on experiments.
2.12 - What are the defining features of an experiment.
2.13 - What are the special challenges in doing cross-cultural research.

Evaluating the Findings
2.14 - Why averages can be misleading.
2.15 - How psychologists use inferential statistics to reach conclusions about their research.
2.16 - How psychologists can combine results from many studies of a question to get a better overall answer.

Keeping the Enterprise Ethical
2.17 - Why psychologists sometimes lie to people taking part in their studies.
2.18 - Why psychologists study nonhuman animals.

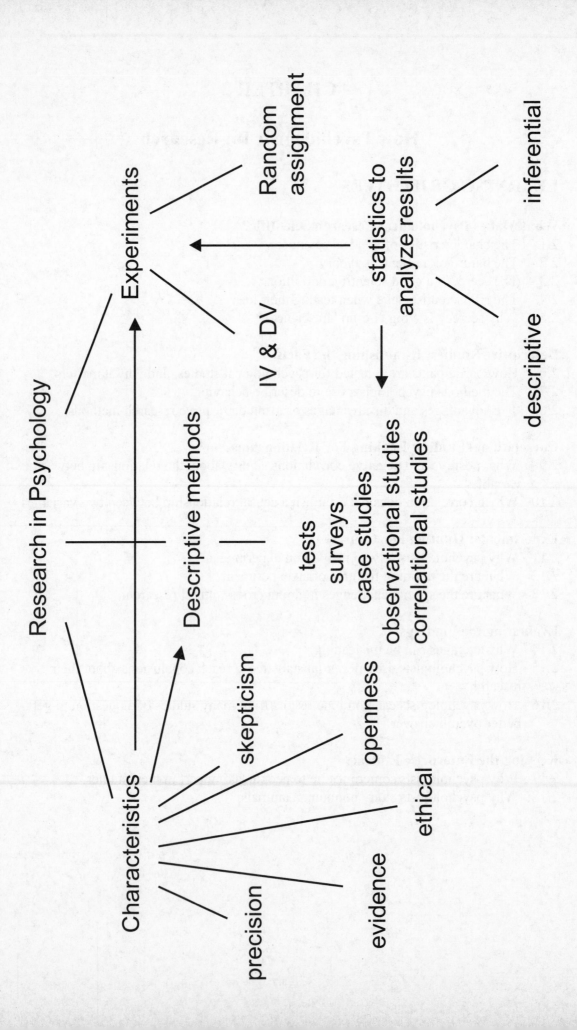

Chapter 2 - Concept Map

Research in Psychology

Characteristics

precision

skepticism

openness

evidence

ethical

Experiments

Random assignment

IV & DV

statistics to analyze results

inferential

descriptive

Descriptive methods

tests

surveys

case studies

observational studies

correlational studies

BRIEF CHAPTER SUMMARY

Chapter 2 discusses the importance of understanding scientific methodology in the psychological context. The text describes the characteristics of scientific research that should be used to evaluate research findings in psychology and in other fields. Three major types of research studies are described: descriptive studies, correlational studies, and experimental studies. Descriptive studies include case studies, observational studies, studies based on psychological tests, and studies based on surveys. Correlational studies are a special category of descriptive studies that describe the strength and direction of relationships between two variables. Correlational research is useful in making predictions from one variable to another, but not very helpful in determining causality. Experimental research is the only method to determine cause and effect relationships, because it is conducted in a highly controlled fashion. The components of experimental research include manipulating independent variables and measuring dependent variables, as well as randomly assigning participants to experimental and control conditions. Potential biases in conducting research are discussed, as well as methods to reduce such bias (e.g., single-blind and double-blind studies). The text explains descriptive and inferential statistics and demonstrates how they help to make research findings meaningful. Finally, the ethical concerns surrounding studying human beings and animals are discussed.

PREVIEW OUTLINE

Before you read the chapter, review the preview outline for each section of the text. After you have read the chapter, close this book and try to <u>recreate</u> the outlines on a blank piece of paper.

I.   **WHAT MAKES PSYCHOLOGICAL RESEARCH SCIENTIFIC?**
    A.   **Why are research methods so important to psychologists?**
        1.   Helps separate truth from unfounded belief
        2.   Helps sort out conflicting views
        3.   Helps correct false ideas that may cause people harm
    B.   **What makes research scientific?**
        1.   Precision
            a.   Start with a theory: organized system of assumptions and principles that purports to explain certain phenomena
            b.   From a hunch or theory, derive a specific hypothesis
            c.   Operational definitions: terms must be defined in ways that can be observed and measured
        2.   Skepticism: accept conclusions with caution but be open to new ideas
        3.   Reliance on empirical evidence rather than on personal accounts
        4.   Willingness to make "risky predictions" and the principle of falsifiability
        5.   Openness in the scientific community so that findings can be replicated

II. DESCRIPTIVE STUDIES: ESTABLISHING THE FACTS

- A. **Case Studies – Detailed descriptions of particular individuals**
  1. Advantages include producing detailed picture of one individual
  2. Disadvantages: rely on possibly inaccurate memories, cannot generalize to all human behavior, do not test hypotheses
- B. **Observational Studies – observing, recording behavior without interfering**
  1. Naturalistic observation: used to find out how people or animals act in their normal environment
  2. Laboratory observation: scientist has greater control but subject might alter his or her behavior
- C. **Tests (assessment instruments) – procedures to measure personality traits, emotional states, aptitudes, interests, abilities, and values**
  1. Types of tests
     - a. Objective tests (inventories) – measures beliefs, feelings, or behaviors of which an individual is aware
     - b. Projective tests – designed to tap unconscious
  2. Characteristics of a good test
     - a. Standardization – uniform procedures for giving, scoring the test
     - b. Norms – established standards of performance
     - c. Reliability – getting the same results from one time to another
       - (1) Test-retest – giving the same test twice
       - (2) Alternate-forms – giving different versions of the same test
     - d. Validity – a test measures what it set out to measure
       - (1) Content validity – test questions ask about a broad array of beliefs and behaviors relevant to what is being measured
       - (2) Criterion validity – predicts other measures of the trait
- D. **Surveys**
  1. Gather information by asking people directly
  2. Potential problems with surveys (e.g., bias in wording, representativeness of sample, volunteer bias, lying or forgetting by subjects)

III. CORRELATIONAL STUDIES: LOOKING FOR RELATIONSHIPS

- A. **Purpose** – to determine whether two variables are related, and if so, how strongly
- B. **Measuring correlations**
  1. Direction of a relationship between variables
     - a. Positive correlation – high values of one variable are associated with high values of the other; low values of one variable are associated with low values of the other

          b.   Negative correlation – high values of one variable are associated with low values of the other and vice versa

      2.   Correlation coefficient indicates the strength of relationship between the two variables; ranges from -1 (strong negative) to +1 (strong positive)

C.   Cautions about correlations

      1.   Benefit – allows someone to predict from one variable to another

      2.   Limitation – cannot show causation

IV.   EXPERIMENTS: HUNTING FOR CAUSES

A.   Purpose of experimentation – to look for causes of behavior because the experiment allows the researcher to control the situation being studied

B.   Experimental variables – the characteristics the researcher is studying

      1.   Independent variable – the characteristic manipulated by the experimenter

      2.   Dependent variable – the behavior the researcher tries to predict

C.   Experimental and control conditions

      1.   Experimental condition – the condition or group in which subjects receive some amount of the independent variable

      2.   Control condition – the condition or group in which subjects do not receive any amount of the independent variable

      3.   Random assignment balances individual differences among subjects between the two groups

D.   Experimenter effects

      1.   Single-blind studies – subjects don't know whether they are in the experimental or control group

      2.   Double-blind studies – neither the experimenter nor the subjects know which subjects are in which group

E.   Culture and Research: Special challenges

      1.   Methods and sampling – need to separate cultural differences from simply translational errors

      2.   Stereotyping – although cultural averages can be found, individual variation still exists within each culture

      3.   Reification – must try to understand why culture is the way it is, not assume differences are inherent

V.   EVALUATING THE FINDINGS

A.   Descriptive statistics: Finding out what's so

      1.   Arithmetic mean compares group scores between two or more groups

      2.   Standard deviation shows how clustered or spread out individual scores are around the mean

B.   Inferential statistics: Asking "So what?"

      1.   Determines the likelihood that the result of the study occurred by chance

2. Statistical significance – the result is expected to occur by chance fewer than 5 times in 100; it does not necessarily indicate real-world importance

3. Statistically significant results allow general predictions to be made about human behavior, though not about any particular individual

C.   Interpreting the findings: What is the best explanation for the findings?

1. Researchers must test a hypothesis in different ways several times
   a. Cross-sectional studies – compare groups at one time
   b. Longitudinal studies – study subjects across the life span

2. Researchers must judge the result's importance with procedures like meta-analysis that combine and analyze data from many studies

VI.   KEEPING THE ENTERPRISE ETHICAL

A.   The ethics of studying human beings

1. American Psychological Association's ethical code
   a. Dignity and welfare of subjects must be respected
   b. People must participate voluntarily and give informed consent
   c. Subjects must be free to withdraw from a study at any time

2. Use of deception: Researchers are required to consider alternatives to deception, show that a study's potential value justifies the use of deception, and debrief subjects about the study's true purpose afterward

B.   The ethics of studying animals

1. Many purposes exist for conducting research using animals (e.g., basic research on a particular species, improve human welfare, practical applications, to study issues that cannot be studied experimentally with human beings)

2. Treatment and regulations have improved due to debates over the issues

RESEARCH METHODS TABLE

Complete this table and compare the differences among the research methods.

RESEARCH METHOD	DEFINITION AND DESCRIPTION	EXAMPLE
CASE HISTORY		
NATURALISTIC OBSERVATION		
LABORATORY OBSERVATION		
TESTS		
SURVEY		
CORRELATIONAL STUDY		
EXPERIMENT		

PRACTICE TEST 1 – Multiple Choice

1.   Introductory psychology students study research methods in order to:
     A.   find proof for their existing beliefs so they can argue against those who disagree.
     B.   be able to critically evaluate psychological findings.
     C.   be able to manipulate statistics to their advantage.
     D.   be able to use their own experiences as scientific proofs.

2.   Which of the following is <u>NOT</u> a characteristic of scientific research?
     A.   Reliance on common sense
     B.   Precision
     C.   Skepticism
     D.   Openness

3.   An organized system of assumptions and principles that purports to explain a specified set of phenomena is called a(n):
     A.   hypothesis.
     B.   operational definition.
     C.   theory.
     D.   risky prediction.

4.   It is important that scientists share their ideas and procedures so that:
     A.   others can replicate their research.
     B.   TV and other media can interview them.
     C.   they can avoid the falsifiability effect.
     D.   the experimental hypothesis can be proven.

5.   Defining a term in ways that can be observed and measured is known as:
     A.   an operational definition.
     B.   a theory.
     C.   common sense.
     D.   objective realism.

6.   Scores on a depression test, changes in time spent sleeping, and food intake each might be:
     A.   hypotheses.
     B.   theories of depression.
     C.   operational definitions of depression.
     D.   empirical evidence.

7. Which of the following violates the principle of falsifiability?
   A. Lack of evidence for a phenomenon is described as predictable since destroying evidence is an alleged characteristic of the phenomenon under study.
   B. Subjects in a study do not represent the larger population being described.
   C. A study uses only volunteer subjects who differ from non volunteers.
   D. An experimenter's expectations subtly influence the outcome of a study.

8. Descriptive research methods:
   A. explain behavior by identifying the causes of the behavior.
   B. allow the researcher to describe and predict behavior.
   C. include the experimental study.
   D. all of the above.

9. Freud based his theory on studying a small number of particular individuals in great detail. This research method is called a(n):
   A. survey.
   B. experiment.
   C. naturalistic observation.
   D. case study.

10. One disadvantage of case studies is that:
    A. they rely on memories, which can be inaccurate.
    B. information may be difficult to interpret.
    C. they cannot be used to generalize about human behavior.
    D. All of the above are disadvantages.

11. Naturalistic observations involve:
    A. giving subjects a series of psychological tests.
    B. assigning research participants to experimental and control groups.
    C. observing subjects in the natural environment.
    D. asking people a series of questions.

12. In the area of test construction, standardization refers to:
    A. the use of uniform procedures in the administration and scoring of a test.
    B. the establishment of standards of performance.
    C. getting the same results over time.
    D. a test measuring what it set out to.

13. _____ validity indicates that the test questions represent fully the trait being measured.
    A. Test-retest
    B. Content
    C. Criterion
    D. Alternate forms

14. Validity is to reliability as:
    A. consistency is to accuracy.
    B. accuracy is to consistency.
    C. criterion is to content.
    D. objective is to projective.

15. You take an intelligence test on Monday and receive a high score. You take it again on Tuesday and receive a low score. This test apparently lacks:
    A. content validity.
    B. criterion validity.
    C. test-retest reliability.
    D. alternate forms reliability.

16. A problem with surveys is that:
    A. their results can by weakened by volunteer bias.
    B. respondents may lie, forget, or remember incorrectly.
    C. biases or ambiguities in the wording of questions may exist.
    D. All of the above are potential problems with surveys.

17. To conduct research on attitudes toward abortion, Dr. Kim distributes surveys to people leaving church after a service. One problem with this survey is that:
    A. people are likely to lie about their attitude.
    B. people are likely to forget their attitude.
    C. the sample is not representative.
    D. the procedures are not uniform.

18. Correlations:
    A. identify the causes of behavior.
    B. determine whether two or more phenomena are related, and if so, how strongly.
    C. can be expressed on a numeric scale from 1 to 10.
    D. require research participants to be observed in a laboratory.

19. The more Jose studies, the more his test scores improve. This is an example of:
    A. a naturalistic observation.
    B. a positive correlation.
    C. a negative correlation.
    D. proof of causation.

20. When recruiting participants to serve in a study, it is most important that the sample be:
    A. diverse.
    B. large.
    C. able to support the hypothesis.
    D. representative.

21. Based on a correlational study showing that those who exercise regularly experience lower rates of depression, which of the following conclusions can be reached?
    A. Exercise causes a reduction in depression.
    B. People who are depressed stop exercising.
    C. There is a relationship between exercise and depression.
    D. Self-esteem influences both exercise and depression levels.

22. Experimentation is:
    A. a type of observational study.
    B. the research method that can most confidently make causal conclusions.
    C. one of the descriptive research methods.
    D. more limited in its conclusions than the other types of methodologies.

23. The independent variable is the variable that:
    A. is manipulated by the researcher.
    B. the researcher tries to predict.
    C. is defined in a way that can be observed and measured.
    D. cannot be controlled.

24. Dr. Kapoor is conducting research on the effects of alcohol on reaction time. She assigns students to two groups. One group receives three ounces of alcohol and the other group receives an alcohol-free beverage that looks, smells, and tastes like alcohol. Following ingestion of the beverage, the reaction time of subjects in both groups is tested. Which of the variables is the dependent variable?
    A. Alcohol
    B. Control group
    C. Alcohol-free beverage
    D. Reaction time

25. In the above study, the group of research participants that receives the alcohol-free beverage is called the:
    A. independent variable group.
    B. control group.
    C. experimental group.
    D. random group.

26. After getting your math exam back, your instructor informs you that the class average was 83% correct. Which of the following is important to keep in mind?
    A.   That more students earned an 83% than any other score.
    B.   It is possible that no one in the class actually got an 83%.
    C.   At least half of the students scored more than 83% correct.
    D.   Almost no students earned less than 30% correct.

27. Inferential statistics:
    A.   summarize individual data into group data.
    B.   combine data from many studies.
    C.   study abilities across the life span.
    D.   permit a researcher to draw conclusions based on evidence.

28. In an experiment assessing a new teaching technique, subjects in the experimental group received a mean score of 84, and subjects in the control group received a mean score of 77. Before the experimenters can say whether the new technique was superior in this study, they must:
    A.   calculate the statistical significance of the results to evaluate the probability that this result could have happened by chance.
    B.   conduct a meta-analysis.
    C.   calculate the statistical significance to determine the real-world importance.
    D.   conduct a longitudinal study to see if the improved learning lasts.

29. Cross-sectional studies differ from longitudinal studies in that cross-sectional studies:
    A.   compare different groups at one time, whereas longitudinal studies examine abilities across the life span.
    B.   examine groups in the laboratory, whereas longitudinal studies examine behavior in the natural environment.
    C.   examine abilities across the life span, whereas longitudinal studies compare different groups at one time.
    D.   cannot establish cause and effect, whereas longitudinal studies can.

30. Meta-analyses are helpful in the interpretation of research findings because they:
    A.   determine which studies are accurate and which are not.
    B.   combine data from many studies.
    C.   establish whether the findings have any real-world importance.
    D.   establish the statistical significance of studies.

31. For ethical purposes, researchers must show they have considered alternative procedures and that they plan to debrief subjects in order to use:
   A.   animals.
   B.   more than one experimental condition.
   C.   informed consent.
   D.   deception.

32. Dr. Ching is conducting a study in which a co-researcher pretends to trip and fall in the presence of research subjects who are taking a reading comprehension test. The subjects have been told the study is on memory, but Dr. Ching is really studying the circumstances under which strangers provide assistance to others. According to ethical principles, Dr. Ching:
   A.   must demonstrate that her study's potential value justifies the use of deception.
   B.   may not continue with this study no matter what she does because it is unethical to be dishonest with the subjects.
   C.   never needs to disclose the true purpose of the study to the subjects.
   D.   needs only show that no harm will come to the subjects.

33. Psychologists use animals in research:
   A.   because sometimes practical or ethical considerations prevent the use of human beings as subjects.
   B.   to discover practical applications.
   C.   to conduct basic research on a particular species.
   D.   All of the above are reasons that animals are used in research.

PRACTICE TEST 2 – Short Answer

1. Research methods are important to psychologists because they help separate truth from _____.

2. "Students who spend more time studying perform better in college." This is an example of a _____.

3. Dr. Sanchez is conducting a study on the effects of anxiety on test performance. She is using subjects' scores on a stress test as her _____ definition of anxiety.

4. Any theory that cannot in principle be refuted violates the _____.

5. Scientists must discuss ideas, testing procedures, and results so their findings can be _____ to reduce fraud and error.

6. Research methods that allow psychologists to describe and predict behavior but not to explain its causes are _____ methods.

7. One important function of replication is to be able to _____ the findings of previous research.

8. Often scientists need a good description of behavior as it occurs in the natural environment before they can explain it. This is the primary purpose of _____.

9. _____ tests measure beliefs, behavior, and feelings of which the person is aware, whereas _____ tests are designed to tap the unconscious.

10. While having a large sample is helpful, it is more important that samples be _____ of the population being studied.

11. At 8:00 a.m. Nobu weighs 179 pounds. He moves the scale slightly and decides to weigh himself again. Though it's only a minute later, he now weighs 177. Nobu's scale lacks the test characteristic of _____.

12. A test that purports to measure personality, but actually measures verbal abilities lacks _____.

13. If SAT scores are able to accurately predict college students' grade point averages, then the SAT demonstrates that it possesses _____.

14. A survey on alcohol use among college students reported that alcohol use among students had dramatically decreased. Later the study reported that the subjects were female students from one expensive Ivy League university. This survey did not use a _____ sample of college students.

15. An experiment is the only way to draw conclusions about _____.

16. A _____ is the numerical measure of the strength and direction of the relationship between two _____.

17. The mean score of a sample does not tell anything about the _____ of the participant responses.

18. When psychologists want to look for causes of behavior, they must use a more controlled method called the _____.

19. In an experiment conducted on the effects of caffeine on alertness, caffeine intake would be the _____ variable, and alertness would be the _____ variable.

20. In the study described in question 19, the subjects who receive caffeinated coffee are in the _____ group whereas those who receive decaffeinated coffee are in the _____ group.

21. Numbers summarizing the data we collect from subjects are called _____ statistics.

22. If the result of a study is unlikely to have happened by chance, then we say the result is statistically _____.

PRACTICE TEST 3 – Essay

1.   Determine which research method is best for each situation below and explain why.

     A.   Determine the favorite foods of adolescents.
     B.   Determine whether a person is introverted or extroverted.
     C.   Determine whether or not frustration causes aggression.
     D.   Determine whether level of education is associated with criminal behavior.
     E.   Determine conversational patterns of men and women.
     F.   Determine why a violinist gave up a flourishing career in business to play in the local symphony.
     G.   Determine the parenting patterns used on a child who is having behavior problems and whose parents cannot control him.

2.   In the following experiments identify: 1) a possible hypothesis, 2) the independent and dependent variables, 3) their operational definitions, and 4) experimental and control conditions.

     A.   A study was conducted on the effects of caffeine on studying. Experimental subjects were given 32 ounces of caffeine. Subjects in the control group were given a decaffeinated beverage that looked and tasted like the beverage consumed by the experimental group. After consuming the drinks, all subjects were provided with a chapter of a text to read and then were tested.

     B.   A study was conducted on the effects of types of music on aggressive behavior. There were three experimental groups: one listened to classical music, the second listened to jazz, and the third listened to heavy metal music. Subjects in the control condition were exposed to a white noise machine for the same period of time. Following exposure to the 45-minute music session, all subjects were put in a situation in which they were able to engage in aggressive behavior (punch a punching bag).

     C.   A study was conducted on the effects of exercise on relaxation. There were two experimental groups of subjects. One group engaged in supervised aerobic exercise for 45 minutes. The second experimental group engaged in sit-ups and push-ups for 45 minutes. The control group engaged in a supervised study session. Following the exposure, all subjects were told to wait in a room for the experimenter to return. During this period, they were hooked up to medical equipment monitoring their heart rate, muscle tension, respiration, and blood pressure.

3. Among the following examples, identify which correlations are most likely positive, negative, or zero.

    A. Height and weight
    B. Smoking and health
    C. Studying and drop-out rates
    D. SAT score and grade point average (GPA)
    E. Education level and height
    F. Smoking and education level
    G. Alcohol intake and reaction time
    H. Alcohol intake and automobile accidents
    I. Delinquency and education level
    J. Weight and schizophrenia

4. After reviewing the ethical guidelines adopted by the American Psychological Association (APA), determine which of the following research practices are ethical or unethical and explain why.

    A. Require psychology students to participate as subjects in a research study.
    B. Tell subjects that once they begin a study as a research subject, they must continue until the research is complete.
    C. Withhold information about the hypothesis and research purposes.
    D. Use animals to check the side-effects of a drug thought to cure depression.
    E. Carry out a study that causes discomfort in people after securing informed consent that includes full information about possible risks.

5. What are the key elements of an experiment? Design your own experiment and label the variables.

CHAPTER 3

Genes, Evolution, and Environment

LEARNING OBJECTIVES

Unlocking the Secrets of Genes

3.1 - What the chemical code in our genes encodes *for*.

3.2 - What a complete map of the human genes reveals—and does not reveal.

The Genetics of Similarity

3.3 - The meaning of evolution.

3.4 - Why some traits become more common during evolution and others become less common.

3.5 - Why some evolutionary psychologists assume the existence of innate "mental modules" in the human mind.

3.6 - Some innate human characteristics.

Our Human Heritage: Language

3.7 - What language enables us to do that other animals cannot.

3.8 - The evidence that infants' brains are equipped with an innate facility for acquiring language.

3.9 - The evidence that learning and environment influence language development.

Our Human Heritage: Courtship and Mating

3.10 - How evolutionary psychologists explain male–female differences in courtship and mating.

3.11 - Some problems with evolutionary theories of courtship and mating preferences.

3.12 - The basic issue that divides evolutionary psychologists and their critics.

The Genetics of Difference

3.13 - What it means to say that a trait is "heritable."

3.14 - Three important facts about heritability.

3.15 - How researchers estimate a trait's heritability.

Our Human Diversity: The Case of Intelligence

3.16 - The extent to which intelligence may be heritable.

3.17 - The most common error in the argument that one group is genetically smarter than another.

3.18 - How the environment nurtures or thwarts mental ability.

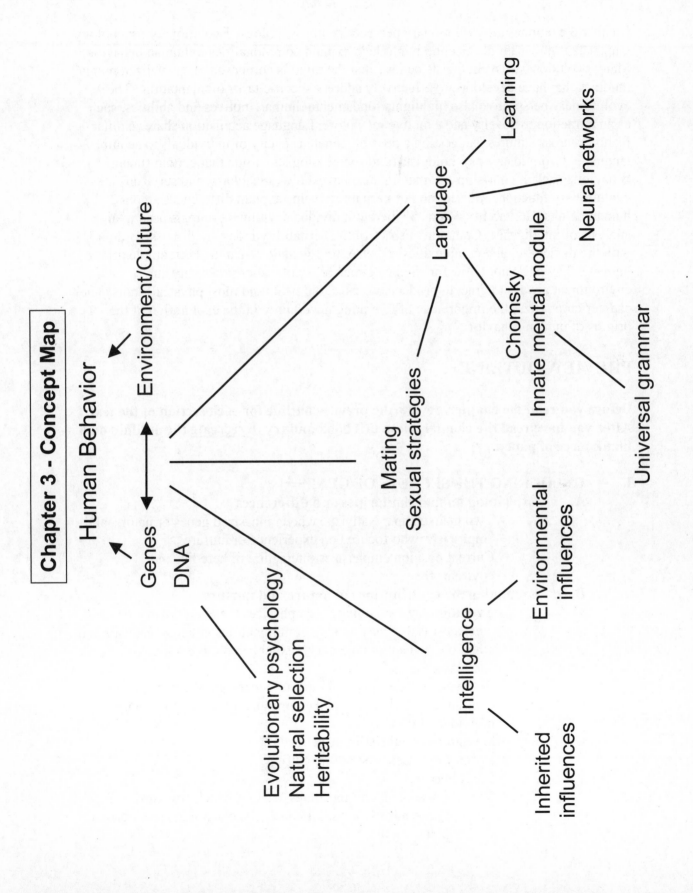

Chapter 3 - Concept Map

Human Behavior

Environment/Culture

Genes

DNA

Evolutionary psychology
Natural selection
Heritability

Mating
Sexual strategies

Intelligence

Environmental
influences

Inherited
influences

Language

Learning

Chomsky
Innate mental module

Neural networks

Universal grammar

BRIEF CHAPTER SUMMARY

Chapter 3 examines the evolutionary perspective in psychology. Evolutionary psychology emphasizes how natural selection might help explain commonalities in human behavior. Many evolutionary psychologists believe that the mind is composed of specialized mental modules that have developed to effectively address specific tasks of adaptation. The evolutionary perspective also highlights fundamental human motives and abilities, such as an attraction to novelty and a motive to explore. Language acquisition shares similar features across cultures, suggesting a possible innate capacity of individuals to acquire language. Evolutionary psychologists (and sociobiologists) argue that certain social behaviors, such as courtship and mating, also have a biological basis and serve an evolutionary function. A discussion of heritability helps explain differences among human beings. Heritability, which applied to individuals within a group, is used in an analysis of intelligence. Common misuses of the heritability index are discussed, along with the difficulties and complexities of behavioral-genetic research. The complexities of human behavior do not allow for simple "either-or" explanations: heredity and environment always interact to produce our psychological (and most physical) traits. The chapter emphasizes the importance of tolerating uncertainty in the exploration of the origins of human behavior.

PREVIEW OUTLINE

Before you read the chapter, review the preview outline for each section of the text. After you have read the chapter, close this book and try to <u>recreate</u> the outlines on a blank piece of paper.

I.   **UNLOCKING THE SECRETS OF GENES**
      A.   **Explaining human similarities and differences**
           1.   Two main camps: Nativists, who emphasized genes or nature, and empiricists, who focused on experience or nurture
           2.   Current position emphasizes interaction of heredity and environment
      B.   **Examining the contributions of nature and nurture**
           1.   **Evolutionary Psychology** – emphasizes the evolutionary mechanisms that may explain commonalities in language, learning, attention, perception, memory, sexual behavior, emotions, and reasoning
           2.   **Behavioral Genetics** – attempts to understand the relative contributions of heredity and environment in order to explain individual differences
      C.   **Definition and characteristics of genes**
           1.   Definition – basic units of heredity
           2.   Characteristics
               a.   Located on chromosomes, each of which contains thousands of genes; all body cells contain 23 chromosome pairs

b.   Chromosomes consist of strands of DNA; genes consist of small segments of this DNA

c.   Some genes are inherited in the same form by everyone; others vary contributing to our individuality

D.   How elements of DNA affect characteristics of the organism
1. Each gene has four basic chemical elements of DNA (A,T,C,G)
2. The order of arrangement helps determine the synthesis of one of the many proteins that affect every aspect of the body

E.   The search for genes that contribute to specific traits
1. It is very difficult to identify a single gene
2. Most traits depend on more than one pair of genes, which makes tracking down the genetic contributions to a trait very difficult
3. Linkage studies – look at genes located close together that may be inherited together across generations
4. Researchers with The Human Genome Project have mapped a rough draft of 3 billion units of DNA
5. Even when a gene is located, its role in physical and psychological functioning is not automatically known

II.   THE GENETICS OF SIMILARITY

A.   Evolutionary psychologists – apply principles of evolution to human psychological qualities and behavior

B.   Evolution and natural selection – General characteristics
1. Definition: evolution is a change in the gene frequencies within a population over many generations
2. Why do frequencies change?
    a.   Variations arise as genes spontaneously mutate and recombine
    b.   Charles Darwin's natural selection: As individuals with a genetically influenced trait become more successful at surviving and reproducing in a particular environment, their genes will become more common in the population and may spread
3. Approach of evolutionary psychology
    a.   Asks what challenges humans faced in prehistoric past and draws inferences about behaviors that might have evolved to solve survival problems – evaluates the inferences using research
    b.   Assumes the human mind evolved as a collection of specialized and independent modules to handle specific survival problems. A particular module may involve several dispersed but interconnected areas of the brain

C.   Innate human characteristics – Common evolutionary history may explain universal abilities such as infant reflexes, interest in novelty, a desire to explore and manipulate objects, an impulse to play, and basic cognitive skills

III. OUR HUMAN HERITAGE: LANGUAGE
A. **The nature of language**
  1. Definition – language is a set of rules for combining elements that are in themselves meaningless into utterances that convey meaning
  2. Humans seem to be the only species that acquires language naturally and that can combine sounds to produce original sentences
  3. Some non human animals can be taught aspects of language
B. **The innate capacity for language**
  1. Noam Chomsky – changed thinking about how language is acquired
      a. Language is not learned bit by bit, but via a language acquisition device, or "mental module" in the brain
      b. Children learn surface structure – the way a sentence is spoken – and deep structure – the meaning of a sentence
      c. Though rules of grammar (syntax) aren't taught to children, they use them to transform surface structures into deep structures
      d. Psycholinguists' arguments to support Chomsky's position
          (1) Children in different cultures go through similar stages of language development – born with a universal grammar
          (2) Children make errors called overregularizations that adults would not, evidence that they are not simply imitating
          (3) Adults do not consistently correct children's syntax yet children learn to speak correctly
          (4) Children not exposed to adult language may invent one of their own
          (5) Infants as young as 7 months can derive simple linguistic rules from a string of sounds
  2. Language may have developed as the human equivalent of mutual grooming, to facilitate the forging of social bonds
  3. Researchers are trying to identify brain modules and genes involved in language acquisition
C. **Learning and language** – experience also plays a role in language
  1. Parents recast or expand on children's sentences, which are then repeated
  2. Biologically-determined critical period for learning language

IV. OUR HUMAN HERITAGE: COURTSHIP AND MATING
A. **Agreement about the role of evolution in simple behaviors, disagreement about complex social behaviors**
B. **Evolution and sexual strategies**

   1. Sociobiologists believes that gender differences in courtship and mating evolved in response to a species' survival needs

   2. Males and females have faced different survival and mating problems, which has led to differences in behaviors

     a. Males compete for fertile females; females "shop" for the male with the best genes since their childbearing is limited

     b. This may explain why males are more promiscuous than females

  C. **Culture and the "genetic leash" – the relative power of biology and culture**

   1. Critics of evolutionary approach argue that

     a. Evolutionary explanations of sexual behaviors are based on stereotypes and actual behaviors often contradict these descriptions

     b. Among humans, sexual behavior is varied and changeable

     c. Responses on surveys are often a poor guide to their actual mating choices

   2. Critics worry that evolutionary arguments will be used to justify inequalities and violence

V. **THE GENETICS OF DIFFERENCE**

  A. **The meaning of heritability**: estimates of the proportion of the total variance in a trait that is attributable to genetic variation within a group

  B. **Facts about heritability**

   1. Heritability estimates apply only to a particular group living in a particular environment, and estimates may differ for different groups

   2. Heritability estimates do <u>not</u> apply to individuals, only to variations within a group

   3. Even highly heritable traits can be modified by environment (e.g., height)

  C. **Computing heritability**

   1. Can't estimate heritability directly; must infer it by studying people whose degree of genetic similarity is known

   2. Researchers study those who share either genes or environments; adopted children, identical twins reared apart, and fraternal twins

VI. **OUR HUMAN DIVERSITY: THE CASE OF INTELLIGENCE**

  A. **Genes and individual differences**

   1. Intelligence quotient – derived from norms provided by standardized tests

   2. IQ tests measure a general quality, though IQ tests have been criticized

   3. The kind of intelligence that produces high IQ scores is highly heritable

4.   Genes might affect intelligence by influencing the total amount of "gray matter"

B.   **The question of group differences**
1.   Focus has been on black-white average differences in IQ scores
2.   Between-group studies: problems and conclusions
    a.   Heritability estimates based on differences <u>within</u> group cannot be used to compare differences <u>between</u> groups
    b.   Black-white IQ differences are influenced by the environment
    c.   Sound methodological studies do not reveal genetic differences between blacks and whites

C.   **The environment and intelligence**
1.   Factors associated with reduced mental ability include poor prenatal care, malnutrition, exposure to toxins, and stressful family circumstances
2.   Healthy and stimulating environments can raise mental performance; experiences such as talking to parents, being encouraged to think things through, and early lessons in the arts (e.g., music, drama) may help

VII.   **BEYOND NATURE VERSUS NURTURE**
A.   **Neither nature nor nurture can entirely explain similarities or differences. Genetic and environmental influences blend and become indistinguishable in the development of any individual**

PRACTICE TEST 1 – Multiple Choice

1. A single gene is likely to influence:
    A. a single trait.
    B. a single preference.
    C. many behaviors.
    D. many individuals.

2. When researchers locate a gene, they:
    A. do not automatically know its role in physical or psychological functioning.
    B. are almost near the final step in understanding the role of that gene.
    C. know exactly what traits are influenced, but not all the behaviors.
    D. know what behavior is influenced, but cannot pinpoint all the traits it applies to.

3. The ability of computer neural networks to learn aspects of language without mental modules or preprogrammed rules suggests that:
    A. computers have an inborn language acquisition device.
    B. children may also learn language features without inborn mental modules.
    C. language is actually a relatively simple behavior.
    D. children can better acquire language by interacting with computers.

4. Genes are:
    A. rod-shaped structures found in every cell of the body.
    B. thread-like strands that make up chromosomes.
    C. one of the four basic elements of DNA.
    D. the basic units of heredity.

5. Chromosomes are:
    A. rod-shaped structures found in every cell of the body.
    B. located on genes.
    C. one of the four basic elements of DNA.
    D. the basic units of heredity.

6. The full set of genes contained in each cell is known as the:
    A. DNA.
    B. chromosome.
    C. genome.
    D. basis.

7. When a sperm and egg unite at conception, the fertilized egg, and all the body cells that eventually develop from it (except for sperm cells and ova) contain:
   A. 46 pairs of chromosomes.
   B. 23 chromosomes.
   C. 46 chromosomes in 23 pairs.
   D. 23 pairs of genes.

8. Which statement describes the relationship among genes, chromosomes, and DNA?
   A. Genes, the basic unit of heredity, are located on chromosomes, which consist of strands of DNA. Genes consist of small segments of DNA molecules.
   B. Genes are composed of chromosomes and DNA.
   C. Chromosomes, the basic unit of heredity, direct the genes and the DNA.
   D. DNA houses both genes and chromosomes in its rod-shaped structures.

9. Parents influence language acquisition by:
   A. speaking to children via surface structure, which children translate to deep structure meaning.
   B. consistently correcting children's syntax.
   C. using universal grammar to help children to acquire inborn mental modules and rules.
   D. recasting and expanding statements, which children then imitate.

10. Evolution describes changes in gene frequencies that take place over:
    A. the lifetime of an individual.
    B. many generations.
    C. a large number of mental modules.
    D. a small number of species.

11. Change in gene frequencies are achieved by:
    A. gene mutations that contribute to survival.
    B. nature adapting to anticipate future conditions.
    C. completely random genetic changes.
    D. species attempting to become more complex.

12. In natural selection, genes that contribute to survival allows members of a species to:
    A. teach their offspring the new genes that contribute to survival.
    B. modify their genetic code over the lifetime of the individual organism.
    C. transmit such random mutations to other species.
    D. produce offspring with similar beneficial genes.

13.   Which of the following is not one of the problems with applying evolutionary theory to human mating preferences?
      A.   Mating varying widely across different cultures.
      B.   Sampling methods have often been limited in scope.
      C.   Much of the data is based on possibly inaccurate questionnaires.
      D.   Evolution cannot account for why females are not more promiscuous.

14.   Specialized and independent components of the brain that handle specific survival problems, such as the need to find food, are called:
      A.   mental modules.
      B.   heritability nodes.
      C.   synapses.
      D.   biological markers.

15.   Psycholinguists suggest that by applying rules that make up the grammar of language, we are able to understand and produce new sentences correctly. These rules are called:
      A.   surface structure.
      B.   overregularizations.
      C.   syntax.
      D.   mental modules.

16.   The phrases "Mitsuko gave the ball to Uyen," and "Uyen received the ball from Mitsuko" have:
      A.   the same surface structure.
      B.   different deep structures.
      C.   the same surface and deep structures.
      D.   the same deep structure.

17.   Though they are learning different languages, Lana from Morocco, Ayse from Turkey, and Paulo from Italy are going through similar stages of language development and combine words in ways that adults never would. This supports the conclusion that:
      A.   language is learned in bits and pieces.
      B.   the syntax of all languages is remarkably similar.
      C.   the brain contains a language acquisition device that allows children to develop language if they are exposed to an adequate sampling of speech.
      D.   language acquisition is primarily the result of imitation of speech.

18.   Chomsky's contribution to the understanding of language acquisition was the idea that:
   A.   language is learned bit by bit, as one might learn a list of U.S. presidents.
   B.   there is a critical period for learning language.
   C.   children go through different stages of language development.
   D.   language is too complex to learn bit by bit, so there must be a "mental module" in the brain that allows young children to develop language.

19.   Which of the following best supports Chomsky's position on language acquisition?
   A.   Children everywhere go through similar stages of linguistic development.
   B.   Children combine words in ways adults never would, which rules out imitation.
   C.   Even children who are profoundly retarded acquire language.
   D.   All of the above support Chomsky's position on language acquisition.

20.   Which of the following reflects the sociobiological view on mating and marriage?
   A.   Marriage and mating behaviors have been learned through reinforcements.
   B.   Males and females have faced different kinds of survival and mating problems and have evolved differently in aggressiveness and sexual strategies.
   C.   Socialization accounts for differences in mating behaviors.
   D.   None of the above reflects the sociobiological position.

21.   "It pays for males to compete for access to fertile females and to try to inseminate as many females as possible; because females can conceive and bear only a limited number of offspring, it pays for them to be selective and look for the best mate." This reflects the position of:
   A.   outdated psychologists.
   B.   an empiricist.
   C.   sociobiology.
   D.   Chomsky.

22.   Critics of the evolutionary approach cite which of the following positions to support their view?
   A.   Though humans and animals may engage in similar behaviors, the motives or origins of the behaviors differ.
   B.   Not all animal and human behavior conforms to the sexual stereotypes.
   C.   Among human beings, sexual behavior is extremely varied and changeable.
   D.   All of the above are arguments used by critics of the evolutionary approach.

23. Heritability:
    A.   estimates the proportion of difference in a trait that is attributable to genetic variation within a group.
    B.   is equivalent in meaning to the term genetic.
    C.   estimates the proportion of a trait that is attributable to genes in an individual.
    D.   estimates the proportion of difference in a trait that is attributable to genetic variation between groups.

24. Heritability can be used to estimate:
    A.   IQ differences between whites and Asians.
    B.   IQ differences among Harvard graduates.
    C.   how much of an individual's IQ is determined by heredity.
    D.   exactly which genes are responsible for intelligence.

25. To study the heritability of a particular trait, which groups of people are studied?
    A.   Adopted children and twins
    B.   Unrelated people
    C.   Biological mothers and daughters
    D.   Husbands and wives

26. Pedro is adopting a child whose biological parents have low IQs. Pedro asks whether this child is also likely to have a low IQ. Which of the following is the best response?
    A.   The child is also quite likely to have a low IQ, since heritability of IQ is high.
    B.   The IQs of the child's biological parents are irrelevant, since environmental influences outweigh heritability.
    C.   While IQ is at least in part heritable, environmental influences can have a great impact; however, it is impossible to make predictions about any individual.
    D.   Nothing is known about the heritability of IQ.

27. Which of the following is a flaw in genetic explanations of black-white differences in IQ?
    A.   Blacks and whites do not grow up, on average, in the same kind of environment.
    B.   Because of racial discrimination and de facto segregation, black children receive less encouragement and fewer opportunities than whites.
    C.   Heritability estimates based on one group (whites) are used to estimate the role heredity plays in differences between groups.
    D.   All of the above are flaws.

28.	Children fathered by black and white American soldiers in Germany after World War II, and reared in similar German communities by similar families, did not differ significantly in IQ. This study
	A.	supports genetic theories explaining black-white IQ differences.
	B.	refutes genetic theories explaining black-white IQ differences.
	C.	has been criticized for methodological errors.
	D.	demonstrates the IQ superiority of blacks over whites.

29.	Two pots of tomatoes were planted with seeds of identical quality. One pot used enriched soil and one pot used impoverished soil. A comparison of the plants from each of these pots is analogous to
	A.	comparing the IQs of two Asian-Americans from similar socioeconomic backgrounds, communities, and school systems.
	B.	looking for a genetic explanation of IQ differences between blacks and whites.
	C.	comparing the IQs of two siblings.
	D.	none of the above

30.	Which of the following is an environmental influence on IQ that can have a negative impact on mental ability?
	A.	Poor prenatal care
	B.	Malnutrition
	C.	Exposure to toxins
	D.	All of the above

31.	Your text mentioned all of the following environmental influences as contributing to intelligence EXCEPT:
	A.	parents reading to their children.
	B.	enrichment classes.
	C.	music lessons.
	D.	sports.

PRACTICE TEST 2 – Short Answer

1. _____ are the basic unit of heredity. They are located on _____.

2. Collectively, the 100,000 or so human genes are referred to as the human _____.

3. It is likely that language development depends on both biological readiness and _____.

4. According to evolutionary psychologists, tendencies to act certain ways and engage in social customs exist because they have contributed to the _____ of our species.

5. As genes become more common or less common in the population, so do the characteristics they influence. This is referred to as _____.

6. Gene frequencies in a population change because genes spontaneously _____.

7. The principle of _____ states that individuals with a particular genetically influenced trait tend to be more successful at staying alive long enough to produce offspring; their genes will become more and more common in the population.

8. Evolutionary psychologists believe that the human mind developed as a collection of specialized and independent _____ to handle specific survival problems.

9. Evolutionary psychologists believe that certain abilities, tendencies, and characteristics evolved because they were useful to our ancestors. Two of these abilities or tendencies include _____ and _____.

10. Language is a set of _____ for combining meaningless _____ into utterances that convey meaning.

11. "Keith kissed Stacy" and "Stacy was kissed by Keith" have the same _____ structure but a different _____ structure.

12. Evolutionary psychologists have suggested that men are more _____ in order to distribute their sperm and genetic material as far as possible.

13. _____ said that language was far too complex to be learned bit by bit. Therefore, there must be an innate mental module for learning language called a language _____ device.

14. One piece of evidence that children have an innate mental module for language is that children in different cultures go through _____ of linguistic development.

15. The basic issue that divides evolutionary scientists and their critics is the _____.

16. Critics of evolutionary approaches to infidelity and monogamy argue that these explanations are based on _____ of gender differences.

17. The proportion of the total variance in a trait that is attributable to genetic variation within a group is called _____.

18. Heritability estimates do not apply to _____.

19. To estimate the heritability of a trait, researchers study _____ and _____ twins.

20. For children and adolescents, heritability estimates of intelligence average around _____ and the estimates for adults are in the _____ range.

21. Genetic explanations for differences in intelligence between blacks and whites are flawed because they use estimates based on a white sample to estimate the role of heredity in _____ differences.

22. Negative environmental influences on mental ability include poor _____ care and _____.

PRACTICE TEST 3 – Essay

1. A. Suppose that you are volunteering at a local drug treatment program. You hear many clients in this program describe their alcoholic family backgrounds and state their belief that their alcoholism is genetic. Using information about genes, chromosomes, and DNA, describe how alcoholism might be genetic.

   B. You attend a lecture in which an author of a self-help book on alcoholism says that alcoholism is fifty percent inherited and, therefore, if you have an alcoholic parent, you have a fifty percent chance of becoming an alcoholic. Discuss the problems with these statements using the facts about heritability.

   C. If you wanted to search for the genes associated with alcoholism, describe the type of study you would conduct and how you would go about collecting your data.

2. Using the approach of evolutionary psychology, expand on the idea that the following characteristics were inherited because they were useful during the history of our species (i.e., they had an evolutionary function).

   A. The feeling of disgust
   B. Intuition
   C. The self-concept
   D. Male promiscuity
   E. Female selectivity

3. Compare and contrast Chomsky's position with the previously accepted position on the acquisition of language. Discuss arguments that support Chomsky's view.

4. A. Describe a study that you would design to evaluate the heritability of intelligence. Describe your conclusions about both hereditary and environmental influences on intelligence. What cautionary statements would you make about the heritability estimate?

   B. Based on your research findings, you are to make recommendations to a federal panel convened to develop a parental training program for low-income families to help them promote intellectual development in their children. Discuss the recommendations you would make to the panel.

CHAPTER 4

The Brain: Source of Mind and Self

LEARNING OBJECTIVES

The Nervous System: A Basic Blueprint
4.1 - The major parts of the nervous system and their primary functions.

Communication in the Nervous System
4.2 - How neurons are structured and how they communicate with one another.
4.3 - The functions of glial cells, the most numerous cells in the brain.
4.4 - Why researchers are excited about the discovery of stem cells in the brain.
4.5 - How learning and experience alter the brain's circuits.
4.6 - What happens when levels of neurotransmitters are too low or too high.
4.7 - Which hormones are of special interest to psychologists, and why.

Mapping the Brain
4.8 - The techniques researchers use for understanding the workings of the brain.
4.9 - The limitations of brain scans as a way of understanding the brain.

A Tour through the Brain
4.10 - The major parts of the brain and some of their major functions.
4.11 - Why it is a good thing that the outer covering of the human brain is so wrinkled.
4.12 - How a bizarre nineteenth-century accident illuminated the role of the frontal lobes.

The Two Hemispheres of the Brain
4.13 - What would happen if the two cerebral hemispheres could not communicate with each other.
4.14 - Why researchers often refer to the left hemisphere as "dominant."
4.15 - Why "left-brainedness" and "right-brainedness" are often exaggerations.

Two Stubborn Issues in Brain Research
4.16 - Why some brain researchers think a unified "self" is only an illusion.
4.17 - Findings and fallacies about sex differences in the brain.

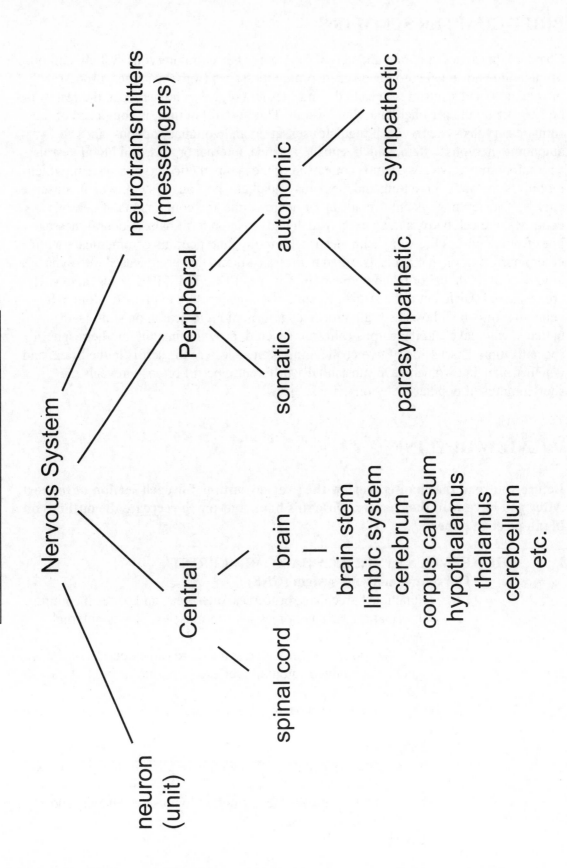

Chapter 4 - Concept Map

Nervous System

neuron (unit)

Central

Peripheral

neurotransmitters (messengers)

spinal cord

brain

brain stem
limbic system
cerebrum
corpus callosum
hypothalamus
thalamus
cerebellum
etc.

somatic

autonomic

parasympathetic

sympathetic

BRIEF CHAPTER SUMMARY

Chapter 4 discusses the brain and nervous system. The central nervous system, composed of the brain and spinal cord, receives incoming messages from the senses, processes that information, and sends messages to the muscles and organs. The nerves in the rest of the body make up the peripheral nervous system. This system, in turn, is composed of the somatic nervous system, which regulates sensation and voluntary actions, and the autonomic nervous system, which regulates glands, internal organs, and blood vessels. The autonomic nervous system is composed of the sympathetic nervous system, which mobilizes the body for action, and the parasympathetic nervous system, which conserves energy. The nervous system is made up of neurons; the key components of neurons are dendrites, the cell body, and an axon, which ends in axon terminals. A neural message goes from dendrites to axon via an electrical impulse, and neurons communicate with other neurons through chemicals called neurotransmitters that are released into synapses. A variety of methods for mapping the brain, such as EEG, TMS, PET scans, and MRI, are discussed. Different brain structures and their functions are explained, along with general issues about how the brain processes information. Research on split-brain patients, who have had the corpus callosum severed, provides insight into hemispheric specialization. Discussion of two challenging issues—where the self is in the brain, and whether men and women have substantially different types of brains—reveals the shortcomings of popular views on these subjects.

PREVIEW OUTLINE

Before you read the chapter, review the preview outline for each section of the text. After you have read the chapter, close this book and try to <u>recreate</u> the outlines on a blank piece of paper.

I. THE NERVOUS SYSTEM: A BASIC BLUEPRINT
   A. The central nervous system (CNS)
      1. Functions – receives, processes, interprets, and stores incoming information; sends out messages to muscles, glands, internal organs
      2. Two components – brain and spinal cord (an extension of the brain which can produce automatic reflexes without the help of the brain)
   B. The peripheral nervous system (PNS) – handles the input and output of the CNS
      1. Functions
         a. Sensory neurons – bring input to CNS from skin, muscles, and organs
         b. Motor neurons – carry output to muscles, glands, and organs
      2. Divisions

        a.   Somatic system (also called skeletal nervous system) – connects to sensory receptors and skeletal muscles

        b.   Autonomic system – regulates blood vessels, glands, organs

             (1)   Sympathetic nervous system – mobilizes body for action

             (2)   Parasympathetic nervous system – slows action

II.   COMMUNICATION IN THE NERVOUS SYSTEM

    A.   Components of the nervous system – include both neurons and glial cells

    B.   The structure of the neuron

        1.   Dendrites – receive messages from other neurons, transmit to cell body

        2.   Cell body – keeps the neuron alive, determines whether neuron fires

        3.   Axon – transmits messages from cell body to neurons, muscles, or glands

        4.   Nerves – bundles of nerve fibers in the PNS

    C.   Neurons in the news

        1.   Neurogenesis – production of new neurons from immature stem cells

        2.   Stem cells – immature cells that renew themselves and have the potential to develop into mature cells

    D.   How neurons communicate

        1.   Synapse – axon terminal, synaptic cleft, membrane of receiving dendrite

        2.   Neural impulses – how neurons communicate

             a.   Electrical impulse, or action potential

             b.   Synaptic vesicles release chemical neurotransmitters

             c.   They excite or inhibit the firing of the receiving neuron

             d.   Neurons either fire or do not fire (all or none principle)

    E.   The plastic brain

        1.   New learning and stimulation promotes neuron growth and synaptic connections

        2.   Unused connections are also pruned away

        3.   Plasticity – brain's ability to change and adapt in response to experience

    F.   Chemical messengers in the nervous system

        1.   Neurotransmitters: Versatile couriers

             a.   Each neurotransmitter binds only to certain types of receptor sites

             b.   Some better understood neurotransmitters and some of their effects

                 (1)   Serotonin – sleep, mood, and other behaviors

                 (2)   Dopamine – movement, learning, memory, emotion

        (3)   Acetylcholine – muscle action, memory, emotion, cognition

        (4)   Norepinephrine – heart rate, learning, memory, emotion

        (5)   GABA – inhibitory neurotransmitter

        (6)   Glutamate – major excitatory neurotransmitter

2.   Endorphins: The brain's natural opiates (endogenous opioid peptides) reduce pain, promote pleasure as well as other behaviors

3.   Hormones: Long-distance messengers

    a.   Produced in endocrine glands and released into the bloodstream

    b.   Some may also be classified as neurotransmitters

    c.   Hormones of interest to psychologists include melatonin (regulates biological rhythms), adrenal hormones (related to emotion and stress), and sex hormones (androgens, estrogens, progesterone)

    d.   Hormones that are of interest to psychologists

        (1) Melatonin – regulates biological rhythms and promotes sleep

        (2) Oxytocin – enhances uterine contractions during childbirth

        (3) Adrenal hormones – involved in emotion and stress

        (4) Sex hormones – include androgens, estrogen, and progesterone

MAPPING THE BRAIN – Methods for studying the brain

    A.   **Lesion method** – damaging or removing section of brain in animals

    B.   **Electrode methods** – detect electrical activity of the neurons

        1.   Electroencephalogram (EEG)

        2.   Needle electrodes and microelectrodes (into a single cell)

    C.   **Transcranial Magnetic Stimulation (TMS)**

        1.   Wire coil around head produces magnetic field

        2.   Produce motor responses or inactivate an area of the brain

    D.   **Positron-Emission Tomography – PET scan**

        1.   Records biochemical changes in the brain as they occur

        2.   Injects a radioactive substance to indicate brain activity

    E.   **Magnetic Resonance Imaging (MRI)**

        1.   Uses magnetic fields and radio frequencies

        2.   New "functional MRI" captures brain changes very quickly

    F.   **Cautions about brain research**

        1.   Findings are difficult to interpret and can be manipulated

        2.   Results don't tell us what is happening inside the person's head

        3.   Each brain, like fingerprints, is unique

III.   **A TOUR THROUGH THE BRAIN**

    A.   **Localization of function** – different brain parts perform different tasks

B.   **The brain stem** – rises out of spinal cord
        1.   Medulla – regulates automatic functions; breathing and heart rate
        2.   Pons – regulates sleeping, waking, and dreaming
        3.   Reticular activating system – network of neurons, extends upward and connects with higher brain areas; screens information, alertness

C.   **The cerebellum** – Atop brain stem; regulates balance and coordination of muscle movement; may play a role in remembering skills, analyzing sensory information

D.   **The thalamus** – Relays motor impulses out of brain, directs incoming sensory messages to higher centers

E.   **The hypothalamus** – associated with survival drives, such as hunger, thirst, emotion, sex and reproduction, body temperature

F.   **Pituitary gland** – "master gland" governed by hypothalamus

G.   **Limbic system** – loosely interconnected structures involved in emotions
        1.   Amygdala – evaluates sensory information to determine its importance
        2.   Hippocampus – allows formation and storage of new memories

H.   **Cerebrum** – site of higher forms of thinking
        1.   Divided into two halves or cerebral hemispheres that are connected by a band of fibers called the corpus callosum
            a.   Each hemisphere controls the opposite side of the body
            b.   Each hemisphere has somewhat different talents (lateralization)
        2.   Cerebral cortex – layers of densely packed cells covering the cerebrum
            a.   Occipital lobes – contain the visual cortex
            b.   Parietal lobes – contain somatosensory cortex
            c.   Temporal lobes – involved in memory, perception, and emotion
            d.   Frontal lobes – contain the motor cortex; responsible for making plans and thinking creatively, Broca's area (speech production)
        3.   Phineas Gage – Damage to prefrontal cortex resulting in personality changes

IV.   **THE TWO HEMISPHERES OF THE BRAIN**
    A.   **Split brains: A house divided**
        1.   Normal brain – the two hemispheres communicate via the corpus callosum
        2.   Split brain refers to surgery in which the corpus callosum is severed
        3.   Daily lives of split-brain patients were not much affected, but effects on perception and memory are observable under experimental conditions

B.   The two hemispheres: Allies or Opposites?
1.   Many researchers believe the left side is dominant because cognitive skills – including language, rational and analytic abilities – originate here
2.   Others point to abilities of the right hemisphere: superior spatial-visual abilities, facial recognition, nonverbal sounds, music appreciation
3.   Differences are relative; in real life, the hemispheres cooperate

V.   TWO STUBBORN ISSUES IN BRAIN RESEARCH
A.   Where is the self?
1.   Most neuroscientists believe that the mind can be explained in physical terms as a product of the cerebral cortex
2.   One theorist suggests the brain consists of independent parts that deal with different aspects of thought; another suggests that a unified self is an illusion and that the brain is independent modules working in parallel
B.   Are there "his" and "hers" brains?
1.   Efforts to identify male-female differences have reflected biases
2.   Some evidence that male and female brains are different, but many conclusions can be drawn and findings often have changed
3.   Problems exists with conclusions drawn by popular writers about sex differences in the brain

VI.   COSMETIC NEUROLOGY: TINKERING WITH THE BRAIN
A.   Neuroethics – interdisciplinary specialty that focuses on the legal, ethical, and scientific implications of research

Complete this chart by identifying the function that corresponds to the brain structure listed in the left column.

BRAIN STRUCTURE	FUNCTION
BRAIN STEM	
Medulla	
Pons	
Reticular Activating System	
CEREBELLUM	
THALAMUS	
Olfactory Bulb	
HYPOTHALAMUS	
PITUITARY GLAND	
LIMBIC SYSTEM	
Amygdala	
Hippocampus	
CEREBRUM	
Left Cerebral Hemisphere	
Right Cerebral Hemisphere	
Corpus Callosum	
Cerebral Cortex	
Occipital Lobes	
Temporal Lobes	
Parietal Lobes	
Frontal Lobes	

PRACTICE TEST 1 – Multiple Choice

1. The function of the central nervous system is to:
   A. receive, process, and interpret incoming information.
   B. send out messages to muscles.
   C. send out messages to glands and organs.
   D. all of the above.

2. The peripheral nervous system:
   A. is composed of the brain and spinal cord.
   B. handles the central nervous system's input and output.
   C. depends exclusively on sensory neurons.
   D. depends exclusively on motor neurons.

3. The _____ receives, processes, interprets, and stores incoming information from the senses and sends out messages destined for the muscles, glands, and internal organs. The _____ handles its input and output.
   A. central nervous system; peripheral nervous system
   B. peripheral nervous system; autonomic nervous system
   C. sympathetic nervous system; parasympathetic nervous system
   D. peripheral nervous system; central nervous system

4. The _____ nervous system is part of the peripheral nervous system.
   A. somatic
   B. sympathetic
   C. autonomic
   D. all of the above

5. One function of the somatic nervous system is to:
   A. carry information from the senses to the CNS and from the CNS to the skeletal muscles.
   B. carry information to the glands and organs.
   C. control the sympathetic and parasympathetic nervous systems.
   D. process information in the brain.

6. The autonomic nervous system is involved with:
   A. voluntary responses.
   B. the nerves connected to the senses and skeletal muscles.
   C. involuntary responses such as the regulation of blood vessels and glands.
   D. sensory nerves.

7. The sympathetic nervous system governs _____ responses, whereas the parasympathetic nervous system governs _____ responses.
   A. voluntary; involuntary
   B. involuntary; voluntary
   C. arousal; relaxing
   D. sensory; motor

8. Neurons:
   A. are the basic units of the nervous system.
   B. are held in place by glial cells.
   C. transmit electrical messages throughout the nervous system.
   D. are characterized by all of the above.

9. The three main parts of the neuron are the:
   A. dendrites, cell body, and axon.
   B. axon, dendrites, and synapse.
   C. synapse, impulse, and cleft.
   D. myelin sheath, dendrites, and synapse.

10. The _____ receive messages from other neurons, whereas the _____ carry messages on to other neurons or to muscle or gland cells.
    A. cell bodies; dendrites
    B. dendrites; axons
    C. axons; dendrites
    D. myelin sheaths; cell bodies

11. Neurons are like catchers and batters. The _____ are like catchers because they receive information; the _____ are like batters because they send on the message.
    A. dendrites; axons
    B. cell bodies; axons
    C. axons; dendrites
    D. dendrites; glials

12. The cell body:
    A. determines whether the neuron should fire.
    B. receives incoming impulses from other neurons.
    C. speeds the conduction of the neural impulse.
    D. connects with the synapse.

13.   When a neural impulse reaches the tip of the axon terminal:
      A.   the neuron fires.
      B.   synaptic vesicles in the synaptic end bulb release neurotransmitters that
           cross the synaptic cleft and lock into receptor sites on the post-synaptic
           neuron.
      C.   the synaptic end bulb sends an electrical current into the dendrites of the
           next neuron.
      D.   the synaptic end bulb locks into the receptor sites on the post-synaptic
           dendrites.

14.   Glial cells are responsible for:
      A.   supplying neurons with nutrients and removing waste.
      B.   transmitting information to other neurons.
      C.   extending the reach of a neuron's axon terminals.
      D.   moving the neuron to various locations throughout the nervous system.

15.   How do neurotransmitters affect the post-synaptic neuron?
      A.   They cause a change in the electrical potential, exciting the neuron and
           causing it to fire.
      B.   They cause a change in the electrical potential, either exciting or inhibiting
           the next neuron.
      C.   They cause a change in the electrical potential, inhibiting the neuron and
           stopping it from firing.
      D.   They do not make contact with the next neuron, remaining in the synapse.

16.   Serotonin, dopamine, acetylcholine, and norepinephrine are:
      A.   adrenal hormones.
      B.   endorphins.
      C.   sex hormones.
      D.   neurotransmitters.

17.   Mood, sleep, appetite, pain suppression, sensory perception, and temperature
      regulation are all influenced by:
      A.   dopamine.
      B.   serotonin.
      C.   endorphins.
      D.   all of the above.

18.   Stem cells are interesting to psychologists because they have the potential to:
      A.   inhibit the neurogenesis of undesirable cells.
      B.   renew themselves and develop into mature cells.
      C.   protect the brain from hazardous toxins.
      D.   bond to the receptor sites from various neurotransmitters.

19. Sleep disorders, epilepsy, and memory problems have all been linked to:
    A.   the loss of the prefrontal cortex.
    B.   excessive production of glial cells.
    C.   axons that have shrunk in length.
    D.   abnormal neurotransmitter levels.

20. Melatonin is involved in:
    A.   regulation of biological rhythms.
    B.   sexual arousal.
    C.   enhancement of memory.
    D.   production of milk during nursing.

21. The _____ is a method for analyzing biochemical activity in the brain that uses injections containing a harmless radioactive element.
    A.   MRI (magnetic resonance imaging)
    B.   PET scan (positron-emission tomography)
    C.   EEG (electroencephalogram)
    D.   TMS (transcranial magnetic stimulation)

22. Brain stem is to _____ as cerebrum is to _____.
    A.   emotions; vital functions
    B.   vital functions; emotions
    C.   higher forms of thinking; vital functions
    D.   vital functions; higher forms of thinking

23. The limbic system includes the:
    A.   cortex and corpus callosum.
    B.   spinal cord and brain.
    C.   cerebellum and brain stem.
    D.   amygdala and hippocampus.

24. The _____ has deep crevasses and wrinkles that enable it to contain billions of neurons without requiring people to have the heads of giants.
    A.   corpus callosum
    B.   cerebral cortex
    C.   cerebellum
    D.   hypothalamus

25. The four distinct lobes of the cortex are the:
    A.   occipital, parietal, temporal, and frontal lobes.
    B.   sensory, auditory, visual, and motor lobes.
    C.   hind, mid, fore, and association lobes.
    D.   front, back, side, and top lobes.

26. Which of the following best summarizes the different hemispheric functions?
    A. The left brain is more active in logic, and the right brain is associated with visual-spatial abilities.
    B. The left brain is more active in artistic and intuitive tasks, and the right brain is more involved in emotional and expressive abilities.
    C. The left brain contains visual-spatial abilities, whereas the right brain is more involved in artistic and creative activities.
    D. The right brain is more dominant, and the left brain is more subordinate.

27. Emotion and stress are influenced by:
    A. oxytocin.
    B. sex hormones.
    C. melatonin.
    D. adrenal hormones.

28. Localization of function refers to the fact that:
    A. personality traits are reflected in different areas of the brain.
    B. information is distributed across large areas of the brain.
    C. different brain parts perform different jobs and store different sorts of information.
    D. brain processes are like holography.

29. The issue of whether there are sex differences in the brain is controversial because:
    A. evidence of anatomical sex differences in humans is contradictory.
    B. findings have flip-flopped as a result of the biases of the observers.
    C. even if anatomical differences exist, we do not know what they mean.
    D. all of the above.

30. Throughout life, new learning results in the establishment of new synaptic connections in the brain, with stimulating environments producing the greatest changes. Conversely, some unused synaptic connections are lost as cells or their branches die and are not replaced. This indicates that the brain:
    A. is more lateralized than scientists once thought.
    B. continues to develop and change in response to the environment.
    C. develops new brain cells on a regular and ongoing basis.
    D. is more holistic than scientists once thought.

31. One limitation of brain scans for locating the center of certain activities is:
    A. the variability of brains between individuals.
    B. that scans cannot pinpoint the specific location of activity.
    C. these activities show up as different colors on different scans.
    D. current technology cannot examine both structure and activity simultaneously.

32. When a 3½-foot iron rod was driven through Phineas Gage's head, he:
    A. died instantly.
    B. lost the ability to form new memories.
    C. experienced a profound change in personality.
    D. was unable to perform complex motor activities.

33. Some researchers have referred to the left hemisphere as dominant because:
    A. it controls the hand most frequently used for writing and other tasks.
    B. of its influence as the primary determinant of personality.
    C. of the role it plays in processing aggression.
    D. it is more involved in complex cognitive skills.

34. Which of the following is true?
    A. Both hemispheres of the brain are typically cooperative for everyday activities.
    B. The left side of the brain is more critical to normal functioning.
    C. The left and right sides of the brain are frequently contradicting each other.
    D. All behaviors and abilities are equally controlled by both parts of the brain.

35. The self may be an illusion because:
    A. the corpus callosum deteriorates over time leading to split personality.
    B. brain scans have demonstrated the self is located in different places in different people.
    C. most people do not have a regulated sense of self.
    D. the different parts of the brain appear to work independently to produce a unifed self.

PRACTICE TEST 2 – Short Answer

1. The nervous system is divided into two main parts: the _____ nervous system, which receives, processes, interprets, and stores incoming information, and the _____ nervous system, which contains all parts of the nervous system outside the brain and spinal cord.

2. The peripheral nervous system is divided into the _____ nervous system, which controls the skeletal muscles and permits voluntary action, and the _____ nervous system, which regulates blood vessels, glands, and internal organs and works more or less without a person's conscious control.

3. The autonomic nervous system is divided into the _____ nervous system, which mobilizes the body for action and increases energy, and the _____ nervous system, which conserves and stores energy.

4. The _____ contains the biochemical machinery for keeping the neuron alive.

5. The _____ of a neuron receive messages from other nerve cells and transmit them toward the cell body. The _____ transmits messages away from the cell body to other cells.

6. Most neurons are insulated by a layer of fatty tissue called the _____ that prevents signals from adjacent cells from interfering with each other and speeds up the conduction of neural impulses.

7. Individual neurons are separated by tiny gaps called the _____.

8. When an electrical impulse reaches the _____ of a neuron, chemical substances called _____ are released into the synapse. Once across the synapse, the molecules fit into sites on the receiving neuron, changing the membrane of the receiving cell.

9. What any given neuron does at any given moment depends on the net effect of all the messages being received from other neurons. The message that reaches a final destination depends on the rate at which individual neurons are firing, how many are firing, what types are firing, and where they are located. It does NOT depend on how strongly neurons are firing because the firing of a neuron is a(n) _____ event.

10. _____ are chemical messengers that reduce pain and promote pleasure. Dopamine, serotonin, and norepinephrine are examples of another type of chemical messenger called _____.

11. Hormones originate primarily in the _____ glands, which deposit them into the bloodstream where they are carried to organs and cells.

12. Neurotransmitters affect a variety of behaviors. Low levels of _____ and _____ may be implicated in severe depression; _____ affects memory and loss of cells producing this neurotransmitter may help account for some of the symptoms of Alzheimer's disease.

13. The three main types of sex hormones that occur in both sexes (though in differing amounts) are _____, _____, and _____.

14. The procedure for recording neural activity by use of electrodes is called a(n) _____.

15. Other methods of investigating living brains are PET scans, which record biochemical changes in the brain as they are happening, and _____ which utilize magnetic fields and radio frequencies to explore the "inner space" of the brain.

16. This dense network of neurons, which extends above the brain stem into the center of the brain and has connections with higher areas, screens incoming information and arouses the higher centers when something happens that demands their attention. Without the _____ system, we could not be alert or perhaps even conscious.

17. The structures of the brain stem include the _____ that is responsible for sleeping, waking, and dreaming, and the _____, that is responsible for bodily functions like breathing and heart rate. Standing atop the brain stem, the _____ contributes to a sense of balance and muscle coordination.

18. The _____ is like a busy traffic officer that directs sensory messages from the spinal cord to higher brain centers.

19. The _____ sits beneath the thalamus and is involved with drives vital for survival, such as hunger, thirst, emotion, sex, and reproduction.

20. The _____ system is strongly linked to emotions.

21. Case histories of brain-damaged people such as H.M. indicate that the _____ enables us to store new information for future use.

22. The cerebral cortex, the layer of cells that covers the cerebrum, is divided into four distinct lobes. The _____ lobes contain the visual cortex, the _____ lobes contain the somatosensory cortex, the _____ contain the auditory cortex, and the _____ lobes contain the motor cortex.

23. A large bundle of nerve fibers called the _____ connects the two cerebral hemispheres.

24. There are two main language areas in the brain. _____ area is involved in language comprehension and is located in the _____ lobe, and _____ area is involved in speech production and is located in the _____ lobe.

25. To examine the issue of sex differences, we need to ask two separate questions: Do physical differences actually exist in male and female brains, and if so, what do they have to do with _____?

26. _____ insulate neurons and protect them from toxic agents.

27. The production of new neurons from immature cells is known as _____ and this process is promoted by cells known as _____.

28. Hormones that are of particular interest to psychologists are _____, _____, _____, and _____.

29. Brain scans can tell us _____ things happen, but not _____ they happen.

30. The _____ of Phineas Gage's brain was damaged when an iron rod was propelled through his head.

31. _____ is more active in logical, symbolic, and sequential tasks.

PRACTICE TEST 3 – Essay

1. You are sitting at your desk trying to study for a test you are very nervous about, and all you can focus on is the stereo playing in the other room. You get up, go to the other room, and turn down the stereo. Beginning with the external stimuli (the sound) and ending with your movement to the other room, describe:
   A. from the standpoint of a single neuron
   B. the brain structures that are involved, in sequence
   C. the nervous system involvement

2. For each scenario, indicate the brain structure(s) most likely to be involved in the behavior that is described.
   A. Dr. Sanchez inserts an electrode into a structure within the brain. As this electrode is activated, the person sweats and shivers, feels hungry and thirsty, and sometimes even seems angry and sexually aroused.
   B. A computer-enhanced image has enabled a research team to observe the flow of information within the nervous system. While watching this flow, the researchers notice that incoming sensory messages are relayed through this center before finally reaching their destination in the cerebral hemispheres.
   C. As a result of a serious automobile accident, Pedro's ability to make plans and show initiative was seriously impaired.
   D. Bjorn's great grandmother has had a serious stroke. As a result, she is unable to speak, though she appears to understand and respond non-verbally to what is being said.
   E. Yuko's elderly neighbor is showing signs of memory loss.
   F. Maria has been unable to continue as a gymnast since the lower rear area of her brain was damaged in a car accident. All tasks requiring balance or coordinated movements are beyond Maria's capacities.

3. As a result of mixing tranquilizers and alcohol, Helen has become what is called "brain dead," and though she does not respond to people, she continues to live without any life-sustaining equipment. Which parts of her brain have been damaged and which parts continue to function?

4. In the descriptions that follow, cortical functions are disrupted in various ways. From the descriptions identify the cortical structures and state their functions.

    A. Removing a tumor from an area just behind her forehead has dramatically altered Denise's personality. Previously outgoing and warm, she is now hostile and needs prodding to get anything done.

    B. Lately Rashad has been experiencing tingling sensations in various body parts and he sometimes "forgets" where his hands and fingers are. Tests reveal a growth near the surface of the brain just under the center of his head.

    C. Hazan has a large blind spot in his visual field and doctors have eliminated the possibility of eye and optic nerve problems.

5. In the examples below, identify whether the phenomena are primarily related to the functioning of the right hemisphere, the left hemisphere, or both.

    A. Ken is being tested for school placement. Part of the test involves putting puzzle pieces together so they form geometric shapes. Ken performs well.

    B. Another portion of the test involves reading simple sentences aloud. Ken garbles the words and says them in an improper sequence.

    C. A third portion of the test requires Ken to respond to sets of photographs, each set containing five pictures of a person posed identically except for facial expression.

    D. The last portion of the test assesses manual dexterity in the non dominant arm and hand. Because Ken is left-handed, he is required to perform all sorts of mechanical tasks with his right hand. He fails this part of the test.

    E. What overall conclusion might be reached about Ken's hemispheric functioning?

CHAPTER 5

Body Rhythms and Mental States

LEARNING OBJECTIVES

Biological Rhythms: The Tides of Experience
5.1 - How biological rhythms affect our physiology and performance.
5.2 - Why you feel out of sync when you fly across time zones or change shifts at work.
5.3 - Why some people get the winter blues.
5.4 - How culture and learning affect reports of "PMS" and estimates of its incidence.

The Rhythms of Sleep
5.5 - The stages of sleep.
5.6 - How sleep gets disrupted and the consequences that result.
5.7 - The mental benefits of sleep.

Exploring the Dream World
5.8 - Freud's theory that dreams are the "royal road to the unconscious."
5.9 - How dreams might be related to your current problems and concerns.
5.10 - How dreams might be related to ordinary daytime thoughts.
5.11 - How dreams could be caused by meaningless brain-stem signals.

The Riddle of Hypnosis
5.12 - Common misconceptions about what hypnosis can do.
5.13 - The legitimate uses of hypnosis in psychology and medicine.
5.14 - Two ways of explaining what happens during hypnosis.

Consciousness-Altering Drugs
5.15 - The major types of psychoactive drugs
5.16 - How recreational drugs affect the brain.
5.17 - How people's prior drug experiences, individual characteristics, expectations, and mental sets influence their reactions to drugs.

Chapter 5 - Concept Map

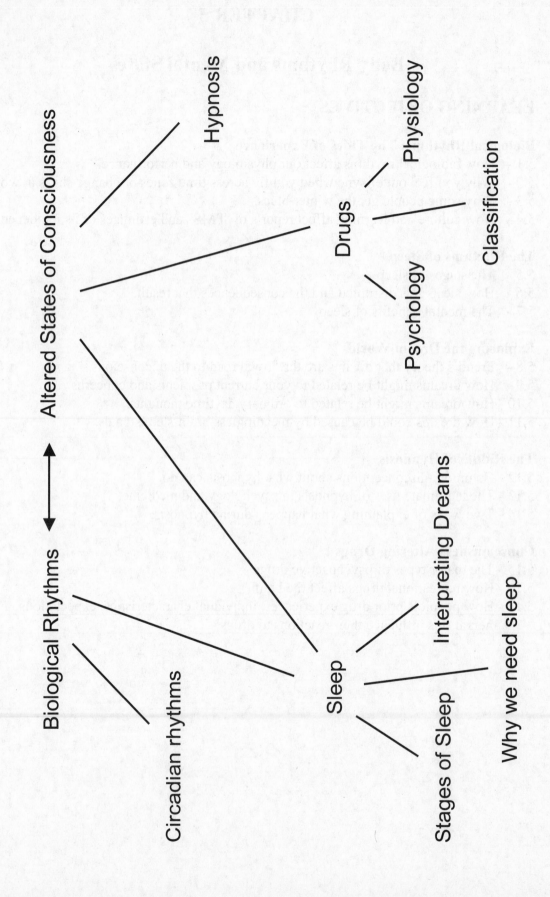

BRIEF CHAPTER SUMMARY

Chapter 5 examines biological rhythms and states of consciousness. Circadian rhythms are biological rhythms that have an approximately 24-hour cycle. The effects of internal desynchronization and hormones are discussed. During the sleep cycle, four stages of non rapid eye movement (NREM) sleep alternate with rapid eye movement sleep (REM) approximately every ninety minutes during the night. Dreaming is more likely to happen during REM sleep. Although the purpose of dreams is not conclusively known, psychologists have proposed several explanations, such as dreams as the "royal road to the unconscious" (Freud), dreams as thinking, dreams as efforts to deal with problems, and the activation synthesis theory. The characteristics of hypnosis are discussed, as are the two principal theories of hypnosis: the dissociative theories (and the hidden observer) and the sociocognitive approach. Several myths about hypnosis (e.g., that hypnosis has enormous effects on memory) are refuted. Classes of consciousness-altering drugs include stimulants, depressants, opiates, and psychedelics.

PREVIEW OUTLINE

Before you read the chapter, review the preview outline for each section of the text. After you have read the chapter, close this book and try to <u>recreate</u> the outlines on a blank piece of paper.

I. **BIOLOGICAL RHYTMS: THE TIDES OF EXPERIENCE**
    A.   **Definitions**
          1.   Consciousness – awareness of oneself and the environment
          2.   Biological rhythms – 5 regular fluctuations in biological systems
          3.   Endogenous rhythms – occur in absence of external cues
    B.   **Circadian rhythms** – occur roughly every 24 hours; exist in plants, animals, insects, and humans
          1.   The body's clock
               a.   Controlled by the suprachiasmatic nucleus (SCN)
               b.   SCN regulates neurotransmitters and hormones (e.g., melatonin)
          2.   When the clock is out of sync
               a.   Change in routine may cause internal desynchronization
               b.   Cycles are affected by environmental and individual factors

C. **Mood and long-term rhythms**
1.   Does the season affect moods? Seasonal affective disorder (SAD) less prevalent than commonly thought
2.   Does the menstrual cycle affect moods?
   a.   Clear support for *emotional* symptoms of premenstrual syndrome (PMS) is lacking
   b.   Research on hormonal (testosterone) influences on men is lacking
   c.   Conclusion – few people of either sex are likely to undergo personality shifts because of hormones

II. **THE RHYTHMS OF SLEEP**
    A. **The realms of sleep** – sleep is not an unbroken state of rest
        1.   Cycle (series of stages) occurs every 90 minutes on average
            a.   Four non-REM stages, each deeper than the previous
                1 – small, irregular brain waves; light sleep
                2 – high-peaking waves called sleep spindles
                3 – delta waves begin; slow with high peaks
                4 – mostly delta waves and deep sleep
            b.   REM sleep (also called paradoxical sleep) is characterized by active brain waves, eye movement, loss of muscle tone, and vivid dreams
            c.   REM and non-REM sleep alternates throughout the night, with REM stages getting longer and closer together, and deeper sleep (stages 3 and 4) getting shorter
    B. **Why we sleep**
            a.   Sleep is recuperative for the body
            b.   Sleep is necessary for normal mental functioning
            c.   Causes of daytime sleepiness
                (1)   Sleep apnea – breathing periodically stops during sleep
                (2)   Narcolepsy – unpredictable daytime attacks of sleepiness
                (3)   Not getting recommended amount of sleep
            d.   Mental benefits of sleep
                (1)   Consolidation – memories stored more effectively
                (2)   Sleep enhances problem solving

III. **EXPLORING THE DREAM WORLD**
    A. **Characteristics of dreams** – inward focus of attention, lucid dreams
    B. **Theories of dreams** – every culture has its theories about dreams
        1.   Dreams as unconscious wishes (Freud)
            a.   Manifest content – what we experience and remember
            b.   Latent content – hidden, symbolic; unconscious wishes
        2.   Dreams as efforts to deal with problems (problem-focused approach)

a.   Reflect ongoing, conscious concerns of waking life

b.   Opportunity for resolving problems

3.   Dreams as thinking (cognitive approach)

     a.   Brain does similar work as when awake, but more unfocused

4.   Dreams as interpreted brain activity (activation-synthesis theory)

     a.   Dreams are the result of neurons firing spontaneously (activation) in the lower brain (in the pons) that are sent to the cortex

     b.   Signals from pons have no meaning, but the cortex tries to make sense of (synthesize) them

IV.   THE RIDDLE OF HYPNOSIS

A.   **Definition** – procedure in which the practitioner suggests changes in the sensations, perceptions, thoughts, feelings, or behavior of the subject

B.   **The nature of hypnosis** – researchers agree on the following:

1.   Responsiveness depends more on person being hypnotized than on the hypnotist's skill

2.   Participants cannot be forced to do things against their will; hypnotic inductions increase suggestibility but only to a modest degree

3.   Feats performed under hypnosis can be performed by motivated people without hypnosis

4.   Hypnosis does not increase the accuracy of memory; it can increase amount of information remembered, but it also increases errors

5.   Does not produce a literal re-experiencing of long-ago events

6.   Hypnosis has been effective for medical and psychological purposes

C.   **Theories of hypnosis** – two competing theories predominate

1.   Dissociation theories – a split in consciousness in which one part of the mind operates independently of the rest of consciousness; hidden observer

2.   The sociocognitive approach

     a.   The effects are a result of the interaction between the hypnotist and the abilities, beliefs, and expectations of the subject

     b.   People are playing the role of a hypnotized person without faking

V.   CONSCIOUSNESS-ALTERING DRUGS

A.   **Altering mood and consciousness**

1.   Efforts to alter mood and consciousness appear to be universal

2.   During the 1960s, many sought to deliberately alter consciousness

B. **Classifying drugs**
    1.   Psychoactive drug – substance affecting perception, mood, thinking, memory, or behavior by changing the body's biochemistry
    2.   Classified according to the drug's effects on central nervous system
        a.   Stimulants – speed up activity in central nervous system; include cocaine, amphetamines, nicotine, caffeine, cocaine
        b.   Depressants (sedatives) – slow down activity in central nervous system; include alcohol, tranquilizers, barbiturates
        c.   Opiates – relieve pain and mimic endorphins; include opium, morphine, heroin, methadone
        d.   Psychedelics – alter normal thought and sometimes produce hallucinations; include LSD, mescaline, psilocybin
        e.   Marijuana – don't fit other classifications

C. **The physiology of drug effects**
    1.   Effects produced by acting on neurotransmitters in a variety of ways
    2.   Some drugs lead to tolerance and withdrawal

D. **The psychology of drug effects** – The effects of a drug depend on more than chemical properties, but also psychological factors
    1.   Experience with the drug refers to the number of times a person has taken it
    2.   Individual characteristics – including body weight, metabolism, initial state of emotional arousal, personality characteristics, and physical tolerance for the drug
    3.   Environmental setting – the context in which a person take the drug
    4.   Mental set – a person's expectations about the drug's effects and reasons for taking it

PRACTICE TEST 1 – Multiple Choice

1.   A circadian rhythm is an example of a:
   A.   biological rhythm.
   B.   mental set.
   C.   psychosomatic pattern.
   D.   psychoactive affect.

2.   As part of a research study, Isamu is living in a comfortable room with a DVD
   and iPod, but there are no windows, clocks, or sounds coming in from outside.
   He is told to eat, sleep, and work whenever he feels like doing so. The purpose of
   this study most likely is to:
   A.   examine sensory deprivation.
   B.   examine the affect of daylight on depression.
   C.   explore endogenous circadian rhythms.
   D.   explore intrinsic motivation.

3.   Circadian rhythms last approximately:
   A.   1 hour.
   B.   12 hours.
   C.   24 hours.
   D.   1 week.

4.   When individuals are unaware of the actual time, their "day" cycle typically
   averages:
   A.   exactly 24 hours.
   B.   about 28 hours.
   C.   slightly more than 24 hours.
   D.   only 12 hours.

5.   Dorlene suffers from extreme depression during the winter months, which doesn't
   let up until the spring. Dorlene most likely could be diagnosed with:
   A.   circadian fragmentation disorder.
   B.   REM desentization disorder.
   C.   winter malady disorder.
   D.   seasonal affective disorder.

6.   Due to stress at work, Pablo has had his sleep disrupted for several weeks and
   hasn't slept at all for the past several days. He may begin to suffer:
   A.   damaged brain cells.
   B.   loss of creativity and attention.
   C.   hallucinations and delusions.
   D.   all of the above.

7. Which of the following can desynchronize circadian rhythms?
   A. An overseas trip
   B. Switching shifts at work
   C. Going on daylight savings time
   D. All of the above

8. Menstrual cycle research on hormones and mood shifts suggests that:
   A. for most people, hormones are reliably and strongly correlated with mood.
   B. hormonal shifts cause mood shifts.
   C. mood changes cause hormonal shifts.
   D. no causal relationship has been established between hormonal shifts and moods.

9. Which of the following conclusions reflects the findings on premenstrual symptoms?
   A. The idea of mood swings as a premenstrual symptom has been questioned since men and women don't differ in the number of mood swings they experience in a month.
   B. For most women, the relationship between cycle stage and symptoms is weak.
   C. There is no reliable relationship between cycle stage and work efficiency.
   D. All of the above.

10. Sleep is necessary:
    A. because of its recuperative properties.
    B. because the brain requires sleep.
    C. to repair cells and remove waste products from the muscles.
    D. for all of the above reasons.

11. The brain waves that occur when you first go to bed and relax are called:
    A. alpha waves.
    B. delta waves.
    C. beta waves.
    D. gamma waves.

12. Fatima is a subject in a sleep study. When her brain emits occasional short bursts of rapid, high-peaking waves called sleep spindles, she is in which stage of sleep?
    A. Stage 1
    B. Stage 3
    C. Stage 2
    D. Stage 4

13. REM sleep is called paradoxical sleep because:
    A. dreams are often paradoxical, and they occur most often in REM sleep.
    B. the brain is extremely active but the body is devoid of muscle tone.
    C. people are easily awakened, even though it is a deep sleep.
    D. the brain is very calm and inactive, but the body is quite active.

14. After the first 30 to 45 minutes of sleep, you have progressed from stage 1 sleep to stage 4 sleep. After this, you most likely:
    A. go into a prolonged non-REM period.
    B. enter REM sleep.
    C. progress back up the ladder from stage 4 to stage 3 to stage 2 to stage 1.
    D. go back to stage 1 and continue through the four stages all night.

15. The most vivid dreams occur during:
    A. the menstrual cycle.
    B. REM sleep.
    C. stage 1 sleep.
    D. non-REM sleep.

16. Serge has lost one night's sleep. He may begin to suffer:
    A. damaged brain cells.
    B. loss of creativity and attention.
    C. hallucinations and delusions.
    D. all of the above.

17. According to the _____, dreams express our unconscious desires.
    A. information-processing approach
    B. psychoanalytic approach
    C. activation-synthesis hypothesis
    D. problem-solving hypothesis

18. Which hypothesis suggests that dreams result from cortical attempts to interpret spontaneous neural activity?
    A. Dreams as thinking
    B. Psychoanalytic
    C. Activation-synthesis
    D. Problem-solving

19. Which of the following statements best describes the effect of hypnosis on memory?
    A. "Age regression" allows one to remember childhood experiences accurately.
    B. Under hypnosis, people can accurately recall events from earlier lives.
    C. Memories recalled under hypnosis are often vivid but inaccurate.
    D. Memory errors usually decrease under hypnosis.

20. Which evidence argues against the credibility of age regression?
    A.   Subjects who were age regressed as part of a study could not accurately recall their favorite comforting object from age three.
    B.   Subjects in a study did not know basic facts about the time period in which they were supposed to have lived in a previous life.
    C.   When people are regressed to an earlier age, brain wave patterns do not resemble those of children.
    D.   All of the above

21. Those who believe that hypnotic state differs from normal consciousness believe:
    A.   that hypnosis involves dissociation.
    B.   the powers of hypnosis are exaggerated.
    C.   that suggestion alone can produce the same results.
    D.   all of the above.

22. Those who say hypnosis is a(n) _____ believe that hypnosis involves role-playing.
    A.   altered state
    B.   deliberate deception
    C.   sociocognitive process
    D.   none of the above

23. Susan, who is normally very modest, is removing some of her clothes under hypnosis. How might this be explained, according to the theory that hypnosis is a social-cognitive process?
    A.   She is in an altered state.
    B.   She has dissociated.
    C.   She is playing the role of a hypnotized person.
    D.   She has relinquished control to the hypnotist.

24. A sleep disorder in which breathing periodically stops, often hundreds of times a night, is known as:
    A.   narcolepsy.
    B.   sleep apnea.
    C.   consolidation.
    D.   interrupted sleep disorder.

25. Psychoactive drugs work primarily by affecting:
    A.   brain structures.
    B.   bodily rhythms.
    C.   neurotransmitters.
    D.   blood flow to the brain.

26. Which of the following are psychoactive drugs?
    A. Tobacco
    B. Opium
    C. Caffeine
    D. All of the above

27. The fact that dreams frequently reflect a person's current concerns supports which interpretation of dreaming?
    A. Activation-synthesis theory
    B. Psychoanalytic theory
    C. Problem-focused approach
    D. Learning integration approach

28. Alcohol, tranquilizers, and sedatives are examples of:
    A. opiates.
    B. depressants.
    C. psychedelics.
    D. stimulants.

29. When George began using drugs, he used only a small amount. After six months, he required more and more to achieve the same effect. George experienced:
    A. withdrawal.
    B. brain damage.
    C. tolerance.
    D. mental set.

30. Gonzalo and Edinam both used the same amount of cocaine, but they each had different reactions. Which of the following differences between them might account for this?
    A. Physical condition
    B. Expectations for the drug
    C. Prior experience with cocaine
    D. All of the above

31. According to the problem-focused approach, dreams reflect:
    A. our ongoing conscious preoccupation of waking life.
    B. the desires, motives, and conflicts of which we are unaware.
    C. an interpretation of random firing of neurons.
    D. the symbol expression of biological rhythms.

32. The cognitive approach to dreaming is similar to the problem-focused approach, EXCEPT it:
    A. asserts that there is also a hidden meaning underlying the content of dreams.
    B. makes no claims about problem solving.
    C. states that dreams produce an increased frequency of neuronal firing.
    D. details how expectations alter how we perceive the message of dreams.

33. Hypnotic suggestions have been successful in:
   A.   increasing the accuracy of memory.
   B.   forcing people to unwillingly perform certain actions.
   C.   helping people reexperience first few years of life.
   D.   reducing the perception of pain.

34. Brain damage is frequently demonstrated when people use recreational drugs with a:
   A.   light or moderate frequency.
   B.   heavy frequency.
   C.   none of the above.
   D.   all of the above.

PRACTICE TEST 2 – Short Answer

1.   Many researchers believe that seasonal affective disorder is produced by one's _____ being out of sync or abnormal levels of _____.

2.   The sleep cycle is an example of a(n) _____ rhythm.

3.   Circadian rhythms are controlled by a biological clock called the _____.

4.   A periodic, more or less regular fluctuation in a biological system is known as a _____.

5.   Internal _____ occurs when your normal routine changes, such as when you must take a long airplane flight over many time zones.

6.   Few people of either sex are likely to undergo personality shifts solely as a result of _____.

7.   The majority of vivid dreams occur during _____.

8.   The short bursts of rapid, high-peaking waves that occur during Stage 2 sleep are known as sleep _____.

9.   REM sleep is called paradoxical sleep because the body is _____ while the brain is _____.

10.   _____ is a sleep disorder in which one's breathing is stopped for several minutes, causing the person in choke and gasp.

11.   Psychoanalytic theory suggests that we must distinguish the obvious, or _____, content of a dream from the hidden, or _____, content that reveals the true meaning of the dream.

12.   The _____ approach to dreaming asserts that dreams reflect the ongoing conscious preoccupations of waking life.

13.   The _____ theory suggests that dreams are the result of spontaneous neural firing.

14.   Hilgard suggests that only one part of consciousness goes along with hypnotic suggestions. The other part is like a _____, watching but not participating.

15.   Some people report that hypnosis has helped them recall long-ago events. These memories are likely to be _____.

16. The _____ explanation of hypnosis suggests that during hypnosis a split in consciousness occurs.

17. Hypnosis has been used effectively for _____ purposes.

18. The _____ explanation regards hypnosis as a form of role playing.

19. _____ drugs affect perception, mood, thinking, memory, or behavior.

20. Recreational drugs produce their effects primarily by altering the _____ in one's brain.

21. Amphetamines, cocaine, caffeine, and nicotine are all examples of _____.

22. Some drugs, such as heroin and tranquilizers can lead to _____, a state in which larger and larger doses are needed to produce the same effect.

23. The psychoactive drugs exert their effects by influencing _____ levels.

24. Several factors influence the way a particular individual reacts to the use of a drug. Two of those factors are _____ and _____.

25. A sleep disorder involving sudden and unpredictable daytime attacks of sleepiness or lapses into REM sleep is known as _____.

PRACTICE TEST 3 – Essay

1.   Dr. Irving is conducting a survey on premenstrual syndrome (PMS). Of the 100 subjects who responded to the survey, 70 per cent indicated that they experience PMS on a regular basis. Compare these findings to the research in the text that argues against PMS and answer the following questions:
   A.   How was PMS defined? What symptoms were included and why is this important?
   B.   What are some of the problems with the self-reporting of PMS symptoms?
   C.   Describe possible influences of expectations and attitudes toward menstruation on the results of the survey.
   D.   Describe the results of research findings from studies that did not reveal their true purpose.

2.   For the ninth grade science project, Megan kept a detailed diary of her sleep experiences during a one-month interval. The information obtained and her conclusions are submitted below. Using actual evidence related to sleep, comment on each of these claims.

   A.   During the period of the study, I awakened myself once during each night at different times. Each time I woke myself up, I felt the same as when I wake up in the morning. This indicates that sleep actually is the same kind of thing all through the night.
   B.   I was allowed to stay up all night twice. It was really hard to keep my eyes open at around 4:00 a.m., but by 6:00 a.m. I felt wide awake. This suggests that the loss of sleep is invigorating.
   C.   After missing sleep two nights in a row, I felt like going to bed extra early the next day. This indicates that we need to catch up on our rest.
   D.   Even though I felt O.K. after missing sleep for two nights, I got a "D" on an exam at school. This suggests that maybe sleep loss has more effects than I thought!
   E.   During the time of the study, I had two dreams and my sister had five. This indicates that we only dream several times a month.

3.　Yuko had a dream that she and her husband had gone horseback riding. He was far ahead of her and, though she was riding as fast as she could, she was unable to catch up. Eventually Yuko lost her way and was unsure where she was going. She dismounted her horse and found that she was in a beautiful valley, and she stopped there and felt very peaceful. Identify which theory would give each of the following interpretations of this dream.

    A.　This dream has little significance or meaning. It represents the attempt of the cortex to make sense of random neuronal firing in the brain stem.

    B.　This dream has little significance. It represents the brain's mental housekeeping. It is sorting, scanning, and sifting new information into "wanted" and "unwanted" categories.

    C.　The dream has great significance. It is likely to be a dream about Yuko's unresolved relationship with her father. She has always felt abandoned by him and could never win his attention or affection, which she has always deeply desired.

    D.　The dream has to do with Yuko's concern that she cannot keep up with her husband's pace. He always has more energy than she does and although she tries, what she would most like to do is "get off the merry-go-round," relax, and take life easier.

4.　You and your friends see a hypnotist at a show. Afterward, your friends ask various questions about hypnosis. Can you be forced to do things against your will under hypnosis? Can you remember long-forgotten memories under hypnosis? Is hypnosis ever used in practical situations, outside of entertainment? Based on your study of hypnosis, what are your answers to your friends' questions?

5.　For each type of drug listed below, indicate the following: 1) the type of drug, 2) the common effects of the drug, and 3) the result of abusing the drug.

    A.　Alcohol
    B.　Tranquilizers
    C.　Morphine
    D.　Amphetamines
    E.　Cocaine
    F.　LSD
    G.　Marijuana

CHAPTER 6

Sensation and Perception

LEARNING OBJECTIVES

Our Sensational Senses
6.1 - Why we experience separate sensations even though they all rely on similar neural signals.

6.2 - What kind of code in the nervous system helps explain why a pinprick and a kiss feel different.

6.3 - How psychologists measure the sensitivity of our senses.

6.4 - How information can be sensed yet not perceived.

6.5 - What happens when people are deprived of all external sensory stimulation.

6.6 - Why we sometimes fail to see an object that we're looking straight at.

Vision
6.7 - How the physical characteristics of light waves correspond to the psychological dimensions of vision.

6.8 - The basics of how the eye works, and why the eye is not a camera.

6.9 - How we see colors, and why we can describe a color as bluish green but not as reddish green.

6.10 - How we know how far away things are.

6.11 - Why we see objects as stable even though sensory stimulation from the object is constantly changing.

6.12 - Why perceptual illusions are valuable to psychologists.

Hearing
6.13 - The basics of how we hear.

6.14 - How we locate the source of a sound.

Other Senses
6.15 - The basics of how we taste, smell, and feel.

6.16 - Why you have trouble tasting your food when you have a cold.

6.17 - Why pain is complicated to understand and treat.

6.18 - How two senses inform us of the movement of our own bodies.

Perceptual Powers: Origins and Influences
6.19 - Whether babies see the world in the way adults do.

6.20 - What happens when people who are born blind or deaf have their sight or hearing restored.

6.21 - How psychological factors affect perception.

Perception without Awareness
6.22 - That perception is often unconscious.

6.23 - Whether "subliminal perception" will help you lose weight or reduce your stress.

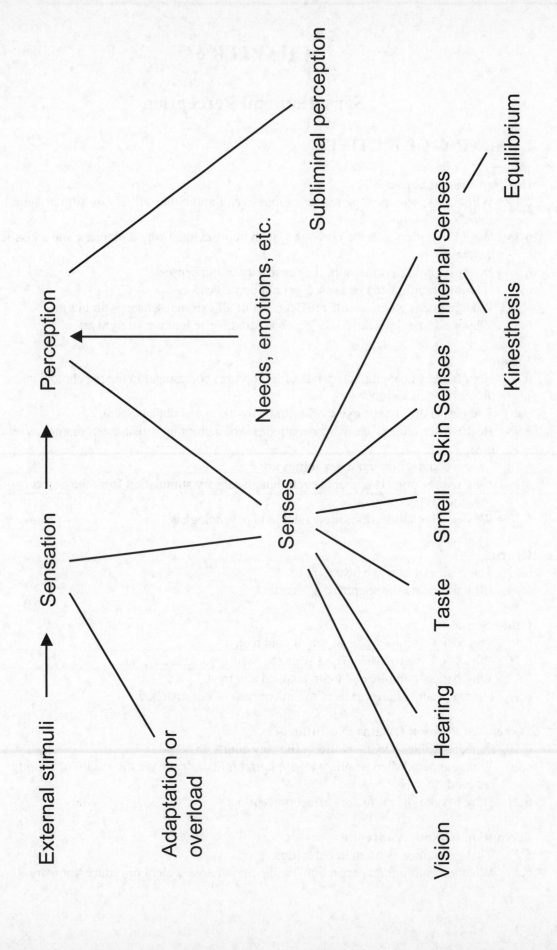

Chapter 6 - Concept Map

External stimuli → Sensation → Perception

Sensation → Senses

Adaptation or overload

Needs, emotions, etc. → Perception

Perception → Subliminal perception

Senses:
- Vision
- Hearing
- Taste
- Smell
- Skin Senses
- Internal Senses
  - Kinesthesis
  - Equilibrium

BRIEF CHAPTER SUMMARY

Chapter 6 examines the processes of sensation and perception for the various senses, and the relationship between them. Receptors in the senses change physical energy into neural energy. The physical characteristics of the stimuli correspond to psychological dimensions of our sensory experience. Psychophysics (how the physical properties of stimuli are linked to psychological experiences), signal detection theory, sensory adaptation, and sensory overload are discussed. After sensation has occurred, perception, the process of organizing and interpreting the sensory information, begins. The general processes of vision, hearing, taste, smell, pain, equilibrium, and kinesthesis are reviewed. For each of these senses, the chapter examines the relevant biological structures and processes (e.g., rods and cones) as well as the relevant theories that explain perception (e.g., trichromatic theory and opponent-process theory to explain how we see color). Perceptual strategies, including depth and distance strategies, visual constancies and form perception strategies, are described. Some perceptual abilities appear to be inborn, whereas others are influenced by psychological, environmental, and cultural factors. The gate control theory of pain and a newer, modified version of the theory are reviewed.

PREVIEW OUTLINE

Before you read the chapter, review the preview outline for each section of the text. After you have read the chapter, close this book and try to <u>recreate</u> the outlines on a blank piece of paper.

I.   **OUR SENSATIONAL SENSES**
    A.   **Definitions**
          1.   Sensation – the detection of physical energy emitted or reflected by physical objects by cells (receptors)
          2.   Perception – organizing sensory impulses into meaningful patterns
    B.   **The riddle of separate sensations** – How can we explain separate sensations?
          1.   There are five widely known senses and other lesser-known senses; all of them evolved to help us survive
          2.   Sense receptors (cells in sense organs) detect a stimulus and convert the energy into electrical impulses that travel along nerves to the brain
          3.   The nervous system encodes the neural messages using anatomical codes and functional codes (Doctrine of specific nerve energies)
    C.   **Measuring the senses**
          1.   Psychophysics – how the physical properties of stimuli are related to our psychological experience of them
          2.   Absolute threshold – the smallest amount of energy a person can detect reliably (50 percent of the time)

3. Difference thresholds – the smallest difference in stimulation that a person can detect reliably; also called just noticeable difference (jnd)
4. Signal-detection theory
   a. Accounts for response bias (tendency to say yes or no to a signal)
   b. Separates sensory processes (the intensity of the stimulus) from the decision process (influenced by observer's response bias)

D. Sensory adaptation
1. Senses designed to respond to change and contrast in the environment
2. Decline in sensory responsiveness occurs when a stimulus is unchanging; nerve cells temporarily get "tired" and fire less frequently
3. Sensory deprivation studies – subjects became edgy, disoriented, confused

E. Sensing without perceiving
1. Selective attention – ability to focus on some parts of the environment and block out others
2. Inattentional blindness – failing to consciously register objects that we are looking straight at

II. VISION

A. What we see
1. Psychological dimensions of visual world – hue, brightness, saturation
2. Physical properties of light – wavelength, intensity, complexity

B. An eye on the world – Parts of the eye
1. Parts of the eye include cornea, lens (focuses light), iris (controls amount of light that gets into eye), and pupil (dilates to let light in)
2. Retina – in the back of the eye where the visual receptors are located
   a. Rods: sensitive to light, not to color
   b. Cones: see color, but need more light to respond

C. Why the visual system is not a camera
1. Eyes are not a passive recorder of external world; neurons build picture
2. Visual system cells have response specialties (feature detectors in animals)
3. Controversy over specialized "face modules" in the brain

D. How we see colors
1. Trichromatic theory – first level of processing – three types of cones
2. Opponent-process theory – second stage of processing (ganglion cells)

E. **Constructing the visual world**
1. Visual perception – the mind interprets the retinal image and constructs the world using information from the senses
2. Form perception – Gestalt descriptions of how we build perceptual units include: figure/ground, proximity, closure, similarity, continuity
3. Depth and distance perception – binocular cues and monocular cues
4. Visual constancies: When seeing is believing
   a. Perceptual constancy – perception of objects as unchanging though the sensory patterns they produce are constantly shifting
   b. Shape, location, brightness, color, and size constancies

III. HEARING
A. **What we hear**
1. Stimulus for sound is a wave of pressure created when an object vibrates, which causes molecules in a transmitting substance (usually air) to move
2. Characteristics of sound
   a. Loudness – intensity (amplitude) of a wave's pressure; decibels
   b. Pitch – frequency (and intensity) of wave; measured in hertz
   c. Timbre – complexity of wave; the distinguishing quality of a sound
3. Psychological properties of sound
B. **An ear on the world – the process of hearing**
1. Sound wave passes into the outer ear through a canal to strike the eardrum
2. Eardrum vibrates at the same frequency and amplitude as the wave
3. The wave vibrates three small bones, then to the cochlea
4. Organ of Corti in the cochlea contains the receptor cells called cilia, or hair cells, which are imbedded in the basilar membrane
5. The hair cells initiate a signal to the auditory nerve, which carries the message to the brain
C. **Constructing the auditory world**
1. Perception is used to organize patterns of sounds to construct meaning
2. Strategies include figure/ground, proximity, continuity, similarity, closure
3. Loudness is a distance cue; using both ears helps estimate direction

IV. OTHER SENSES
A. **Taste: Savory sensations**
1. Chemicals stimulate receptors on tongue, throat, and roof of mouth

<ul>
<li>a.   Papillae – bumps on tongue – contain taste buds</li>
<li>b.   Replaced every 10 days – number declines with age</li>
</ul>

2.   Four basic tastes: salty, sour, bitter, sweet – and a new one (umami)

- a.   Each taste produced by a different type of chemical
- b.   Flavors are a combination of the four, but unclear how this occurs
- c.   Taste is heavily influenced by smell, temperature and texture of food, culture, and individual differences

B.   Smell: The sense of scents

1.   Receptors are specialized neurons (5 million) in a mucous membrane in upper part of nasal passage that respond to chemical molecules in the air

2.   Signals travel from receptors to the brain's olfactory bulb by the olfactory nerve to the higher regions of the brain

3.   The psychological impact of odors may be because olfactory centers in the brain are linked to areas that process memories and emotions

C.   Senses of the skin

1.   Skin protects the innards, it helps identify objects, it is involved in intimacy, and it serves as a boundary

2.   Skin senses include: touch, warmth, cold, and pain

D.   The mystery of pain

1.   Pain differs from other senses in that the removal of the stimulus doesn't always terminate the sensation

2.   Gate-control theory of pain – for years, the leading explanation

- a.   To experience pain sensation, impulses must pass a "gate" of neural activity that sometimes blocks pain messages
- b.   The theory correctly predicts that thoughts and feelings can influence pain perception
- c.   Limitations of gate-control theory – Cannot explain pain that occurs without injury or disease or phantom limb pain

3.   Updating the gate-control theory

- a.   The brain not only responds to incoming pain signals, but it is also capable of generating pain on its own
- b.   Chronic, pathological pain involves glial cells
- c.   Experience of pain influenced by individual differences as well as cultural beliefs

E.   The environment within

1.   Kinesthesis – tells us about location and movement of body parts using pain and pressure receptors in muscles, joints, and tendons

2.   Equilibrium – gives information about body as a whole

3.   Normally, kinesthesis and equilibrium work together

V.   PERCEPTUAL POWERS: ORIGINS AND INFLUENCES
A.   Inborn abilities

1.   Studies show that experience during a critical period may ensure survival and the development of skills already present at birth
2.   Research concludes that infants are born with many perceptual abilities

B.   **Critical periods** – exist in various senses (sight, hearing, smell)

C.   **Psychological and cultural influences**
1.   Perceptions affected by needs, beliefs, emotions, expectations
2.   Culture and experience also influence perception

VI.   **PERCEPTION WITHOUT AWARENESS**

A.   **Subliminal perception – How persuasive?**
1.   Evidence exists that simple visual images can affect your behavior even when you are unaware that you saw it (priming effects)
2.   However, there is little evidence for subliminal persuasion

VII.   **EXTRASENSORY PERCEPTION: REALITY OR ILLUSION?**

A.   **Research basis for confirmation and disconfirmation**
1.   Most reports come from anecdotal accounts
2.   Some studies under controlled conditions found positive results, but methodological problems existed and results were not replicated
3.   Conclusion is that there is no supporting scientific evidence

PRACTICE TEST 1 – Multiple Choice

1.   The detection of physical energy by receptors in the sense organs is known as:
        A.   perception.
        B.   sensory overload.
        C.   sensation.
        D.   sensory adaptation.

2.   The eyes, ears, tongue, nose, skin, and internal body tissues all contain:
        A.   anatomical codes.
        B.   functional codes.
        C.   sense receptors.
        D.   sense organs.

3.   Perception differs from sensation in that:
        A.   perception allows us to organize and interpret sensations.
        B.   perception is the raw data coming in from the senses.
        C.   sensation is an organizing and interpretive process; perception is not.
        D.   perception can be measured; sensations cannot.

4.   Which theory argues that light and sound produce different sensations because they stimulate different regions of the brain?
        A.   Signal detection theory
        B.   Trichromatic theory
        C.   Doctrine of specific nerve energies
        D.   Opponent-process theory

5.   Which of the following best accounts for the fact that light and sound produce different sensations due to the specific cells that are firing, how many are firing, the rate at which they are firing, and the patterning of each cell's firing?
        A.   Anatomical codes
        B.   Functional codes
        C.   Doctrine of specific nerve energies
        D.   Feature detectors

6.   Inattentional blindness refers to:
        A.   the childhood loss of vision.
        B.   a total loss of perceptual ability.
        C.   failure to register objects we are looking at.
        D.   underdevelopment of one's cones and rods.

7.   _____ stimulate different nerve pathways, which go to different places in the brain, whereas focusing on the number, rate, and pattern of the firing of particular cells in response to certain stimuli describes _____.
   A.   Anatomical codes; functional codes
   B.   Neural codes; cellular codes
   C.   Functional codes; anatomical codes
   D.   Psychophysics; transduction

8.   Signal detection theory takes into account:
   A.   observers' response tendencies.
   B.   sensory differences among species.
   C.   the role of feature detectors.
   D.   which cells are firing, how many cells are firing, and the rate at which they fire.

9.   As a research participant, Betsy is asked to compare lights within several pairs of lights and indicate whether one is brighter than the other. Betsy is being asked to detect:
   A.   the absolute threshold.
   B.   the j.d.n.
   C.   the difference threshold.
   D.   Weber's Law.

10.   Researchers have found that sensory deprivation may:
   A.   lead to confusion and grouchiness.
   B.   produce a restless, disoriented feeling.
   C.   cause hallucinations.
   D.   cause all of the above.

11.   Maria enjoys the wonderful smells from the kitchen when she first arrives at her mother's house, but she no longer notices them after a while. What accounts for this?
   A.   Sensory adaptation
   B.   Selective attention
   C.   Absolute thresholds
   D.   Difference thresholds

12.   In class, Jonah is completely focused on the professor's words, though there are noises and distractions all around him. This is best explained by:
   A.   sensory adaptation.
   B.   selective attention.
   C.   sensory deprivation.
   D.   sensory overload.

13. Humans experience the wavelength of light as:
    A.   hue or color.
    B.   brightness.
    C.   saturation or colorfulness.
    D.   wave complexity.

14. The fovea contains:
    A.   only rods.
    B.   only cones.
    C.   an equal number of rods and cones.
    D.   more rods than cones.

15. Rods are to cones as:
    A.   bright light is to dim light.
    B.   the iris is to the pupil.
    C.   black and white vision is to color vision.
    D.   none of the above.

16. The visual receptors are located in the:
    A.   cornea.
    B.   pupil.
    C.   lens.
    D.   retina.

17. The optic nerve connects:
    A.   rods and cones.
    B.   the cornea with the brain.
    C.   the pupil and the lens.
    D.   the retina with the brain.

18. Which theory of color vision suggests that one type of cone responds to blue, another type of cone to green, and a third to red?
    A.   Doctrine of specific nerve energies
    B.   Opponent-process theory
    C.   Trichromatic theory
    D.   Feature detector theory

19. Which theory of color vision best explains negative afterimages?
    A.   Trichromatic theory
    B.   Opponent-process theory
    C.   Doctrine of specific nerve energies
    D.   Weber's Law

20.   Perceptual illusions are valuable to psychologists because they:
      A.   let us know how gullible the average person is.
      B.   tell us about the perceptual strategies of the mind.
      C.   help us detect the early warning signs of inattentional blindness.
      D.   give us hints about which sense modality is most frequently used.

21.   The slight difference in sideways separation between two objects as seen by the left eye and the right eye is called:
      A.   a binocular cue.
      B.   a depth cue.
      C.   retinal disparity.
      D.   all of the above.

22.   As you watch a door opening, its image changes from rectangular to trapezoidal, yet you continue to think of the door as rectangular. What explains this phenomenon?
      A.   Perceptual constancy
      B.   Retinal disparity
      C.   Monocular depth cues
      D.   Selective attention

23.   When we hear a sound, we will often rotate our heads to:
      A.   locate the source of a sound.
      B.   discover the distance of a sound.
      C.   figure out the loudness of a sound.
      D.   calculate the frequency of a sound.

24.   The part of the ear that plays the same role in hearing as the retina plays in vision is called the:
      A.   cochlea.
      B.   eardrum.
      C.   organ of Corti.
      D.   auditory nerve.

25.   Rods and cones are to vision as the _____ is/are to hearing.
      A.   cilia or hair cells
      B.   eardrum
      C.   basilar membrane
      D.   cochlea

26.   The cilia are embedded in the _____ of the _____.
      A.   cochlea; auditory nerve
      B.   basilar membrane; cochlea
      C.   eardrum; cochlea
      D.   cochlea; basilar membrane

27. When you bite into a piece of bread or an orange, its flavor is a result of:
    A. a combination of the four basic tastes: salty, sour, bitter, and sweet.
    B. a combination of the four basic tastes: salty, smooth, pungent, and sweet.
    C. the activation of specific taste receptors.
    D. the taste receptors located in a specific part of the tongue.

28. How does the sense of smell differ from the senses of vision and taste?
    A. Smell does not have receptor cells.
    B. Although vision and taste have limited numbers of basic cell types, smell may have as many as a thousand.
    C. Smell uses anatomical coding and not functional coding, whereas vision and taste use both.
    D. There are fewer basic smells than basic tastes or colors.

29. When compared to placebo recordings, research on the use of subliminal messages to help one lose weight or reduce stress have shown that subliminal messages:
    A. are extremely effective in all cases.
    B. have no effectiveness beyond what you would expect from a placebo.
    C. work better than a placebo, but only if the placebo and subliminal message are both visual.
    D. are less effective than visual placebos and more effective than auditory placebos.

30. Phantom pain:
    A. does not exist.
    B. is strictly psychological.
    C. may occur because a matrix of neurons in the brain is generating pain signals.
    D. is a result of the increase in pain fibers.

31. Calan is trying to balance on her left leg while holding her right foot with her left hand. Her ability to balance relies on the sense of _____, and her ability to grab her foot relies on the sense of _____.
    A. equilibrium; kinesthesis
    B. kinesthesis; equilibrium
    C. touch; equilibrium
    D. coordination: touch

32. Malga can touch her finger to her nose with her eyes shut. What allows her to do this?
    A. The olfactory sense
    B. Kinesthesis
    C. Equilibrium
    D. ESP

33. Which group is studied to evaluate whether perceptual abilities are inborn?
    A. Cats
    B. People who first gained sensation as an adult
    C. Babies and infants
    D. All of the above

34. The concept of priming is:
    A. the subliminal or explicit exposure to information, and then assessing if memory or performance is affected by this information.
    B. the experiencing of one sensation (such as the sound of a bee) with different sense (such as a particular smell).
    C. a habitual way of perceiving, based on expectations.
    D. the focus of attention on some stimuli at the expense of others.

35. Besides taste, the most important factor in determining our perception of food is its:
    A. color.
    B. temperature.
    C. texture.
    D. odor.

36. Hiroaki was born without vision. Thanks to a recent surgery, he has been given vision for the first time. Which of the following is most likely during the early days following the surgery?
    A. He will suffer from extreme inattentional blindness.
    B. He will have trouble seeing.
    C. His vision will be perfectly normal.
    D. His other four basic senses will be enhanced.

37. When a stimulus is below a person's absolute threshold for detecting it, we say that the stimulus is:
    A. subliminal.
    B. unconditioned.
    C. conditioned.
    D. primed.

PRACTICE TEST 2 – Short Answer

1. _____ is the process by which sensory impulses are organized and interpreted.

2. The two basic kinds of code used by the nervous system to convey sensations are _____ and _____ codes.

3. You've been talking to your best friend as she's been discussing her new hair color. Despite the fact you're looking straight at her, you fail to notice that she's not wearing glasses for the first time during the entire time you've known her. This phenomenon is referred to as _____.

4. The smallest amount of energy that a person can detect reliably is known as the _____ threshold.

5. The smallest difference between two stimuli that a person can reliably detect is the _____.

6. Signal-detection theory holds that responses in a detection task consist of both a _____ process and a _____ process.

7. When a stimulus is unchanging or repetitious, receptors may stop firing so that we no longer notice it. This process is referred to as sensory _____.

8. Joseph wants to better understand how people perceive depth. He uses two lines that are of the same length, one with branches facing outward and one with branches facing inward. He discovers that most people think the line with the outward branches is longer. Joseph is using a _____ to study depth perception.

9. Although located in the eye, the structure known as the _____ is actually part of the brain.

10. The visual receptors sensitive to low levels of light are called _____; receptors sensitive to color are called _____.

11. _____ cells are responsive to specific patterns, such as horizontal versus vertical lines.

12. When a sound reaches our ears, it typically reaches each ear at _____. This fact helps us locate the direction of a sound.

13. The reason food tastes different when we are sick is because _____.

14. Our tendency to perceive objects as stable and unchanging even when the sensory patterns they produce are changing is referred to as perceptual _____.

15. An opponent-process cell that fired in response to red would turn _____ in response to green.

16. The receptors for hearing are hair cells embedded in the _____, in the interior of the _____.

17. When deaf people receive cochlear implants to allow them to process auditory signals, most of them tend to find sounds _____.

18. The four basic tastes are _____, _____, _____, and _____. A possible fifth basic taste is _____.

19. People's responses to particular odors are affected by both _____ and individual differences.

20. The skin senses include _____, _____, _____, and _____.

21. The _____ theory of pain holds that pain depends on whether neural impulses get past a point in the spinal cord and reach the brain.

22. _____ tells us where our body parts are located, and _____ tells us the orientation of the body as a whole.

23. A widely used procedure for studying depth perception in children is the _____ procedure.

24. Certain psychological influences affect perception. These include needs, beliefs, _____, and _____.

25. Researchers have shown even when the labels are mismatched with the tapes for subliminal messages, improvements in memory and self-esteem could still be achieved. This demonstrates that the improvements were due to _____.

26. New evidence on pain suggests that chronic pain also involves _____ cells.

27. _____ is the term for when people don't "see" or register a particular object even though it is right in front of them.

PRACTICE TEST 3 – Essay

1. Explain the phenomena listed below in terms of the concept listed after it.

    A. A nurse notices that patients perform worst on auditory tests – tests of auditory thresholds – when they are tired as a result of losing sleep. Analyze the effects of their performance using signal detection theory.
    B. John is looking all over for his glasses when his wife points them out at the top of his head. Explain this behavior using principles of sensory adaptation.
    C. Malcolm is studying for a test in psychology while the T.V. is blaring and his roommate is on the phone in the same room. Discuss this in relation to sensory overload.

2. Describe the process of vision, starting from a light wave and going to the eye and then the brain, including all relevant structures.

3   Assume that you are developing a color-generating device that will reproduce the colors in the human color spectrum. Explain which colors you need and why, according to the two theories of color vision listed below.

    A. Trichromatic theory
    B. Opponent-process theory

4. Describe the procedure for the visual cliff and what it is intended to measure.

5. Psychological factors can influence what we perceive and how we perceive it. Identify the psychological factors that could influence the following perceptions.

    A. You had an argument with your sister. As you are walking home from school, she drives past you. You saw her look at you but figured that she did not stop because she is angry with you.
    B. You think that your neighbor is an unethical character. One day you see him entering his house during the day and you are certain that he is sneaking around so that no one will see him.
    C. You are expecting your best friend to come visit you and you are very excited. Every time you hear something, you run to the door, certain that there was a knock.

CHAPTER 7

Learning and Conditioning

LEARNING OBJECTIVES

Classical Conditioning
7.1 - Four important features of classical conditioning.
7.2 - What is actually learned in classical conditioning.

Classical Conditioning in Real Life
7.3 - How classical conditioning might explain your irrational fear of heights or mice.
7.4 - How you might be conditioned to like certain tastes and odors and be turned off by others.
7.5 - How sitting in a doctor's office can make you feel sick and placebos can make you feel better.
7.6 - How technology is helping researchers study the biological basis of classical conditioning.

Operant Conditioning
7.7 - How the consequences of your actions affect your future behavior.
7.8 - What praising a child and quitting your nagging have in common.

Principles of Operant Conditioning
7.9 - Four important features of operant conditioning.
7.10 - How operant principles help explain superstitious behavior.
7.11 - What it means to "shape" behavior.
7.12 - Some biological limits on operant conditioning.

Operant Conditioning in Real Life
7.13 - When punishment works in real life and why, often, it does not.
7.14 - Some effective alternatives to punishment.
7.15 - How reinforcement can be misused.

Learning and the Mind
7.16 - How you can learn something without any obvious reinforcement.
7.17 - How we often learn not by doing but by watching.

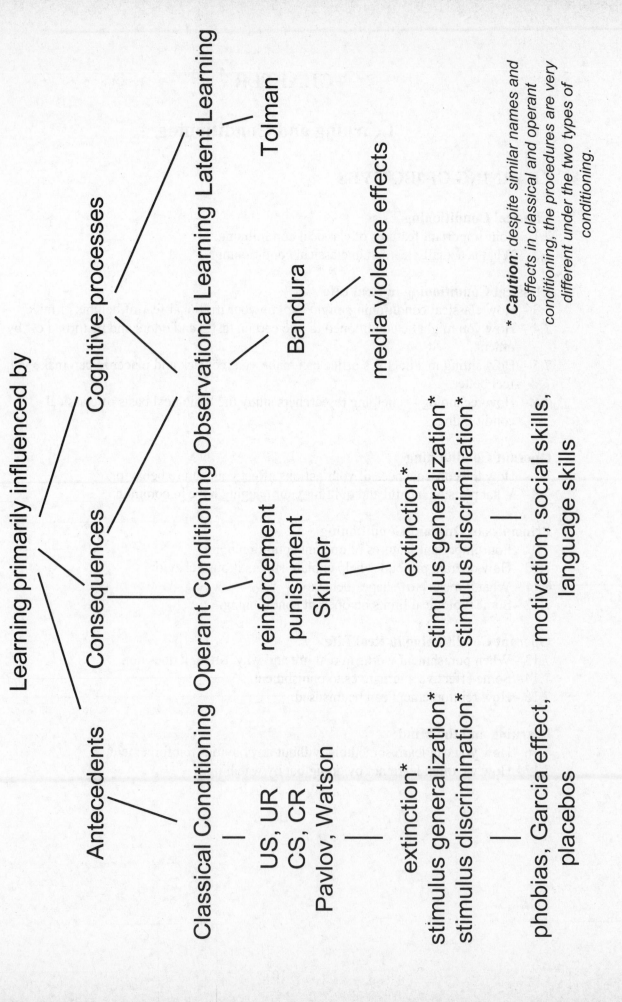

Chapter 7 - Concept Map

Learning primarily influenced by

Antecedents

Consequences

Cognitive processes

Classical Conditioning   Operant Conditioning   Observational Learning   Latent Learning

US, UR
CS, CR
Pavlov, Watson

extinction*
stimulus generalization*
stimulus discrimination*

phobias, Garcia effect,
placebos

reinforcement
punishment
Skinner

extinction*
stimulus generalization*
stimulus discrimination*

motivation, social skills,
language skills

Bandura

media violence effects

Tolman

* **Caution**: *despite similar names and effects in classical and operant conditioning, the procedures are very different under the two types of conditioning.*

BRIEF CHAPTER SUMMARY

Chapter 7 explores how we learn to make lasting changes in our behaviors due to our learning history. Two types of conditioning are discussed, as well as some theories that have attempted to go beyond basic conditioning models. Both types of conditioning suggest that psychology can be explained in terms of behavior and stimuli alone, without reliance on hypothetical mental processes. Classical conditioning explains how we learn many simple behaviors, such as fears and preferences. Operant conditioning explains how we learn complex behaviors as a result of the consequences of our actions. These consequences can take the form of positive reinforcement, negative reinforcement, positive punishment, or negative punishment. In addition, when reinforcement is not continuous (intermittent), learning is more long-lasting. Biological limitations to conditioning also are discussed. Social-cognitive theories expand behavioral principles to suggest the role that mental processes may play in the acquisition of new behaviors. Observational learning and latent learning are two social-cognitive theories of learning.

PREVIEW OUTLINE

Before you read the chapter, review the preview outline for each section of the text. After you have read the chapter, close this book and try to <u>recreate</u> the outlines on a blank piece of paper.

I. **INTRODUCTION TO LEARNING**
   A. **Definitions**
      1. Learning – any relatively permanent change in behavior due to experience
      2. Behaviorism – an approach to psychology that emphasizes the study of observable behavior and the role of the environment as a determinant of behavior
      3. Conditioning – a basic kind of learning that involves associations between environmental stimuli and the organism's responses
   B. **Types of learning:** Classical and Operant conditioning; Social-cognitive learning theories

II. **CLASSICAL CONDITIONING – began with the research of Ivan Pavlov**
   A. **New Reflexes from old – terminology**
      1. Unconditioned stimulus (US) – elicits a reflexive response in the absence of learning
      2. Unconditioned response (UR) – elicited by a stimulus in the absence of learning
      3. Conditioned stimulus (CS) – when an initially neutral stimulus comes to elicit a conditioned response after being paired with a US
      4. Conditioned response (CR) – response that is elicited by a CS
      5. Classical conditioning (also called Pavlovian or respondent conditioning) – procedure by which a neutral stimulus is regularly

paired with a US and the neutral stimulus becomes a CS, which elicits a CR that is similar to the original, unlearned one

B. **Principles of classical conditioning**
1. Extinction – repeatedly presenting the conditioned stimulus without the unconditioned stimulus it was originally paired with, until the learned response disappears
2. Spontaneous recovery – reappearance of a learned response after its apparent extinction
3. Higher-order conditioning – a procedure in which a neutral stimulus becomes a conditioned stimulus through association with an already established conditioned stimulus
4. Stimulus generalization – after conditioning, the tendency to respond to a stimulus that resembles one involved in the original conditioning
5. Stimulus discrimination – the tendency to respond differently to two or more similar stimuli

C. **What is actually learned in classical conditioning?**
1. The stimulus to be conditioned should precede the unconditioned stimulus because the CS serves as a signal for the US
2. Many psychologists say that the learner learns *information* (more than simply an association between two stimuli); that the CS predicts the US
3. Rescorla introduced and tested cognitive concepts; organism as information seeker who forms a representation of the world

III. **CLASSICAL CONDITIONING IN REAL LIFE – recognized by John B. Watson**
A. **Learning to like** – conditioning positive emotions (e.g., used in advertising)
B. **Learning to fear** – conditioning negative emotions
1. We're biologically primed to learn some things more easily than others
2. Phobias (irrational fears) can be learned through conditioning (e.g., Little Albert) and unlearned through counterconditioning
C. **Accounting for taste** – taste aversions are often classically conditioned
D. **Reacting to medical treatments** may generalize to a range of other stimuli

IV. **OPERANT CONDITIONING**
A. **Introduction to operant conditioning** (also called instrumental conditioning)
1. Behavior becomes more likely or less likely, depending on its consequences; emphasis is on environmental consequences
2. Whereas classical conditioning involves responses controlled only by antecedents, operant conditioning involves responses controlled primarily by consequences

B.   **The birth of radical behaviorism – Thorndike and Skinner**
C.   **The consequences of behavior**
   1.   A **neutral consequence** neither increases nor decreases the probability that the response will recur
   2.   **Reinforcement** makes a response more likely to recur
   3.   **Punishment** makes a response less likely to recur
   4.   Primary and secondary reinforcers and punishers – can be very powerful
      a.   Primary reinforcers satisfy physiological needs
      b.   Primary punishers are inherently unpleasant
      c.   Secondary reinforcers (and punishers) are reinforcing (and punishing) through association with other (primary) reinforcers
   5.   Positive and negative reinforcers and punishers
      a.   Positive reinforcement – something pleasant follows a response
      b.   Negative reinforcement – something unpleasant is removed
      c.   Positive punishment – something unpleasant occurs
      d.   Negative punishment – something pleasant is removed

V.   PRINCIPLES OF OPERANT CONDITIONING
A.   **Factors that influence the effect of consequences**
   1.   Extinction – learned response weakens when the reinforcer is withheld
   2.   Spontaneous recovery – the return of a response that has been extinguished
   3.   Stimulus generalization – a response occurs to stimuli that resemble the stimuli present during the original learning
   4.   Stimulus discrimination – the ability to distinguish between similar stimuli and to respond only to the one that results in the reinforcer
   5.   Discriminative stimulus signals whether a response will pay off
   6.   Learning on schedule – the pattern of delivery of reinforcements
      a.   Partial or intermittent schedules – reinforcing only some responses (which can result in learning superstitious behaviors)
      b.   For a response to persist, it should be reinforced intermittently, which will make the response more difficult to extinguish
   7.   Shaping – gradually reinforcing responses that are more similar to the desired response (successive approximations to the desired response)
   8.   Biological limits on learning: limitations of genetic predispositions and physical characteristics, instinctive drift

B.   **Skinner: The man and the myth**
   1.   Did not deny the existence of consciousness; said that it cannot explain behavior, and that aspects of consciousness are learned behaviors
   2.   Controversial idea that free will is an illusion (determinism)

VI.   OPERANT CONDITIONING IN REAL LIFE
   A.   **General problems** – if reinforcers, punishers, and discriminative stimuli in life remain the same, it is difficult to change behaviors
   B.   **Behavior modification** – operant conditioning programs used in real life

   C.   **The pros and cons of punishment**
   1.   When punishment works – for behaviors that can't be ignored or rewarded – with some criminals (consistency matters more than severity)
   2.   When punishment fails
      a.   Punishment is often administered inappropriately or mindlessly
      b.   The recipient often responds with anxiety, fear, or rage
      c.   Effects can be temporary; may depend on punisher being present
      d.   Most misbehavior is hard to punish immediately
      e.   Punishment conveys little information about desired behavior
      f.   A punishment may be reinforcing because it brings attention
   3.   Alternatives to punishment – avoid abuse, give information about desirable behavior, try extinction, reinforce the alternate, desirable behaviors
   D.   **The problem with reward**
   1.   Misuses of reward – rewards must be tied to the desired behavior
   2.   Why rewards can backfire – people work for intrinsic as well as extrinsic reinforcers, and extrinsic rewards can interfere with intrinsic motivation if used incorrectly

VII.   LEARNING AND THE MIND
   A.   **Latent learning**
   1.   Tolman and Honzik's experiment with latent learning
   2.   Learning can occur even when there is no immediate response and when there is no obvious reinforcement
   B.   **Social-cognitive learning theories**
   1.   Added higher-level cognitive processes to the idea of how people learn
   2.   Humans have attitudes, beliefs, and expectations that affect how they acquire information, make decisions, and reason
   C.   **Learning by observing** – called observational learning

1. Vicarious conditioning occurs from observing a model
2. Supported by Bandura's studies with children learning social behaviors

D. **The case of media violence**
1. Some people become more aggressive after exposure to violent images in the media, but most do not

2. Aggressive individuals tend to be drawn to violent images and are more affected by them

LEARNING THEORIES

Complete the following chart by providing responses under each model of learning.

	OPERANT CONDITIONING	CLASSICAL CONDITIONING	SOCIAL-COGNITIVE THEORIES
INDICATE WHAT IS LEARNED			
EXAMPLES			
IDENTIFY KEY FIGURES			
LIST KEY TERMS			
LIST PRINCIPLES			

PRACTICE TEST 1 – Multiple Choice

1.   Every time Steve's brother sees a Volkswagen, he yells "slugbug" and hits Steve really hard in the arm. The pain inflicted on the arm causes Steve to automatically flinch. Eventually, Steve starts to flinch as soon as he hears the word "slugbug." In this example, the word "slugbug" is a(n):
A.   unconditioned stimulus.
B.   unconditioned response.
C.   conditioned stimulus.
D.   conditioned response.

2.   Every time Steve's brother sees a Volkswagen, he yells "slugbug" and hits Steve really hard in the arm. The pain inflicted on the arm causes Steve to automatically flinch. Eventually, Steve starts to flinch as soon as he hears the word "slugbug." In this example, the pain on the arm is a(n):
A.   unconditioned stimulus.
B.   unconditioned response.
C.   conditioned stimulus.
D.   conditioned response.

3.   An unconditioned stimulus always elicits a(n):
A.   unconditioned stimulus.
B.   unconditioned response.
C.   conditioned stimulus.
D.   conditioned response.

4.   A conditioned response is always elicited by a(n):
A.   unconditioned stimulus.
B.   unconditioned response.
C.   conditioned stimulus.
D.   conditioned response.

5.   If the CS is repeatedly presented without the US, what will happen?
A.   Extinction
B.   Stimulus discrimination
C.   Stimulus generalization
D.   Higher-order conditioning

6.   If a stimulus similar to the conditioned stimulus is repeatedly presented without being followed by the unconditioned stimulus, it will stop eliciting the conditioned response. The differential responses to the conditioned stimulus and the similar stimulus demonstrate:
A.   extinction.
B.   stimulus discrimination.
C.   stimulus generalization.
D.   higher-order conditioning

7. When Chantel watches the news, most of the stories involving cruise ships discuss the ship sinking or being involved in some other type of disaster. Because cruise ships were so frequently paired with words such as death and injury, cruise ships now make Chantel nervous and she refuses to go on a cruise. Development of this fear is an example of:
   A. extinction.
   B. stimulus discrimination.
   C. stimulus generalization.
   D. higher-order conditioning

8. Conditioning is most likely to take place when the neutral stimulus:
   A. precedes the unconditioned stimulus.
   B. precedes another neutral stimulus.
   C. follows the unconditioned stimulus.
   D. follows the unconditioned response.

9. Which of the following is most likely to result in successful conditioning?
   A. If food and a whistle are presented separately just as often as they are presented together
   B. If a whistle follows food consistently
   C. If a whistle is sounded just once prior to the delivery of food
   D. If a whistle reliably predicts the delivery of food

10. When you were growing up, every time your mother saw a mouse, she screamed loudly. Her loud screams always startled and frightened you. Now as an adult, every time you see a mouse, you feel a strong irrational fear. Which of the following accounts for your fear?
    A. Classical conditioning
    B. Spontaneous recovery
    C. Operant conditioning
    D. Conditioned taste aversion

11. When you were growing up, every time your mother saw a mouse, she screamed loudly. Her loud screams always startled and frightened you. Now as an adult, every time you see a mouse, you feel a strong irrational fear. Your irrational fear is a(n):
    A. negative reinforcer.
    B. extinguished behavior.
    C. unconditioned stimulus.
    D. conditioned response.

12.   When you were young, you had lemon meringue pie for the first time and were violently ill later that same day. Ever since then, just the thought of lemon meringue pie is enough to make you sick to your stomach. This example illustrates the:
   A.   Skinner principle.
   B.   Garcia effect.
   C.   Thorndike law.
   D.   Bandura observation.

13.   When you were young, you had lemon meringue pie for the first time and were violently ill later that same day. Ever since then, just the thought of lemon meringue pie is enough to make you sick to your stomach. In this example, the pie is a(n):
   A.   unconditioned stimulus.
   B.   unconditioned response.
   C.   conditioned stimulus.
   D.   conditioned response.

14.   Maggie has been undergoing intensive chemotherapy. One of the side effects of chemotherapy is a feeling of nausea. Every single time Maggie is in the hospital parking lot, she goes and gets chemotherapy shortly thereafter. What is most likely to happen with the hospital parking lot?
   A.   The chemotherapy will make her think of the parking lot.
   B.   The parking lot will reduce any nausea caused by the treatment.
   C.   Maggie is likely to feel nauseous at just the sight of the parking lot.
   D.   The parking lot will probably have no effect on Maggie.

15.   Every time Jake takes a pill prescribed by his doctor, he tells himself, "This will make me better." Indeed, the pills do cause him to feel better. Since the sight and effect of the pill are consistently paired with his statement "This will make me better," what is most likely to happen when Jake is unknowingly given a fake pill (i.e., placebo)?
   A.   The pill will not make him feel any better because it is fake.
   B.   Jake's statement will work as a CS to make him feel better.
   C.   Jake will not tell himself that "This will make me better."
   D.   The chemicals of the pill itself will make him feel better.

16.   Classical conditioning research involving functional MRI associated certain images with pleasant smells like peanut butter or vanilla. Exposure to these images revealed increased activity in which two brain areas linked to motivation and emotion?
   A.   Amygdala and prefrontal cortex
   B.   Hippocampus and orbitofrontal cortex
   C.   Corpus callosum and Broca's area
   D.   Thalamus and occipital lobes

17. Reinforcement always _____ the future frequency of behavior it follows, whereas punishment always _____ the future frequency of behavior it follows.
    A. increases; increases.
    B. increases; decreases.
    C. decreases; increases.
    D. decreases; decreases.

18. When a stimulus or event is presented following a response, and this response is weakened and less likely to occur again, this is called:
    A. positive reinforcement.
    B. negative reinforcement.
    C. positive punishment.
    D. negative punishment.

19. When a stimulus or event is removed following a response, and this response is strengthened and more likely to occur again, this is called:
    A. positive reinforcement.
    B. negative reinforcement.
    C. positive punishment.
    D. negative punishment.

20. Whenever your Dad catches you studying, he says "good job, I'm proud of you." As a result, you study more often in the future. Whenever your Mom catches you not studying, she will nag you until you start studying again. As soon as you start studying, she stops nagging you. As a result, you study more often in the future. In these examples, your Dad's praise functions as _____ and the removal of your Mom's nagging functions as _____.
    A. reinforcement; reinforcement.
    B. reinforcement; punishment.
    C. punishment; reinforcement.
    D. punishment; punishment.

21. Kiandra's teacher tells her parents. "Kiandra's misbehavior is just for attention. You should just ignore her and it should stop." Kiandra's teacher is attempting to apply what principle?
    A. Negative reinforcement.
    B. Extinction.
    C. Stimulus generalization.
    D. Intermittent reinforcement.

22. When Taliza throws a tantrum in the supermarket, her father tries to talk to her calmly or to ignore her behavior. Sometimes, he does not have the patience to be calm and he just gives her a cookie to quiet her down. He has put Taliza on:
   A. continuous reinforcement.
   B. intermittent reinforcement.
   C. negative reinforcement.
   D. stimulus generalization.

23. Every time Luis comes up to bat during a baseball game, he taps the side of his foot three times with his baseball bat for luck. Periodically, after tapping the side of his foot, Luis will hit a homerun. Luis points out how this is proof that tapping his foot is important. What behavioral principle can account for this superstitious behavior?
   A. Stimulus generalization
   B. Intermittent reinforcement
   C. Extinction
   D. Negative reinforcement

24. Deanna is able to ignore her son's constant quiet requests for candy. Eventually, her son gets slightly louder and Deanna gives him a piece of candy to make him quiet. Soon, Deanna learns to ignore his slightly loud requests, so her son gets extremely loud and Deanna once again gives him candy to quiet him down. Now her son is extremely loud all the time. Which principle is illustrated by this example?
   A. Shaping
   B. Classical conditioning
   C. Punishment
   D. Spontaneous recovery

25. Operant conditioning works best when you:
   A. apply the consequences after a long delay.
   B. deliver reinforcers regardless of what behavior was occurring.
   C. capitalize on an organism's inborn tendencies.
   D. maximize the occurrence of spontaneous recovery.

26. The most important factor in making punishment effective is:
   A. how consistent it is.
   B. that you administer it only when angry.
   C. to make sure it is physical in nature.
   D. delivering the punishment in a public setting.

27. One disadvantage of punishment is:
    A.   the effects of punishment are long lasting.
    B.   that punishment conveys little information about what one should do.
    C.   most misbehavior is too easy to punish immediately.
    D.   all of the above.

28. One way to avoid the use of punishment is to:
    A.   teach problem-solving skills instead.
    B.   extinguish the undesired behavior.
    C.   reinforce alternative or incompatible behavior.
    D.   all of the above.

29. Koichi is a struggling artist who loves his work. He becomes well known and people are now commissioning him to paint and will pay him regardless of the work's quality. He finds that his passion for his work has decreased. What has happened?
    A.   Intrinsic rewards have interfered with extrinsic rewards.
    B.   He has been put on a token economy and does not like it.
    C.   Extrinsic rewards have interfered with intrinsic motivation.
    D.   His love for work has been extinguished through the absence of rewards.

30. Tolman's experiments demonstrating latent learning showed that:
    A.   learning can occur though it may not be immediately expressed.
    B.   rats are capable of insight.
    C.   extrinsic rewards can reduce intrinsic motivation.
    D.   personality characteristics interact with environmental influences.

31. Bandura's study with children who watched the short film of two men playing with toys demonstrated which of the following?
    A.   Children must be rewarded every single time to imitate models.
    B.   Children were likely to imitate the aggressive behaviors shown in the film.
    C.   Children will only imitate other children, not adults.
    D.   Aggression cannot be learned through imitation.

PRACTICE TEST 2 – Short Answer

1.   Whenever you imagine yourself standing at the edge of a great height, you become very nervous. In this case, your fearful thought is called a _____.

2.   When a neutral stimulus is paired with an unconditioned stimulus that elicits some reflexive unconditioned response, the neutral stimulus comes to elicit a similar or related response. The neutral stimulus is then called a _____.

3.   If a conditioned stimulus is repeatedly presented without the unconditioned stimulus, the conditioned response eventually disappears. This is called _____.

4.   The process by which a neutral stimulus becomes a conditioned stimulus by being paired with an already established conditioned stimulus is known as _____ conditioning.

5.   Julie developed a conditioned fear response to the cocker spaniel that bit her. She is now afraid of all dogs. This is called stimulus _____.

6.   In stimulus _____, different responses are made to stimuli that are similar (but not identical) to the conditioned stimulus.

7.   Many theorists believe that the conditioned stimulus (CS) elicits a conditioned response (CR) because the CS _____ the US, not simply because they are associated with one another.

8.   Every time Jorge visits his family, his Mom bakes an apple pie. His family visits are always pleasurable, so the smell of apple pie is consistently paired with pleasant experiences. As a result, the smell of apple pie alone is enough to put Jorge in a good mood. In this example, the apple pie is a _____ and the good feeling is a _____.

9.   In _____ conditioning, behavior becomes more or less likely to occur depending on its _____.

10.   A response may be strengthened or may be more likely to occur again as a result of a stimulus known as a _____.

11.   Alex joins his friends at a party. His friends encourage him to drink too much and unwisely his listens, despite his inexperience with alcohol. Alex then spends the next 5 hours vomiting. Ever since that night, Alex feels sick to his stomach if he even smells alcohol. Alex's nausea can be explained by _____ conditioning.

12. There is a greater biological readiness to associate sickness with _____ than with sights or sounds.

13. In _____ reinforcement or punishment, something is given following a desired or undesired response; in _____ reinforcement or punishment, something is taken away or withdrawn following a desired or undesired behavior.

14. Frequently, people confuse _____ reinforcement with _____ because both involve unpleasant stimuli.

15. The placebo effect probably involves the classical conditioning of a patient's _____.

16. Responses are more resistant to extinction when they are not always followed by a reinforcer. Such schedules are called _____ schedules of reinforcement.

17. In _____, you initially reinforce a tendency in the right direction, then gradually require responses that are more and more similar to the final, desired response.

18. An alternative to punishment is a combination of _____ and _____.

19. Punishment tells someone what _____, but it does not communicate _____.

20. Regardless of the strength of the reinforcer, human beings cannot be taught to live underwater without a life support system. This fact demonstrates the _____ limits on learning.

21. Learning that is not immediately displayed in an overt response is called _____.

22. In _____ learning, the learner observes a model making certain responses and experiencing the consequences.

23. If you receive a reward for doing a task well, your intrinsic motivation is likely to _____.

24. Recent classical conditioning experiments involving functional MRI have helped to explain why we may feel full after eating but may find a surge in motivation to eat more when presented with a different type of food. This phenomenon is known as the _____.

PRACTICE TEST 3 – Essay

1.   In the following examples, identify the unconditioned stimulus, unconditioned response, conditioned stimulus, and conditioned response.

   A.   When your father is angry with you, he calls you by both your first and middle names. Every time you hear him call you that way, you become anxious.

   B.   Jody is allergic to the pollen of flowers, which causes her the sneeze. One day her friend brings home some plastic flowers and Jody starts sneezing at the sight of them, despite the lack of pollen.

   C.   Your true love wears a certain perfume. Every time you smell that perfume, you feel happy inside.

   D.   You had a terrifying car accident at the corner of Park Place and Main Street. Now every time you approach that corner, you feel anxious.

2.   In the following examples identify the principles of classical conditioning, such as stimulus discrimination, stimulus generalization, extinction, etc.

   A.   While caring for your friend's dog, you notice that it displays a cowering posture as you roll up a newspaper. You try this several more times with magazines or stacks of notebook paper and the dog displays the same behavior. You become convinced that this dog is generally afraid of rolled-up paper.

   B.   Sara, a dog breeder, has been phobic about Doberman pinschers since one attacked her. After the attack, she felt tense and apprehensive whenever she walked by a Doberman, even if the dog was in a cage or on a leash, though she was never uncomfortable with any other type of dog. Recently Sara has been experiencing a change in her feelings toward Dobermans. She was given four Doberman puppies to sell and since being around them for several months, she is no longer fearful of Dobermans.

   C.   At a red light, Chris and Ximena automatically tensed and felt chills when they heard the screech of tires behind them. Later, while watching a car race, Chris and Ximena remarked that the screeching of tires was having little effect on them at that time.

   D.   After Masato got food poisoning from roast chicken, he vowed he would never return to that restaurant nor would he ever eat chicken again. All he wanted was to go home and eat his mother's cooking. As Masato entered the kitchen, he became nauseated when he saw the turkey sitting on the table.

3.   Identify whether the consequences in the following examples are positive or negative reinforcement, or positive or negative punishment. Indicate the probable effects of the consequences, according to operant theories of learning.

   A.   A buzzer sound continues until a seat belt is fastened, which makes you more likely to fasten your seatbelt.
   B.   Whenever Monica picks up a cigarette, her roommate complains and insults her, which results in Monica picking up the cigarette less often.
   C.   Whenever Nobu does the dishes, his girlfriend compliments and kisses him. Nobu finds himself doing dishes more and more.
   D.   Whenever Fred skis down the most difficult slopes, he always has a bad fall. Now Fred avoids the difficult slopes.

4.   Identify the problem or problems in the following examples and, using principles of learning theories, suggest the changes needed.

   A.   Ten-year-old Eliza Jane is expected to keep her room clean. Her parents check her room weekly and in the past year, her room was clean on 20 occasions. Eliza Jane's parents praised her lavishly on 10 of those occasions that her room was clean and on the other 10 occasions, Eliza Jane received no reinforcement. This technique has not been working well since on any given day, the room is likely to be a mess.
   B.   Baby Ari is not yet sleeping through the night. Every time the baby cries, one of his parents picks him up. His parents decide that after checking to make sure the baby is O.K., they will just let him cry. Ari cries and cries for five nights in a row. On the first four nights, his parents kept to their agreement, but on the fifth night, they couldn't stand it any longer and picked him up. Now Ari is crying more than ever.
   C.   Sue is always in trouble in class. Her teacher has tried everything he knows to make her behave: talking to her privately, having her stay after class, and scolding her in public. Regardless of what he does, her misbehavior continues.

5.   Below is an application of punishment. Identify the problems demonstrated in this example and suggest a more effective approach.

A parent discovers crayon marks and scribbling on a recently painted wall. Tommy, 18-months old, is angrily pulled from the playpen, and brought before the wall. He is harshly told, "No! No! No!" and given a sharp slap on the back of his hand. He is still crying when placed in the crib for a nap. Things become quiet for a time, and then the sound of movement is heard. A quick check shows Tommy is not in his crib. A search locates Tommy in the office room. He has doodled in various places with pens and pencils from the desk.

118

CHAPTER 8

Behavior in Social and Cultural Context

LEARNING OBJECTIVES

Roles and Rules
8.1 - How social roles and cultural norms regulate behavior without our being aware of it.
8.2 - The power of roles and situations to make people behave in ways they never would have predicted for themselves.
8.3 - How people can be entrapped into violating their moral principles.

Social Influences on Beliefs and Behavior
8.4 - Two general ways that people explain their own or other people's behavior—and why it matters.
8.5 - Three self-serving biases in how people think about themselves and the world.
8.6 - Why most people will believe outright lies and nonsensical statements if they are repeated often enough.
8.7 - Whether certain fundamental political and religious attitudes have a genetic component.

Individuals in Groups
8.8 - Why people in groups often go along with the majority even when the majority is dead wrong.
8.9 - How "groupthink" can lead to bad, even catastrophic, decisions.
8.10 - How crowds can create "bystander apathy" and unpredictable violence.
8.11 - The conditions that increase the likelihood that some people will dissent from the majority opinion, take risks to help others, or blow the whistle on wrongdoers.

Us versus Them: Group Identity
8.12 - How people in a multicultural society balance ethnic identity and acculturation.
8.13 - What causes ethnocentric, "us–them" thinking and how to decrease it.
8.14 - How stereotypes benefit us and how they distort reality.

Group Conflict and Prejudice
8.15 - The four major causes and functions of prejudice.
8.16 - Four indirect ways of measuring prejudice.
8.17 - Four conditions necessary for reducing prejudice and conflict.

The Question of Human Nature
8.18 - How social psychologists explain the persistence of evil.
8.19 - What "the banality of evil" tells us about human behavior.

Chapter 8 - Concept Map

Social and Cultural Psychology

group behavior
- behavior across groups
  - prejudice
  - stereotypes
  - ethnocentrism
  - group conflict
- behavior within the group
  - conformity
  - groupthink
  - social loafing
  - deindividuation
  - diffusion of responsibility

society's roles and norms
- obedience

social cognition
- attributions
  - situational or dispositional
- attitudes
  - persuasion

BRIEF CHAPTER SUMMARY

Chapter 8 examines some of the major topic areas in the fields of social psychology and cultural psychology, which collectively study the individual in a social and cultural context. The influence of the social context begins with norms or rules that people are expected to follow. Each of us fills many social roles that are governed by norms about how a person in that position should behave. The roles we fill and the rules that govern those roles heavily influence our behavior, as demonstrated by two classic studies (Milgram's investigation of obedience and Zimbardo's prison study). These studies show how situational forces can override our own beliefs and values. The social context also influences thought processes. Attributions—the way we explain why events happen—influence our responses to the world. Certain types of attributional errors and tendencies can occur that may cause misinterpretations of events (e.g., fundamental attribution error, self-serving bias). Attitudes are a fundamental concept, and attempts to change our attitudes are persistent. To resist unwanted persuasion, one must think critically about information from all sources. The presence and influence of other group members can lead to behaviors such as groupthink, conformity, deindividuation, and social loafing. The importance of group and ethnic identities, and interactions among groups, are discussed. Stereotypes help us organize new information, but they also can distort reality (e.g., the tendency to exaggerate differences between groups). The origins of prejudice, attempts to measure prejudice accurately, and efforts to reduce prejudice are discussed. Finally, the chapter raises the question of human nature and its influence on behavior. Studying individuals in a social context helps to identify the normal social influences that contribute to behaviors we often mistakenly think result from individual or personality factors.

PREVIEW OUTLINE

Before you read the chapter, review the preview outline for each section of the text. After you have read the chapter, close this book and try to <u>recreate</u> the outlines on a blank piece of paper.

I.   **ROLES AND RULES**
    A.   **Definitions**
        1.   Social psychology and cultural psychology – fields that examine the influence of social and cultural environment on individuals and groups
        2.   Norms – rules about how we are supposed to act
        3.   Roles – positions in society that are regulated by norms about how people in those positions should behave
    B.   **The obedience studies by Milgram**
        1.   Subjects thought they were in an experiment about learning and were instructed to shock another subject when an error was made
        2.   All participants gave some shock; two-thirds obeyed the experimenter and went to the highest shock level ("severe shock") despite cries of pain

3. Subsequent study variations found that more disobedience occurred when the experimenter left the room, the victim was right there in the room, etc.
4. Conclusion: obedience is a function of the situation, not of personalities
5. Evaluating the obedience study: some considered the study unethical, but the Milgram study highlighted the danger of unquestioning obedience

C. **The prison study by Zimbardo**
1. When college students were randomly assigned to be prisoners or guards, prisoners became passive and panicky, while some guards became abusive
2. Behavior depends on social roles, which can overrule personality, values

D. **Why people obey**
1. People obey because they believe in the authority's legitimacy and to avoid negative outcomes and gain positive ones
2. Why do people obey when it's not in their interest or violates their values?
   a. Allocating responsibility to the authority
   b. Routinization – defining the activity as routine; normalizing it
   c. Wanting to be polite – people lack the words to disobey
   d. Entrapment – commitment to course of action is escalated

II. **SOCIAL INFLUENCES ON BELIEFS AND BEHAVIOR**
A. **Social cognition** – how the social environment influences thoughts, beliefs, etc.
B. **Attributions** – explanations we make for behavior
1. Types of attributions and biases
   a. Situational attributions – identify the cause of an action as something in the environment or situation
   b. Dispositional attributions – identify the cause of an action as something in the person, such as a trait or motive
   c. Fundamental attribution error – tendency to overestimate dispositional factors and underestimate the influence of the situation when explaining someone else's behavior
   d. Self-serving bias – tendency to take credit for good actions and rationalize mistakes when explaining one's own behavior
   e. Just-world hypothesis – the need to believe the world is fair; that good people are rewarded and bad people are punished
C. **Attitudes** – beliefs that may be explicit or implicit
1. Not always based on reason; can be based on conformity, habit, rationalization, economic self-interest, generational events

2.   Attitudes can change to achieve consistency; to reduce cognitive dissonance (when two attitudes or an attitude and a behavior conflict)

3.   Recent research suggests a possible role of genetics in attitude formation

4.   Attitudes are also influenced by other people trying to persuade us

    a.   Friendly persuasion – enhanced by the familiar, repetition (validity effect), arguments by admired persons

    b.   Coercive persuasion suppresses ability to reason, to think critically, and to make good choices; person's access to information is severely controlled, often by a powerful leader

III.   INDIVIDUALS IN GROUPS

    A.   Conformity

        1.   Asch's conformity study – comparing line segments

        2.   People conform for a variety of reasons including identification with group members, popularity, self-interest, and to avoid punishment

        3.   Conformity has good and bad sides, but it can suppress critical thinking

    B.   Groupthink – the tendency for all members of the group to think alike and suppress disagreement; often results in faulty or even disastrous decisions

        1.   Occurs when a group's need for total agreement overwhelms its need to make the wisest decision

        2.   Groupthink more likely when group has illusion of invulnerability, biased information seeking, self-censorship, pressures on dissenters to conform, and an illusion of unanimity

        3.   Groupthink can be counteracted if doubt and dissent are encouraged and if decisions are made by a majority rather than by unanimity

    C.   The anonymous crowd

        1.   Diffusion of responsibility

            a.   The more people who are around when a problem occurs, the less likely one of them will offer assistance

            b.   Individuals fail to act because they believe someone else will do so

            c.   May explain why crowds of people fail to respond to an emergency

        2.   Social loafing – individuals work less and let others work harder – more likely to occur when members are not accountable, etc.

        3.   Deindividuation – losing all awareness of individuality and sense of self; people more likely to conform to the norms of the specific group situation

            a.   Increases willingness to do harm, break the law (e.g., riots)

            b.   Can also increase friendliness and self-disclosure

D. **Altruism and dissent**

    1.   Altruism – the willingness to take selfless or dangerous action for others

    2.   Reasons for altruistic action include a combination of personal convictions and situational influences

    3.   Steps involved in dissent, and altruism

        a.   The individual perceives the need for intervention or help

        b.   Cultural norms encourage taking action

        c.   The situation increases the likelihood of taking responsibility

        d.   The costs of doing nothing outweigh the costs of getting involved

        e.   The individual has an ally

        f.   The individual becomes entrapped; once initial steps have been taken, most people will increase their commitment

IV. **US VERSUS THEM: GROUP IDENTITY**

    A. **Social identities** – part of a person's self-concept that is based on identification
with a nation, ethnic group, gender, or other affiliations

    B. **Ethnic identity**

        1.   Ethnic identity – close identification with a religious or ethnic group

        2.   Acculturation – identification with the dominant culture

    C. **Ethnocentrism** – the belief that one's own culture is superior to others

        1.   Influence of social identities

            a.   Social identities create "us" or ingroup, versus "them" categories

            b.   Us-them identities are strengthened when the groups compete

            c.   Interdependence in reaching mutual goals (cooperation) can reduce competitiveness and hostility

    D. **Stereotypes**

        1.   Summary impression of a group in which all members of that group are viewed as sharing common traits that may be positive, negative, or neutral

        2.   Stereotypes help us process new information, retrieve memories, organize experience, make sense of differences, and predict how people will behave

        3.   Stereotypes can distort reality (e.g., exaggerate differences between groups, underestimate differences within other groups)

V. **GROUP CONFLICT AND PREJUDICE**

    A. **Prejudice** – a negative stereotype and a strong, unreasonable dislike or hatred of a group or its individual members

    B. **The origins of prejudice**

1. Psychological causes – such as warding off doubt or fear
2. Social causes – fitting in with peers and important others
3. Economic causes– such as justifying a majority group's dominance
4. Cultural and national causes– prejudice bonds people with their culture and nation

    C.   **Defining and measuring prejudice**
1. Difficult to define prejudice and sexism
2. Explicit prejudice may be declining, but implicit prejudice may be slower to change
3. Four ways of measuring prejudice includes measures of social distance, measures of behavior (e.g., nonverbal behavior or aggression), brain activity, and speed of associations (e.g., Implicit Associations Test)

    D.   **Reducing conflict and prejudice**
1. Appealing to moral or intellectual arguments are not sufficient
2. Conditions that must be met in order to reduce prejudice or group conflict:
   a. Both sides must have equal legal status, economic opportunities, and power
   b. The larger culture must endorse egalitarian norms and provide moral support and legitimacy for both sides
   c. Both sides must have opportunities to work and socialize together, formally and informally
   d. Both sides must cooperate, working together for common goal

VI.   **THE QUESTION OF HUMAN NATURE**
    A. Under certain conditions, good people often can be induced to do bad things and everyone is affected by the rules of their culture (banality of evil)

PRACTICE TEST 1 – Multiple Choice

1. Rules that regulate "correct" behaviors for a manager or an employee are called:
   A. norms.
   B. occupational roles.
   C. social rules.
   D. depersonalization.

2. In his obedience experiments, Milgram found that people were more likely to disobey the experimenter and refuse to administer shock when:
   A. the experimenter stayed in the room.
   B. the subject administered shocks directly to the victim in the same room.
   C. authority figures, rather than "ordinary" people, ordered subjects to continue.
   D. the subject worked with a peer who helped administer shocks.

3. In Milgram's obedience studies, the person most likely to disobey was a subject who:
   A. felt very upset about administering shocks to another person.
   B. worked with peers who refused to continue administering shocks.
   C. had strong moral and religious principles.
   D. heard the victim scream that his heart was bothering him.

4. In the typical obedience experiment, what percentage of the subjects administered the maximum amount of shock to the victim?
   A. Only 1 to 2 percent
   B. Approximately two-thirds
   C. 30 percent
   D. All of the subjects

5. The primary lesson of the Zimbardo prison study was:
   A. to demonstrate that certain personality types should not be in positions of authority.
   B. that people's behavior depends largely on the roles they are asked to play.
   C. that students are very suggestible and are not good research subjects.
   D. how quickly people are corrupted by power.

6. Which conclusion is shared by the prison study and the obedience study?
   A. The personality of people influenced their behavior more than the roles they were asked to play.
   B. What people will do depends upon the situation they were put it.
   C. Social roles and obligations have small influence on behavior.
   D. All of the above

7.   Which of the following causes people to obey when they really would rather not?
     A.   Entrapment
     B.   Good manners
     C.   Routinization
     D.   All of the above

8.   When Nicole's husband Pat forgot to run an errand, she attributed his forgetting to his selfishness. When Keith's wife Stacy forgot to run an errand, he attributed her forgetting to her being preoccupied with problems at work. Nicole made a(n) _____ attribution, whereas Keith made a(n) _____ attribution.
     A.   dispositional; situational
     B.   situational; dispositional
     C.   self-serving; external
     D.   external; self-serving

9.   "Kazumi bicycles to school because she is athletic" is an example of:
     A.   a dispositional attribution.
     B.   the self-serving bias.
     C.   the fundamental attribution error.
     D.   a situational attribution.

10. "Jennifer bicycles to school because no one will drive her" is an example of:
     A.   a dispositional attribution.
     B.   the self-serving bias.
     C.   the fundamental attribution error.
     D.   a situational attribution.

11. In attributing causes to other people's behaviors, the tendency to overestimate the effects of personality factors and underestimate the effects of situational factors is called:
     A.   a dispositional attribution.
     B.   the just-world hypothesis.
     C.   the fundamental attribution error.
     D.   the self-serving bias.

12. I believe that I got an A in geometry because I'm a hard worker, but I got a D in biology because the teacher doesn't like me. This demonstrates:
     A.   the just-world hypothesis.
     B.   the self-serving bias.
     C.   the fundamental attribution error.
     D.   blaming the victim.

13. "People get what they deserve" is an example of:
    A. the just-world hypothesis.
    B. a situational attribution.
    C. the fundamental attribution error.
    D. the self-serving bias.

14. When Hortense was diagnosed with cancer, she believed that she must have done something wrong to have deserved such an illness. Her belief is an example of:
    A. a situational attribution.
    B. guilt.
    C. the just-world hypothesis.
    D. an internal attribution.

15. In contrast to the actual results of the basic Milgram experiment, most psychiatrists and nonprofessionals thought people would:
    A. stop delivering shock early in the experiment.
    B. deliver the maximum amount of shock.
    C. figure out that the shocks were not real.
    D. check on the welfare of the victim.

16. Research suggests that religious affiliation is _____ and a person's depth of religious feeling is _____.
    A. heritable; also heritable.
    B. not heritable; also not heritable.
    C. not heritable; heritable
    D. heritable; not heritable.

17. Acculturation is identification with:
    A. a religious or ethnic group.
    B. the dominant culture.
    C. negative stereotypes.
    D. an influential leader.

18. The idea that repetition increases the perception that familiar statements are true demonstrates:
    A. cognitive dissonance.
    B. generational identity.
    C. the validity effect.
    D. coercive persuasion.

19. Grant is being given a test to see how fast he can match black faces with positive or negative words. Grant is most likely being given a(n):
   A. Thematic Aptitude Test.
   B. Matching to Sample Test.
   C. Implicit Association Test.
   D. Multiphasic Personality Test.

20. People are likely to conform:
   A. in order to keep their jobs, win promotions, or win votes.
   B. if they wish to be liked.
   C. if they want to avoid being unpopular.
   D. for all the reasons listed above.

21. In close-knit groups, members tend to think alike and suppress dissent. This is called:
   A. group polarization.
   B. validity effect.
   C. diffusion of responsibility.
   D. groupthink.

22. Geraldo's boss always likes to be right and to be the "expert" on any topic. Whenever their work team meets, he becomes irritated with whoever disagrees with him. If anyone tries to speak up to him, others in the group quickly change the subject to be sure no one challenges him. What is occurring in this situation?
   A. Groupthink
   B. Diffusion of responsibility
   C. Social loafing
   D. Deindividuation

23. A woman was stabbed and none of the numerous onlookers called for help. What accounts for this?
   A. Social loafing
   B. Mere-repeated exposure effect
   C. Diffusion of responsibility
   D. Deindividuation

24. The willingness to take selfless or dangerous action on behalf of others is called:
   A. interdependence.
   B. individuation.
   C. altruism.
   D. all of the above.

25. Which of the following is <u>NOT</u> one of the factors that predicts altruism?
    A. An altruistic personality
    B. An ally
    C. Perceiving the need for help
    D. Entrapment

26. The belief that one's own culture or ethnic group is superior to all others is called:
    A. ethnic separatism.
    B. prejudice.
    B. social norms.
    D. ethnocentrism.

27. The tendency to hold positive attitudes toward people and things we know well is known as:
    A. validity effect.
    B. implicit attitude acceptance.
    C. familiarity effect.
    D. deindividuation.

28. Stereotypes can be helpful because they help us:
    A. increase the accuracy of our opinions about particular individuals.
    B. see the differences between groups.
    C. rapidly process new information and organize experience.
    D. do all of the above.

29. Students are shown a slide of a white male committing a crime against a black male. Later, when they are asked what they saw, most reported seeing a black male committing a crime against a white male. This error is a result of the fact that stereotypes:
    A. produce selective perception.
    B. accentuate differences between groups.
    C. underestimate differences within other groups.
    D. help us process new information.

30. Stereotypes distort reality by:
    A. accentuating differences between groups.
    B. producing selective perceptions.
    C. underestimating differences within other groups.
    D. propagating all of the above.

31. An unreasonable negative feeling toward a category of people is called:
    A. ethnocentrism.
    B. a stereotype.
    B. prejudice.
    D. social identity.

32. Which of the following is most likely to lead to evil actions?
    A. Adherence to roles and entrapment
    B. Lack of a developed conscience
    C. Mental illness
    D. Lack of altruistic orientation

33. In the discussion of attitudes and behavioral genetics, the textbook mentions all of the following traits as being highly heritable EXCEPT:
    A. religiosity.
    B. political conservatism.
    C. openness to experience.
    D. preference for cognitive consistency.

34. Groupthink typically does NOT involve which of the following?
    A. Pressure on dissenters to conform.
    B. An illusion of invulnerability.
    C. Diffusion of responsibility.
    D. Self-censorship.

35. Which of the following is NOT mentioned by the text as a situational factor involved in deciding to dissent or act courageously?
    A. Cultural norms encourage you to take action.
    B. You do not become entrapped.
    C. The cost-benefit ratio supports getting involved.
    D. You have an ally.

36. One way of decreasing prejudice is by getting people exposed to another group's rules, food, customs, and attitude. This approach is referred to as:
    A. equality theory.
    B. contact hypothesis.
    C. jigsaw theory.
    D. exposure hypothesis.

37. Which of the following is not a critical condition for reducing prejudice and conflict?
    A. Both sides must cooperate to work towards a common goal.
    B. Both sides must be provided with moral, legal, and economic support.
    C. Both sides must have equal legal status and economic opportunities.
    D. Both sides must have their fundamental attribution errors corrected.

38. The banality of evil suggests that:
    A. even ordinary people are capable of both extreme cruelty and goodness.
    B. evil acts are most likely to occur in an average person than an unusual person.
    C. undesirable actions are more common than desirable actions.
    D. negative consequences are not of particular interest to psychologists.

PRACTICE TEST 2 – Short Answer

1. _____ are positions in society regulated by norms that describe how people in those positions should behave.

2. In the typical obedience study by Milgram, psychologists were surprised to find that _____ of the subjects administered shocks to the highest level possible.

3. In the prison study, the "prisoners" became panicky and helpless and some of the guards became tyrannical and cruel. Their behavior probably depended on the _____ they were asked to play.

4. The obedience studies and the prison study demonstrate the power of social roles to influence behavior. Some of the reasons that people obey authority, even when it's not in their own interest or may violate their own values, are the rules of good and the idea of _____, which occurs when commitment to a course of action is escalated.

5. In regards to the basic Milgram experiment, psychiatrists predicted that most participants would stop at _____ volts. In reality, most participants delivered _____ volts.

6. A _____ attribution identifies the cause of an action as something in the environment.

7. The tendency to overestimate _____ factors and underestimate the influence of the _____ when explaining someone else's behavior describes the _____ attribution error.

8. The _____ occurs when people take credit for positive actions and attribute the bad ones to the situation.

9. The need to believe that the world is fair, and that good people are rewarded and bad people are punished, is called the _____.

10. According to the textbook, political _____ is not heritable, but political _____ has high heritability.

11. The more a statement is repeated, the more people will believe that it is true. This is known as the _____ effect.

12. Laura feels very close to the other members of her local church and is quick to mention the church in her self-descriptions. Laura has a strong _____.

13. _____ refers to a behavior performed when carrying out an order from someone in authority. In contrast, _____ refers to behavior or attitudes that occur as a result of real or imagined group pressure.

14. Certain historical decisions have been made by strong leaders who discouraged disagreement, preferred unanimous decisions, and did not get opinions from people outside the group. These decisions were a result of _____.

15. Rather than bystander apathy, _____ may account for why individuals in crowds fail to respond to an emergency.

16. One reason for social loafing in a work group may be that the work is _____.

17. The concept of _____ often occurs in large groups and increases a person's willingness to do harm to someone else, to cheat, and to break the law. It may also be a primary reason for mob violence.

18. Four indirect ways of measuring prejudice include _____, _____, _____, and _____.

19. People have _____ identities based on their nationality, ethnic heritage, occupation, and social roles.

20. "We" are good, noble, and humane; "they" are bad, stupid, and cruel. Such beliefs reflect _____.

21. One way stereotypes distort reality is that they _____ differences between groups and _____ differences within other groups.

22. According to research on behavioral genetics, some core attitudes stem from personality traits that are highly heritable, such as the personality trait _____.

23. Identification with the dominant culture is known as _____.

PRACTICE TEST 3 – Essay

1.   Identify the influences and effects of roles and norms in the Zimbardo prison study and the Milgram obedience study.

2.   A group of students were asked to explain the source of a person's grades. They provided the explanations below. Examine each explanation and identify the explanatory device it relies upon (i.e., terms related to attribution theories).

    A.   Grades result from a person's intelligence and self-discipline. When these are high, grades are good and vice versa.

    B.   Grades depend on doing the right things. A person should earn good grades for reading instructions, meeting deadlines, turning in assignments. If a person does not do these things, he or she deserves bad grades.

    C.   Grades depend on quality teaching and educational materials. If the teacher is good, students should be motivated and do well.

    D.   Grades depend on luck. Sometimes it doesn't matter whether a person has studied or not if the test is tricky.

3.   Dr. Wong requires a group project in her sociology class. She wants each group to design a federally funded project to reduce the number of homeless and provide appropriate services for those who remain homeless. She is aware of all the principles of group behavior and she wants to reduce the likelihood of social loafing, diffusion of responsibility, groupthink, and deindividuation. She wants to increase cooperation and independent action. Develop a set of instructions she should use to meet all of her goals for this assignment.

4.   Jan and her sister are having a debate about the Agyflops, people from a country located in the Pacific Ocean. Jan's sister does not like the Agyflops and is explaining why to Jan. Most of her reasons are based on stereotypes. For each statement Jan's sister makes, indicate which stereotype-related problem it exemplifies.

    A.   "When I visited Agyflopia, everyone was so unfriendly. No one smiled."

    B.   "They are so different from us. Americans are so direct, but you never know what the Agyflops are thinking."

    C.   "I guess that there are many Agyflops in school with us, but they never seem to speak correctly and they always seem so stupid."

5.   Why is prejudice so hard to eliminate? You are the principal of a school with students from many different backgrounds. Design a program that attempts to improve relationships and reduce prejudice.

CHAPTER 9

Thinking and Intelligence

LEARNING OBJECTIVES

Thought: Using What We Know
9.1 - The basic elements of thought.
9.2 - Whether the language you speak affects the way you think.
9.3 - How subconscious thinking, nonconscious thinking, and mindlessness help us—and can also cause trouble.

Reasoning Rationally
9.4 - Why algorithms and logic can't solve all of our problems.
9.5 - The difference between deductive and inductive reasoning.
9.6 - The importance of heuristics and dialectical reasoning in solving real-life problems.
9.7 - How cognitive development affects the ways in which people reason and justify their views.

Barriers to Reasoning Rationally
9.8 - How biases in reasoning impair the ability to think rationally and critically.
9.9 - Why people worry more about rare but vivid disasters than about dangers that are far more likely.
9.10 - How the way a decision is framed affects the choices people make.
9.11 - Why people often value fairness even above rational self-interest.
9.12 - How the need to justify the expenditure of time, money, and effort affects how people think about a group they joined or a product they bought.

Measuring Intelligence: The Psychometric Approach
9.13 - Both sides of the debate about whether a single thing called "intelligence" actually exists.
9.14 - How the original purpose of intelligence testing changed when IQ tests came to America.
9.15 - The difficulties of designing intelligence tests that are free of cultural influence.

Dissecting Intelligence: The Cognitive Approach
9.16 - Which kinds of intelligence are not measured by standard IQ tests.
9.17 - The meaning of "emotional intelligence" and why it might be as important as IQ.
9.18 - Some reasons that Asian children perform much better in school than American students do.

Animal Minds
9.19 - Whether animals can think.
9.20 - Whether some animal species can master aspects of human language.

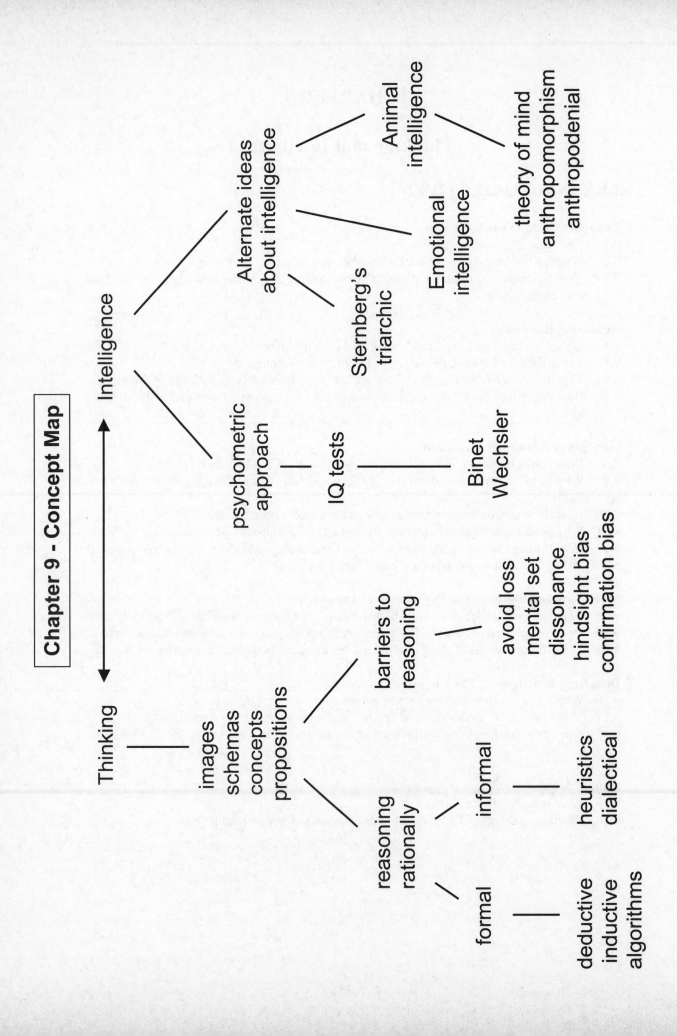

Chapter 9 - Concept Map

Thinking ◄────────────► **Intelligence**

Thinking

images
schemas
concepts
propositions

barriers to reasoning
- avoid loss
- mental set
- dissonance
- hindsight bias
- confirmation bias

reasoning rationally

formal
- deductive
- inductive
- algorithms

informal
- heuristics
- dialectical

Intelligence

psychometric approach

IQ tests
- Binet
- Wechsler

Alternate ideas about intelligence

Sternberg's triarchic

Emotional intelligence

Animal intelligence
- theory of mind
- anthropomorphism
- anthropodenial

BRIEF CHAPTER SUMMARY

Chapter 9 examines the elements and processes of thinking. Concepts, propositions, schemas, and images are all elements of thought. Deductive and inductive reasoning are types of formal reasoning that are useful for well-specified problems that have a single correct answer. Dialectical reasoning and reflective judgment are types of informal reasoning that are useful for more complex problems that require critical thinking. Several cognitive biases affect rational thinking and cause cognitive errors and distortions. Examples include the availability heuristic, the hindsight bias, and the confirmation bias. Intelligence is a characteristic that is difficult to define but is related to one's ability to think. Theorists examine intelligence using two approaches: the psychometric approach, which attempts to measure intelligence through tests; and the cognitive approach, which examines the aspects or domains of intelligence. Sternberg's triarchic theory and other multifaceted approaches are described. Intellectual achievement as measured by test scores is heavily influenced by such factors as motivation and attitude. Finally, psychologists also are interested in the cognitive abilities of nonhumans. Psychologists have long studied and debated whether or not animals have the cognitive capacity for language. Research has been conducted on primates (e.g., bonobos), dolphins, parrots, and other animals.

PREVIEW OUTLINE

Before you read the chapter, review the preview outline for each section of the text. After you have read the chapter, close this book and try to <u>recreate</u> the outlines on a blank piece of paper.

I. **THOUGHT: USING WHAT WE KNOW**
    A.   **The elements of cognition**
        1.   Thinking – mental manipulation of internal representations of objects, activities, and situations
        2.   Concepts – a mental category that groups objects, relations, activities, abstractions, or qualities having common properties
            a.   Basic concepts – those with a moderate number of instances
            b.   Prototype – most representative example of a concept
            c.   Whorf's theory: language molds thought
        3.   Proposition – units of meaning made of concepts that express unitary idea
        4.   Cognitive schemas – mental network of knowledge, beliefs, expectations
        5.   Mental images – mental representations, often visual
    B.   **How conscious is thought?**
        1.   Subconscious processes – outside of awareness but can be made conscious
        2.   Nonconscious processes – remain outside of awareness

3. Implicit learning – learning without the conscious intention to do so
4. Mindlessness – inflexibly acting, speaking, making decisions out of habit

II. REASONING RATIONALLY
A. **Reasoning** – mental activity that involves operating on information in order to reach conclusions; drawing inferences from observations or facts
B. **Formal reasoning: Algorithms and logic**
   1. Algorithms – procedures guaranteed to produce a solution (a recipe)
   2. Deductive reasoning – if the premises are true, the conclusion must be true
   3. Inductive reasoning – the conclusion probably follows from the premises, but could conceivably be false
C. **Informal reasoning: Heuristics and dialectical thinking**
   1. Heuristics – rules of thumb that don't guarantee an optimal solution
   2. Dialectical reasoning – comparing different views to resolve differences
D. **Reflective judgment** – critical thinking; the ability to evaluate and integrate evidence, relate evidence to theory or opinion, and reach conclusions

III. BARRIERS TO REASONING RATIONALLY
A. **Exaggerating the improbable (affect and availability heuristics)** – judging the probability of an event by how easy it is to think of examples
B. **Avoiding loss (framing effect)** – making decisions based on avoiding loss
C. **Fairness bias** – avoiding loss and economic rationality
D. **Hindsight bias** – believing that an outcome was known all along
E. **Confirmation bias** – paying attention to what confirms our beliefs
F. **Mental sets** – using rules that worked in the past
G. **Cognitive consistency** – motivation to reduce *cognitive dissonance* that occurs when a person simultaneously holds two cognitions that are inconsistent or holds a belief that is inconsistent with the person's behavior. Attempts to reduce dissonance are especially high under the following conditions:
   1. Need to justify a choice (postdecision dissonance)
   2. Need to justify behavior that conflicts with your view of yourself
   3. Need to justify your efforts
H. **Overcoming our cognitive biases:** biases are not always bad; biases usually diminish when decisions have serious consequences, and knowledge can reduce its impact

IV. MEASURING INTELLIGENCE: THE PSYCHOMETRIC APPROACH
A. **Intelligence** – ability to profit from experience, acquire knowledge, think

abstractly, act purposefully, or adapt to changes in the environment

Factor analysis – statistical method for analyzing the intercorrelations among various measures or test scores

g factor – many believe in a general ability that underlies all other abilities

Psychometric approach – traditional approach that focuses on how well people perform on standardized mental tests

B. **The invention of IQ tests**
   1. Binet measured children's mental age (MA) – intellectual development relative to other children's; intelligence quotient (IQ) and Stanford-Binet
   2. Wechsler developed test for adults (WAIS) and children (WISC)

C. **Culture and testing**
   1. Scores are influenced by expectations which shape stereotypes, which can affect scores by creating doubt, called stereotype threat

V. **DISSECTING INTELLIGENCE: THE COGNITIVE APPROACH**
   A. **The triarchic theory of intelligence** – Robert Sternberg identifies three aspects:
      1. Componential intelligence – includes metacognition
      2. Experiential intelligence – includes creativity in new situations
      3. Contextual intelligence – includes tacit knowledge (practical knowledge)
   B. **Domains of intelligence**
      1. Emotional intelligence – understanding one's own and others' emotions
   C. **Motivation, hard work, and intellectual success**
      1. Terman study showed motivation was determining factor in life success
      2. Stevenson study found that Asian students far outperformed American students on math tests and the gap is increasing
         a. Differences could not be accounted for by educational resources or intellectual abilities
         b. American parents had lower standards for their children's performance and were more likely than Asian parents to believe math ability was innate
         c. American students did not value education as much

VI. **ANIMAL MINDS**
   A. **Animal intelligence** – subject of study in cognitive ethology
      1. Cognitive ethologists say animals anticipate future events, make plans, coordinate their activities with others of their species
      2. Even complex actions may involve pre-wired behavior, not cognition
      3. Theory of mind – beliefs about the way minds work

B.   **Animals and language**
1.   Primary ingredient in human cognition is language
2.   Criteria for language
    a.   Meaningfulness – adequate ability to refer to things, ideas, feelings
    b.   Displacement – permits communication about objects not present
    c.   Productivity – ability to produce and comprehend new utterances
3.   By these criteria, animals communicate but do not have language
4.   Early efforts to teach language had success which was followed by skepticism and recognition of methodological problems in the research
5.   Newer research better controlled; has found that with training animals can use symbols, signs, understand some words, learn without formal training
6.   Some evidence shows non primates (e.g., dolphins, parrots) can acquire aspects of language

C.   **Thinking about the thinking of animals**
1.   Controversy about how to interpret study findings and research on animal cognition
2.   Concerns amongst researchers regarding anthropomorphism and anthropodenial

PRACTICE TEST 1 – Multiple Choice

1. The ability to think:
    A. is defined as the physical manipulation of the environment.
    B. confines us to the immediate present.
    C. allows for the mental manipulation of internal representations of objects, activities, and situations.
    D. incorporates all of the above.

2. A mental category that groups things that have common properties is called a:
    A. concept.
    B. symbol.
    C. proposition.
    D. schema.

3. Relationships between concepts are expressed by:
    A. super concepts.
    B. symbols.
    C. propositions.
    D. schemas.

4. Propositions are:
    A. complicated networks of knowledge.
    B. prototypes.
    C. units of meaning made up of concepts.
    D. composed of schemas.

5. Processes that are automated, such as typing or driving, are called _____, whereas making decisions without stopping to analyze what we are doing makes use of _____.
    A. subconscious processes; nonconscious processes
    B. mindlessness; subconscious processes
    C. nonconscious processes; mindlessness
    D. subconscious processes; mindlessness

6. Nonconscious processes refer to:
    A. processes that can be brought into consciousness when necessary.
    B. decisions that are made without thinking very hard.
    C. processes that are outside awareness but affect behavior.
    D. the practice of operating on information in order to reach conclusions.

7.   "All cats have fur. This animal is a cat. Therefore, it has fur." This is an example of:
      A.   deductive reasoning.
      B.   dialectical reasoning.
      C.   inductive reasoning.
      D.   divergent thinking.

8.   Inductive reasoning:
      A.   is used when the premises provide support for the conclusion, but the conclusion still could be false.
      B.   is often used in scientific thinking.
      C.   allows for a specific conclusion.
      D.   incorporates all of the above.

9.   When information is incomplete or many viewpoints compete, it is necessary to use:
      A.   informal reasoning.
      B.   formal reasoning.
      C.   inductive reasoning.
      D.   deductive reasoning.

10.   According to Kitchener and King, quasi-reflective judgment is characterized by:
      A.   the assumption that a correct answer always exists.
      B.   emphasizing the reception of truth through the senses or authorities.
      C.   the understanding that some judgments are more valid than others.
      D.   paying attention only to evidence that fits what someone already believes.

11.   When asked about his views on abortion, Danny responds, "That's what I was brought up to believe." According to Kitchener and King, he is in what stage of reflective thought?
      A.   Quasi-reflective
      B.   Prereflective
      C.   Reflective judgment
      D.   None of the above

12.   People are more likely to take risks:
      A.   for a potentially more rewarding solution than for a smaller sure gain.
      B.   if the risks are perceived as a way to avoid loss.
      C.   when the results are explained in terms of lives saved not lives lost.
      D.   none of the above.

13. Which of the following helps to explain the popularity of lotteries and why people buy earthquake insurance?
    A.   Confirmation bias
    B.   Loss aversion
    C.   Availability heuristic
    D.   Hindsight bias

14. Regarding languages in which objects are labeled as either masculine or feminine, researchers have discovered that:
    A.   while many aspects of an object are affected by the label, color perception in not influenced by the language.
    B.   cultures tends to exclusively favor either masculine or feminine labels for all objects.
    C.   assigned labels affect the other kinds of attributes native speakers assign to an object.
    D.   the perception of an object is largely unaffected by the vocabulary and grammar of the native language.

15. Though Allison lives comfortably in a city with a high crime rate, she is afraid to visit California because of a potential earthquake. Which cognitive bias does this represent?
    A.   Loss aversion
    B.   Availability heuristic
    C.   Cognitive dissonance
    D.   Confirmation bias

16. Chester and Koichi are in a very boring class. It is a required course for Chester, but Koichi chose to take this course, and it is too late to withdraw. What of the following is most likely to happen?
    A.   Chester is likely to try to reduce dissonance by saying he likes the class.
    B.   Koichi is likely to try to reduce dissonance by saying he likes the class.
    C.   Koichi is not likely to experience any dissonance.
    D.   Both are likely to experience dissonance.

17. The g factor refers to:
    A.   a general mental ability that underlies all specific abilities.
    B.   a technique using factor analysis.
    C.   the psychometric approach to intelligence.
    D.   all of the above.

18. One reason deductive and inductive reasoning cannot solve all our problems is that:
    A. they depend on knowing all the relevant information, which may not always be available.
    B. deductive reasoning usually comes to the opposite conclusion of inductive reasoning.
    C. they are usually very difficult to calculate, which results in the development of faulty premises.
    D. Dialectical reasoning is a superior method for resolving the premises of all logic.

19. If you were to use a heuristic, you would:
    A. figure out a possible logical conclusion based on the available premises.
    B. figure out the only logical conclusion based on the available premises.
    C. compare opposing ideas and viewpoints to arrive at the best solution.
    D. use a rule of thumb to suggest a plan of action.

20. Componential, experiential, and contextual refer to:
    A. Gardner's domains of intelligence.
    B. aspects of metacognition.
    C. the triarchic theory of intelligence.
    D. divergent thinking.

21. Though Shalini has never traveled overseas before, she is coping well with and adapting well to new situations on her trip to Europe. Which type of intelligence is involved?
    A. Componential
    B. Contextual
    C. Experiential
    D. Metacognitive

22. Which of the following are measured on most intelligence tests?
    A. Experiential intelligence
    B. Componential intelligence
    C. Contextual intelligence
    D. All of the above

23. Based on the studies comparing Asian and American school children, which of the following contributes to achievement?
    A. Whether skills are seen as innate or learned
    B. Standards for performance
    C. Expectation for involvement in outside activities
    D. All of the above

24. When you try to find the best solution by comparing and contrasting opposing facts or ideas, you are using:
    A.   heuristic reasoning.
    B.   inductive reasoning.
    C.   dialectical reasoning.
    D.   deductive reasoning.

25. Cognitive ethology refers to the study of cognitive processes in:
    A.   humans.
    B.   children.
    C.   the elderly.
    D.   nonhumans.

26. Which of the following best summarizes the current thinking on language ability in nonhumans?
    A.   Most mammals are able to use the basics of language.
    B.   Though animals have greater cognitive abilities than is often thought, scientists are divided on this issue.
    C.   Animals do not demonstrate any of the aspects of human language.
    D.   Only primates (chimpanzees and gorillas) have shown any type of language abilities.

27. The bonobo named Kanzi can use a sign to represent food that is not present in the room. This represents which feature of language?
    A.   Meaningfulness
    B.   Productivity
    C.   Displacement
    D.   Creativity

28. Which of the following statements is most likely to be effective in persuading people to try a new treatment?
    A.   This treatment has proven successful with 90% of clients.
    B.   This treatment has failed to show improvement in 10% of clients.
    C.   This treatment has helped 90% of clients and failed 10% of clients.
    D.   All of the above

29. Betsy has been placed in a situation where she has to share $100 with Horace. She and Horace have been told they are allowed three attempts to figure out how to share the money, otherwise neither one of them will receive any money. On the third and final attempt, Horace offers to give her $15 and keep $85 for himself. If Betsy is similar to the average, what is her likely reaction?
    A.   She will happily accept the $15 because it is better than nothing at all.
    B.   She will accept the $15, but be quite upset about it.
    C.   She will accept the $15 and calmly decide to take more money next time.
    D.   She will reject the $15 and take nothing instead.

30. When Alfred Binet invented the IQ test, its purpose was to:
    A.   detect the presence or absence of innate intelligence.
    B.   identify slow learners so that they could be given remedial work.
    C.   figure out what types of jobs would be best suited for those in the military.
    D.   construct an intelligence distribution so that children could be ranked into categories.

31. In America, the IQ test became used as a means of:
    A.   classifying individuals according to some presumed natural ability.
    B.   helping bring below average individuals up to the average intelligence.
    C.   diagnosing systemic flaws in educational approaches.
    D.   identifying teachers who need help refining their teaching techniques.

32. Which of the following is a problem with developing a culture-fair intelligence test?
    A.   Cultures vary in the amount of mental age each is capable of.
    B.   Cultures have different proportions of males and females.
    C.   Cultures differ in terms of problem-solving strategies used.
    D.   None of the above

33. Caitlin often discusses topics that are insensitive to those around her, resulting in them becoming very frustrated by her. Despite some obvious facial cues and changes in the body language of others, she typically doesn't notice the effect she is having on others. Caitlin is probably low in:
    A.   componential intelligence.
    B.   experiential intelligence.
    C.   tacit intelligence.
    D.   emotional intelligence.

PRACTICE TEST 2 – Short Answer

1. Thinking can be defined most simply as the _____ manipulation of information.

2. One unit of thought is the _____, a mental category grouping objects, relations, activities, abstractions, or qualities that share certain properties.

3. Horse, shoe, chair are all examples of _____ concepts that have a moderate number of instances.

4. When using inductive reasoning, it is always possible that _____ will turn up and prove you wrong.

5. While nonconscious processes remain outside of awareness, _____ processes can be brought into consciousness when necessary.

6. "Intuition" and "insight" are thought to be a result of _____ processes.

7. In deductive reasoning, if the premises are true, the conclusion _____ be true, in inductive reasoning, if the premises are true, the conclusion _____ be true.

8. Inductive reasoning and deductive reasoning are types of _____ reasoning. Problems requiring this type of reasoning can be solved by applying a(n) _____, a set of procedures guaranteed to produce a solution.

9. Juries must weigh opposing viewpoints. They would be most likely to use _____ to reach a verdict in a case.

10. Critical thinking requires that people ask questions, analyze assumptions, tolerate uncertainty, and resist oversimplification. These abilities require _____ judgment.

11. The idea that any judgment is as good as any other and is purely subjective would be most likely to occur in the _____ stage of reflective judgment.

12. One kind of rigidity that can hamper problem solving is biases due to _____, a tendency to approach problems in a particular way due to prior experience with similar problems.

13. That a person might be more afraid of an airplane crash than something much more likely to occur, like a car accident, may be a result of the _____.

14. When faced with incomplete information, it is often helpful to rely on rules of thumb that have worked in the past that are known as _____.

15. The language theorist who proposed that language influences how people think was _____.

16. Roger is trying to figure out whether or not he should buy a new car. He compares it to other models and considers the arguments for and against this particular model. Roger is using _____ reasoning.

17. IQ tests have been criticized for being _____ in favor of certain groups.

18. Some people believe that a(n) _____ ability underlies the many specific abilities tapped by intelligence tests, whereas others believe that there are and independent intelligences.

19. According to Sternberg's _____ theory, a person who easily adapts to the demands of new environments exhibits _____ intelligence.

20. Sternberg has identified three facets of intelligence: _____, _____, and _____.

21. Mayumi has a great deal of knowledge about her own cognitive processes and can effectively monitor and control those processes. She would be described as being very good at _____.

22. People tend to prefer questions framed in terms of _____ and tend to avoid questions framed in terms of _____.

23. The cross-cultural study by Stevenson found that American parents had _____ standards for their children's performance and for schools than Asian parents.

24. The three criteria for language are: meaningfulness, _____, and _____.

25. Attributing human emotions to certain animal behavior is an example of _____.

26. In industrial societies, when people are asked to divide resources, they will typically reject any offer in which they would receive less than _____ percent of the resources, even if it means they will receive nothing as a result.

PRACTICE TEST 3 – Essay

1. List a prototype for each of the concepts listed below.
    A. Clothing
    B. Animal
    C. Pet
    D. Relative

2. In each of the following examples, indicate what type of reasoning is most suitable for each problem and explain why.
    A. A navigator must determine the ship's position from the knowledge of a standard formula and the position of the North Star.
    B. A psychologist must determine if nonconformity facilitates creativity.
    C. A scientist must decide whether to pursue a career in teaching or research.
    D. A couple must decide if they are going to have a child.

3. Identify the cognitive biases in each of the following situations.
    A. Richard would rather drive 1,000 miles than fly because it is safer.
    B. Not only did you choose to go to this party 45 minutes away, but you convinced three other friends to go along. Even though no one is enjoying the party, you say you are having a good time.
    C. Jennifer doesn't want to get married and Craig does. When discussing the issue, Jennifer brings up only troubled relationships she knows of and cannot think of any of the happy relationships.

4. In the following examples identify what type of intelligence is being described, according to Sternberg's theory.
    A. Dr. Morris can go into a big organization and quickly identify the problem and select effective strategies for its solution.
    B. Dr. Mazeroll works with people in psychotherapy and knows which strategies are working and when she needs to try something different.
    C. Regardless of what group of people Nicholas finds himself with, he is able to quickly adjust to the situation, handle himself appropriately, and feel comfortable with himself.

5. Do animals have cognitive abilities? Make a case for and against this question.

CHAPTER 10

Memory

LEARNING OBJECTIVES

Reconstructing the Past
10.1 - Why memory does not work like a camera—and how it does work.
10.2 - Why errors can creep into our memories of even surprising or shocking events.

Memory and the Power of Suggestion
10.3 - How memories of an event can be affected by the way someone is questioned about it.

In Pursuit of Memory
10.4 - Whether you can know something without knowing that you know it.
10.5 - Why the computer is often used as a metaphor for the mind.

The Three-Box Model of Memory
10.6 - How the three "boxes" in the three-box model of memory operate.
10.7 - Why short-term memory is like a leaky bucket.
10.8 - Why a word can feel like it's "on the tip of your tongue" and what errors you are likely to make when you finally recall it.
10.9 - The difference between "knowing how" and "knowing that."

The Biology of Memory
10.10 - Changes that occur in the brain when you store a short-term versus a long-term memory.
10.11 - Where in the brain memories for facts and events are stored.
10.12 - Which hormones can improve memory.

How We Remember
10.13 - How memory can be improved, and why rote methods are not the best strategy.
10.14 - Why memory tricks, although fun, are not always useful.

Why We Forget
10.15 - The problem with remembering everything.
10.16 - The major reasons we forget even when we'd rather not.
10.17 - Why most researchers are skeptical about claims of repressed and "recovered" memories.

Autobiographical Memories
10.18 - Why the first few years of life are a mental blank.
10.19 - Why human beings have been called the "storytelling animal."

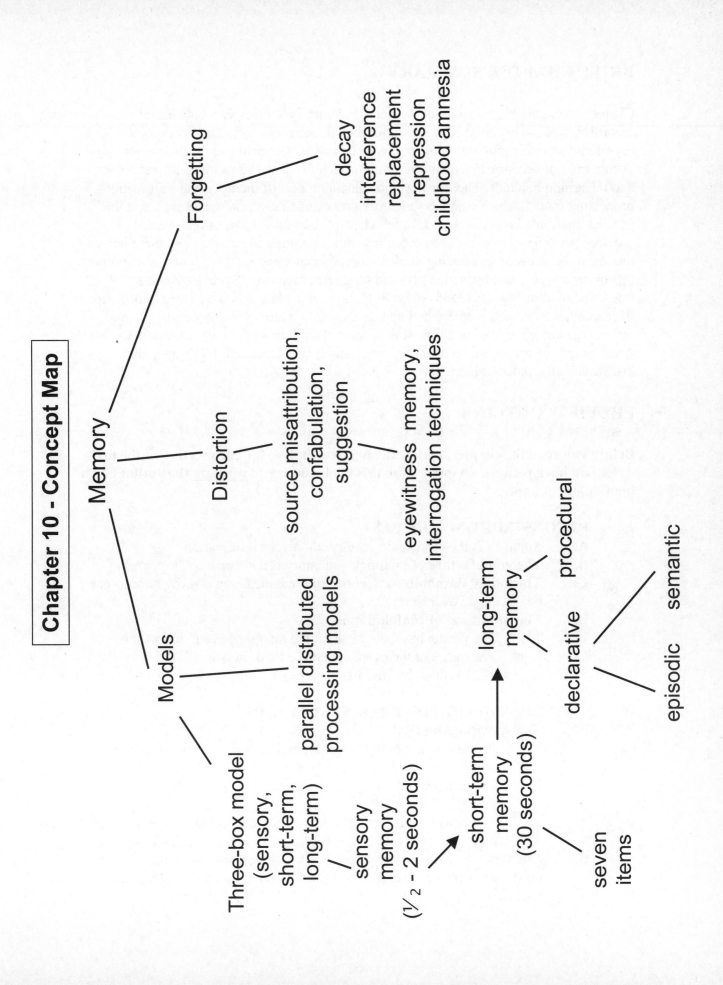

Chapter 10 - Concept Map

Memory

Forgetting
- decay
- interference
- replacement
- repression
- childhood amnesia

Distortion
- source misattribution, confabulation, suggestion
- eyewitness memory, interrogation techniques

Models

Three-box model (sensory, short-term, long-term)

parallel distributed processing models

sensory memory (½ - 2 seconds)

short-term memory (30 seconds)

seven items

long-term memory

declarative

procedural

episodic   semantic

BRIEF CHAPTER SUMMARY

Chapter 10 examines the nature of memory. Memory is not simply a videotaped recording that can be replayed at any time. Rather, our memories often incorporate outside information into our recollections so that what we recall is a reconstruction of events and not necessarily a memory of them. Memory is tested using recall, retrieval, and relearning methods. There are two prominent models of memory: the information-processing model, which compares memory processes to computer processes, and the parallel distributed processing model, which states that knowledge is represented as connections among thousands of processing units operating in parallel. The three-box model, an information-processing model, suggests that there are three types of memory: sensory memory, short-term memory, and long-term memory. Psychologists are interested in knowing what kinds of brain changes take place when we store information. Research has examined memory and its relationship to neurons, brain structures, and hormones. There are several different theories that explain why we forget: decay theory, replacement theory, interference theory, repression, cue-dependent forgetting, and theories about childhood amnesia.

PREVIEW OUTLINE

Before you read the chapter, review the preview outline for each section of the text. After you have read the chapter, close this book and try to <u>recreate</u> the outlines on a blank piece of paper.

I. **RECONSTRUCTING THE PAST**
   A. **Memory** is the capacity to retain and retrieve information
   B. **The manufacture of memory** – memory is a *reconstructive* process
   C. **The fading flashbulb** – memories of dramatic (even positive) events can be inaccurate over time
   D. **The conditions of confabulation**
      1. The person has thought about the imagined event many times
      2. The image of the event contains a lot of details
      3. The event is easy to imagine

II. **MEMORY AND THE POWER OF SUGGESTION**
   A. **The eyewitness on trial**
      1. People fill in missing pieces from memories, which can lead to errors
      2. Errors especially likely when ethnicity of suspect differs from witness
      3. The power of suggestion: the way a question is asked or the more often a story is told can influence what and how much is recalled
   B. **Children's testimony** – children are most suggestible when there's pressure to conform to expectations, and when they want to please the interviewer

III. **IN PURSUIT OF MEMORY**
   A. **Measuring memory**
      1. Explicit memory is conscious recollection
      2. Two ways of measuring explicit memory: recall and recognition
      3. Implicit memory is unconscious retention in memory
   B. **Models of memory**
      1. Three-box model (information-processing)
         a. Sensory register – retains information for a second or two
         b. Short-term memory (STM) – holds limited amount for 30 seconds
         c. Long-term memory (LTM) – accounts for longer storage
      2. Parallel distributed processing (connectionist) model
         a. Information is processed simultaneously, or in parallel
         b. Considers knowledge to be connections among thousands of units

IV. **THE THREE-BOX MODEL OF MEMORY**
   A. **Sensory register: Fleeting impressions**
      1. Includes separate memory subsystems for each of the senses
      2. Compares a stimulus to information already contained in long-term memory; it then goes to short-term-memory or it vanishes
   B. **Short-term memory: Memory's scratch pad**
      1. Holds information up to about 30 seconds as an encoded representation
      2. Working memory – holds information retrieved from long-term memory for temporary use
      3. The leaky bucket – holds seven (plus or minus two) chunks of information
   C. **Long-term memory: Final destination** – capacity is unlimited
      1. Organization in long-term memory
         a. Information is organized by semantic categories
         b. Network models – contents is a network of interrelated concepts
      2. The contents of long-term memory
         a. Procedural memories – knowing how
         b. Declarative memories – knowing that; includes semantic and episodic memories
      3. From short-term to long-term memory – three-box model has been used to explain the serial position effect

V. **THE BIOLOGY OF MEMORY**
   A. **Changes in neurons and synapses**
      1. In STM, changes within neurons temporarily alter neurotransmitter release
      2. LTM changes involve permanent structural changes in the brain
      3. Long-term potentiation; consolidation

B. **Locating memories**
    1. Areas in frontal lobes very active during short-term memory tasks
    2. Formation of declarative memories involve hippocampus
    3. Procedural memories involve the cerebellum
    4. Different brain involvement for implicit and explicit memory tasks
    5. A memory is a cluster of information distributed across areas of the brain
C. **Hormones, emotion, and memory**
    1. The adrenalin connection – hormones released during stress enhance memory, but high levels interfere with ordinary learning
    2. Sweet memories – the effect of these hormones may be due to glucose

VI. **HOW WE REMEMBER**
  A. **Effective encoding**
    1. Some encoding is effortless; some is effortful
    2. Rehearsal – review or practice of material while you are learning it
      a. Maintenance rehearsal – maintains information in STM only
      b. Elaborative rehearsal – associating new information with stored knowledge
    3. Deep processing – processing of meaning
  B. **Mnemonics** – strategies for encoding, storing, and retaining information

VII. **WHY WE FORGET**
  A. **The decay theory** – memories fade with time; doesn't apply well to LTM
  B. **Replacement** – new information wipes out old information
  C. **Interference** – retroactive interference (new information interferes with old) or proactive interference (old information interferes with new)
  D. **Cue-dependent forgetting** – lack of retrieval cues; mood-congruent memory
  E. **Repression** – traumatic memories are blocked from consciousness (also called psychogenic amnesia); lack of evidence to support the idea of repressed memories

VIII. **AUTOBIOGRAPHICAL MEMORIES**
  A. **Childhood amnesia: The missing years**
    1. May occur because brain areas involved in formation or storage of events are not well developed until a few years after birth
    2. Cognitive explanations have also been offered: lack of a sense of self; impoverished encoding; a focus on routine; children's ways of thinking
  B. **Memory and narrative: The stories of our lives**
    1. Narratives are a unifying theme to organize the events of our lives
    2. Themes serve as a cognitive schema that guides what we remember

PRACTICE TEST 1 – Multiple Choice

1. The reconstructive nature of memory refers to:
   A. the alteration of remembered information to help make sense of it.
   B. the capacity to retain and retrieve information.
   C. the ability to retrieve from memory previously encountered material.
   D. vivid, detailed recollections of circumstances.

2. Eyewitness testimony is influenced by:
   A. the fact that the details of events are often inferred rather than observed.
   B. memory errors that increase when the races of the suspect and witness differ.
   C. the wording of questions.
   D. all of the above.

3. Why does the tendency to reconstruct memories present a particularly serious problem in the courtrooms?
   A. Witnesses will lie to cover their memory errors.
   B. Reconstructed memories are almost always wrong.
   C. Witnesses who have reconstructed testimony will fail lie detector tests.
   D. Witnesses sometimes can't distinguish between what they actually saw and what they have reconstructed.

4. Researchers have discovered which of the following about memory?
   A. Memory operates like a videocamera, accurately encoding all that you see.
   B. People's memory can only be altered by extreme stress and hypnosis.
   C. Altering a single word in a question can change people's memory of an event.
   D. People's memory for trivial events can be distorted, but memories of important events can't be changed.

5. Unconsciously remembered material that continues to have an impact on behavior is:
   A. semantic memory.
   B. implicit memory.
   C. explicit memory.
   D. declarative memory.

6. Comparing the mind to a computer and speaking in terms of inputs and outputs reflects the:
   A. parallel distributed processing model of memory.
   B. cognitive model of memory.
   C. information-processing model of memory.
   D. connectionist model of memory.

7.   According to the "three-box" model, which is the first step in memory?
      A.   Short-term memory
      B.   Retrieval
      C.   Storage
      D.   Sensory register

8.   Which of the following is NOT a basic memory process?
      A.   Encoding
      B.   Retrieval
      C.   Storage
      D.   Perception

9.   When experiencing a tip of your tongue state, the word you want to recall and the word you incorrectly recall are likely to be:
      A.   similar in sound or look.
      B.   completely different from one another.
      C.   words that travel parallel neural pathways.
      D.   involved in the production of procedural memory.

10.   Which of the following brain structures is most critical in the storage of facts and events?
      A.   Brain stem
      B.   Hippocampus
      C.   Corpus callosum
      D.   Thalamus

11.   Which of the following describes the function of sensory memory?
      A.   It holds information that has been retrieved from LTM for temporary use.
      B.   It acts as a holding bin until we select items for attention.
      C.   It retains information for up to 30 seconds.
      D.   It aids in the retrieval of information from short-term memory.

12.   By most estimates, information can be kept in STM for _____ without rehearsal.
      A.   one-half to two seconds
      B.   up to 10 seconds
      C.   up to 30 seconds
      D.   up to 5 minutes

13.   One way to increase the amount of information held in STM is to:
      A.   group information into chunks.
      B.   form echoes and icons.
      C.   reduce interference.
      D.   use all of the above methods.

14.   You call information and ask for the phone number of your favorite restaurant. How long do you have to dial the number before you forget?
         A.   10 seconds
         B.   Up to 10 minutes
         C.   Up to 30 seconds
         D.   3 to 5 minutes

15.   What could you do to extend the time that you remember this information?
         A.   Maintenance rehearsal
         B.   Deep processing
         C.   Elaborative rehearsal
         D.   All of the above

16.   Which of the following helps transfer information from short-term memory to long-term memory?
         A.   Deep processing
         B.   Chunking
         C.   Elaborative rehearsal
         D.   All of the above

17.   Information is stored by subject, category, and associations in:
         A.   the sensory register.
         B.   short-term memory.
         C.   the sensory memory.
         D.   long-term memory.

18.   You recall from the chapter on learning that B.F. Skinner was involved in the development of operant conditioning. Your ability to remember this information demonstrates which type of memory?
         A.   Declarative
         B.   Procedural
         C.   Implicit
         D.   All of the above

19.   Learning to type, swim, or drive is a function of which type of memory?
         A.   Semantic
         B.   Episodic
         C.   Procedural
         D.   Declarative

20.   Semantic and episodic memories:
         A.   are types of declarative memories.
         B.   are types of implicit memories.
         C.   are examples of procedural memories.
         D.   demonstrate the primacy effect.

21. Which of the following brain structures is not involved in memory?
    A. Frontal lobes
    B. Hypothalamus
    C. Amygdala
    D. Prefrontal cortex

22. Which of the following can enhance memory?
    A. Epinephrine and norepinephrine
    B. Glutamate and serotonin
    C. Gamma-aminobutyric acid and aspartic acid
    D. Adenosine and glycine

23. Physiologically, short-term memory involves changes in _____, whereas long-term memory involves:
    A. the neuron's ability to release neurotransmitters; permanent structural changes in the brain.
    B. permanent structural changes in the brain; changes in the neurons.
    C. the hippocampus; the cortex.
    D. long-term potentiation; changes in the neuron's ability to release neurotransmitters.

24. One of the shortcomings of using mnemonics is that they:
    A. only help with recognition, not recall.
    B. only help with recall, not recognition.
    C. are often no more effective than rote rehearsal.
    D. are often no more effective than deep processing.

25. Pat learned to speak Italian at home as a child. Now when she studies Spanish, she can recall only the Italian words. This is an example of:
    A. retroactive interference.
    B. motivated forgetting.
    C. proactive interference.
    D. decay.

26. Decay theory does not seem to explain forgetting in long-term memory as evidenced by the fact that:
    A. it is not uncommon to forget an event from years ago while remembering what happened yesterday.
    B. it is not uncommon to forget an event from yesterday while remembering what happened years ago.
    C. people who took Spanish in high school did not do well on Spanish tests 30 years later.
    D. people generally don't remember high school algebra by the time they go to college.

27. The idea that you will remember better if you study for a test in the same environment in which you will be tested is an example of:
   A. state-dependent memory.
   B. elaborated rehearsal.
   C. cue-dependent memory.
   D. deja-vu.

28. Jocelyn is convinced that she remembers an event that occurred when she was six months old. This is impossible because:
   A. parts of the brain are not well developed for some years after birth.
   B. cognitive processes are not in place at that age.
   C. at that age encoding is much less elaborate.
   D. all of the above are reasons.

29. Why is it difficult to remember events earlier than the third or fourth year of life?
   A. The brain systems involved in memory take up to three or four years to develop.
   B. Adults use different schema than children.
   C. Children use different encoding methods than adults.
   D. All of the above

30. Cognitive researchers are interested in the stories humans tell about their lives because:
   A. most problems of adulthood can be traced back to repressed childhood conflicts.
   B. such stories can be used to overcome childhood amnesia.
   C. they reveal that almost all of our memories are false or significantly distorted.
   D. recollections are influenced by one's present mood and expectations.

31. If you had perfect recall for every event, it is likely:
   A. you'd be less efficient due to all the distracting memories.
   B. you'd become more successful at managing every aspect of your life.
   C. your recognition skills would be seriously impaired.
   D. your cerebral cortex would be significantly larger than the average individual.

32. When people have suffered a very traumatic experience, they:
   A. typically repress the experience deep into their unconscious.
   B. often have great difficulty forgetting intrusive memories of the experience.
   C. encode the memory with such great detail that it will always be recalled without error.
   D. experience decreased retroactive interference and increased proactive interference.

PRACTICE TEST 2 – Short Answer

1.   Research in which volunteers often eliminated or changed details of a story that did not make sense to them, and then added other details to make the story coherent, demonstrates that memory is a(n) _____ process.

2.   In reconstructing their memories, people often draw on many sources. They may incorporate information from family stories, photographs, or videos in a new integrated account. Later they may not be able to separate the original experience from what they added after the fact. This phenomenon is called _____ misattribution.

3.   False memories can be as _____ over time as true ones.

4.   Eyewitness accounts of events are heavily influenced by _____ comments made during an interrogation.

5.   In the study involving questioning about broken headlights, researchers changed the recall of participants simply by switching the words _____ and _____.

6.   Simon is watching a scary scene in a movie, which is causing stress and emotional arousal. He is more likely to vividly remember that scene later because of the hormones released by his _____.

7.   Models of memory that borrow heavily from the language of computer programming are referred to as _____ models.

8.   _____ memory holds information for a second or two, whereas _____ holds information for about 30 seconds.

9.   We overcome the limits of short-term memory by grouping small bits of information into larger units, or _____.

10. One way that words are organized in long-term memory is by the _____ categories to which they belong.

11. _____ memories are internal representations of the world, independent of any particular context, whereas _____ memories are internal representations of personally experienced events. Both are types of _____ memories.

12. _____ rehearsal will keep information in short-term memory, but to remember things for the long haul, it is better to use _____ rehearsal which involves associating new items of information with material that has already been stored.

160

13.   The hormones released by the adrenal glands during stress and emotional arousal, including _____, enhance memory.

14.   The _____ theory of forgetting holds that memory traces fade with time if they are not "accessed" now and then.

15.   A type of interference in which new information interferes with the ability to remember old information is called _____ interference. _____ interference is when old information interferes with the ability to remember new information.

16.   Often, when we need to remember, we rely on _____ cues, items of information that can help us find the specific information we're looking for. The type of memory failure that occurs when we lack these cues is called _____ forgetting.

17.   If your emotional arousal is especially high at the time of an event, you may remember that event best when you are in the same emotional state. This is referred to as _____ memory.

18.   Memories from before the age of two are not likely to be real memories because of childhood _____.

19.   When we are happy, we are more likely to recall happy memories, but when we are sad, we are more likely to recall sad memories. This phenomenon is known as _____.

PRACTICE TEST 3 – Essay

1. Identify and describe the three basic processes involved in the capacity to remember.

2. Imagine that you watched a baseball game yesterday and presently retain many details about the game. According to the "three-box" theory, what kind of sequence have such details followed?

3. The home team brings in a new pitcher in the fifth inning. In each situation below, suggest the type of memory most likely to be the most relevant to the example.

   A. Her warm-up style indicates the fluid and coordinated movements of an experienced athlete.
   B. After several batters are walked, she tells the umpire that the calls are no better this week than last week.
   C. As the third batter steps up, the pitcher indicates to the umpire that improper attire is being worn.

4. While searching the attic, Henry discovers his senior-year diary, written over 30 years ago and not seen since.
   A. According to decay theory, what will have been forgotten and why?
   B. The first page contains the title "Happy Times as a Senior." He tries hard to remember but is not successful until he begins reading a description of his homeroom. This triggers a flood of memories. What variable related to forgetting best explains this experience?
   C. Henry finds another section entitled "Worst Times as a Senior." He is sure there were very few but begins to change his mind as he reads. This time there is no flood of memories, but many descriptions of unhappy moments. Henry wonders whether he was overly imaginative or whether senior year was pretty awful. What variables that influence memory best explain this?

5. For finals week, you had to be prepared for exams in English, math, Spanish, Italian, and history. How should the sequence of study be arranged to minimize the possibility of interference?

CHAPTER 11

Emotion, Stress, and Health

LEARNING OBJECTIVES

The Nature of Emotion
11.1 - Which facial expressions of emotion most people recognize the world over.
11.2 - Which parts of the brain are involved with different aspects of emotion.
11.3 - How mirror neurons generate empathy, mood contagion, and synchrony.
11.4 - Which two hormones provide the energy and excitement of emotion.
11.5 - How thoughts create emotions—and why an infant can't feel shame or guilt.

Emotion and Culture
11.6 - Why people from different cultures disagree on what makes them angry, jealous, or disgusted.
11.7 - Why some psychologists question whether there are primary and secondary emotions.
11.8 - How cultural rules affect how people display or suppress their emotions.
11.9 - Why people often do "emotion work" to convey emotions they do not feel.
11.10 - Whether women are really more "emotional" than men.

The Nature of Stress
11.11 - How your body responds to physical, emotional, and environmental stressors.
11.12 - Why being "stressed out" increases the risk of illness in some people but not others.
11.13 - How psychological factors affect the immune system.
11.14 - When having a sense of control over events is beneficial and when it is not.

Stress and Emotion
11.15 - Which emotion may be most hazardous to your heart.
11.16 - Whether chronic depression leads to physical illness.
11.17 - Why confession is often as healthy for the body as it is for the soul.

Coping with Stress
11.18 - Ways of calming the body when you are feeling stressed.
11.19 - The difference between emotion-focused and problem-focused coping.
11.20 - How to reduce stress by rethinking and reappraising your problems.
11.21 - The importance and limitations of social support.

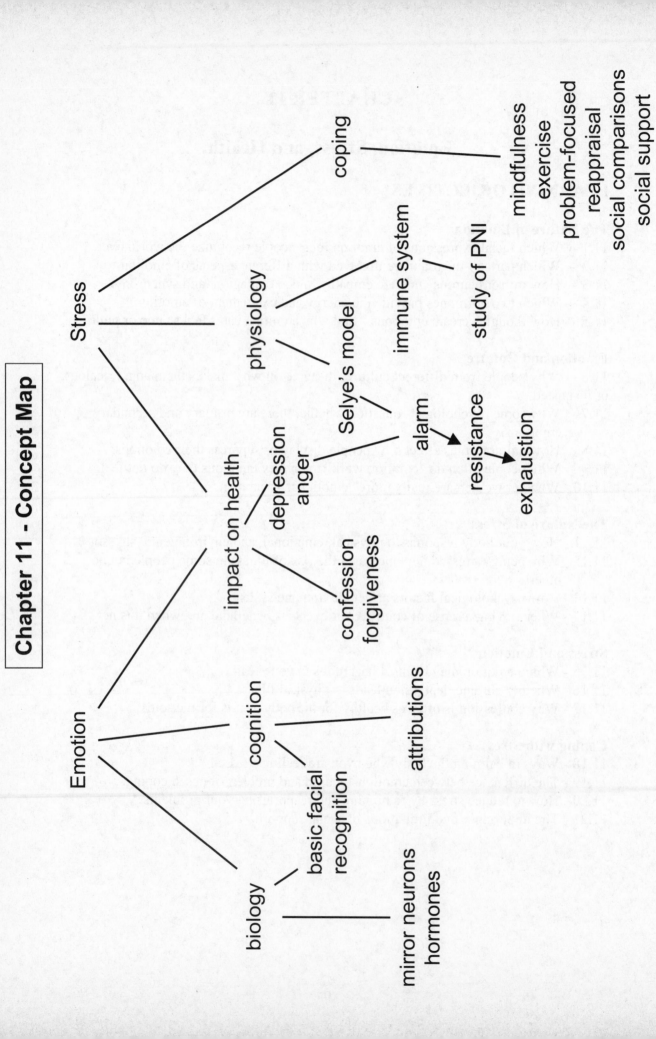

Chapter 11 - Concept Map

Emotion

Stress

biology

cognition

impact on health

physiology

coping

basic facial recognition

mirror neurons hormones

attributions

depression anger

confession forgiveness

Selye's model

immune system

study of PNI

alarm → resistance → exhaustion

mindfulness
exercise
problem-focused
reappraisal
social comparisons
social support

BRIEF CHAPTER SUMMARY

Chapter 11 explores the components of emotion, stress, and health. Emotions have a physical component that involves facial expressions, brain activity, and hormonal activity. There is evidence for seven universal facial expressions. Specific parts of the brain (e.g., amygdala, prefrontal cortex) are associated with aspects of emotion (e.g., approach or avoidance). The physiological component does not result directly in the experience of emotion; events are interpreted, and our perception of events influences our emotional experience. Cultural display rules govern how and when primary emotions may be expressed. Research on gender differences in emotions suggests that men and women experience similar emotions, though they differ somewhat in their physiological responses and their perceptions and expectations about emotional experiences. Emotion and stress have parallels in their physiology, appraisal, and expression. Hans Selye began the modern era of stress research and identified a stress response cycle (alarm phase, resistance phase, and exhaustion phase). Stress is no longer considered a purely biological condition that leads directly to illness, but rather an interaction between aspects of the individual and aspects of the environment. The area of psychoneuroimmunology examines the relationship among psychological processes, the nervous and endocrine systems, and the immune system. The current view of the relationship between stress and illness considers aspects of the external stressor, characteristics of the individual, emotional style of the individual, and perceived coping abilities. Optimistic and pessimistic explanatory styles, and internal versus external locus of control have been researched extensively and play a significant role in physical and psychological health. Several coping methods are reviewed, including solving the problem, thinking about the problem differently, and drawing on social support.

PREVIEW OUTLINE

Before you read the chapter, review the preview outline for each section of the text. After you have read the chapter, close this book and try to <u>recreate</u> the outlines on a blank piece of paper.

I.   **EMOTION AND THE BODY**
   A.   **Primary emotions** are considered to be universal and biologically based, whereas secondary emotions are more culture-specific
           Secondary emotions include emotions that develop with cognitive maturity and vary across individuals and cultures
   B.   **The face of emotion**
           1.   Darwin said facial expressions of emotion had survival functions
           2.   Ekman has found seven universal facial expressions of emotion: anger, happiness, fear, surprise, disgust, sadness, and contempt
           3.   Facial feedback – facial expressions can influence feelings
           4.   Research on babies shows they use emotions to communicate

5.   Facial expressions may have different meanings depending on the context and the culture
    a.   Familiarity affects the ability to read facial expressions
    b.   Expressions can mean different things at different times
    c.   People often use facial expressions to lie about their feelings

C.   **The brain and emotion**
    1.   **Left prefrontal cortex** – associated with motivation to approach others
    2.   **Right prefrontal cortex** – associated with withdrawal from others
    3.   **Amygdala** – gives quick appraisal of sensory information, especially important for anger and fear
    4.   **Mirror neurons** – involved in empathy, imitation, and reading emotions

D.   **The energy of emotion** – hormones produce the energy to respond to alarm signals
    1.   Epinephrine and norepinephrine produce state of arousal
    2.   Emotions differ from one another biochemically

E.   **Biology and Deception: Can lies be detected in the brain and body?**
    1.   The polygraph machine and lie detection – based on idea that lying associated with increased autonomic nervous system activity (increased heart rate, respiration)
    2.   Most researchers see polygraph tests as invalid because no physiological response is uniquely associated with lying
    3.   Other physiological approaches to catching liars include the Computer Voice Stress Analyzer, MRI, and Guilty Knowledge Test

II.   **EMOTION AND THE MIND**
    A.   **How thoughts create emotions**
        1.   Attributions and emotion – how perceptions and explanations of events (attributions) affect emotions
            a.   Appraising events for their personal implications affects emotions
            b.   Cognitions involved range from immediate perceptions of an event to general philosophy of life
        2.   Thoughts and emotions operate reciprocally, each influencing the other
    B.   **Cognitions and emotional complexity** – people can learn how their thinking affects their emotions and then they can learn to change their thinking

III.   **EMOTION AND CULTURE**
    A.   **How culture shapes emotions** – are some emotions specific to culture?

        1.   Language and emotion – words for certain emotional states exist in some languages and not in others (e.g., schadenfreude)

        2.   Culture affects which emotions are defined as "primary" and what individuals feel emotional about

B.   Culture and emotional expression

        1.   Display rules – cultural rules govern how, when emotions are expressed

        2.   Emotion work – how, when to show an emotion we don't feel

IV.   THE NATURE OF STRESS

A.   Hans Selye's General Adaptation Syndrome:

        1.   Alarm phase – the body mobilizes to meet threat

        2.   Resistance phase – resists or copes with a stressor which makes the body more susceptible to *other* stressors

        3.   Exhaustion phase – occurs if the stressor persists; body's resources are depleted and vulnerability to illness increases

B.   Current Approaches

        1.   "Fight or flight" response initiates activity along the HPA axis for increased energy; long-term activation can be harmful

        2.   Responses to stress differ across individuals

C.   The Immune System: PNI

        1.   Researchers study mechanisms that link mind and body; interdisciplinary specialty is called psychoneuroimmunology (PNI)

        2.   PNI researchers study psychological factors (e.g., feeling crowded) that influence the immune system, such as white blood cells (which recognize foreign substances and destroy or deactivate them)

V.   STRESS AND THE MIND

A.   Optimism and pessimism

        1.   Pessimistic style associated with lower achievement, illness, slower recovery from trauma, self-destructive behavior

        2.   Optimistic style associated with "positive illusions" (not denial), active problem solving, persistence, better health habits

        3.   Optimism can be learned, such as by counting one's blessings

B.   The sense of control

        1.   Locus of control – your expectation of whether you can control the things that happen to you

                a.   Internal locus of control – those who believe they are responsible for what happens to them

                b.   External locus of control – those who believe they are victims of circumstances

        2.   The benefits of control

          a.   Difficult events more tolerable if more predictable or controllable

          b.   Feeling in control reduces chronic pain, improves adjustment to surgery and illness, speeds up recovery from diseases

    3.   The limits of control

          a.   Trying to control the uncontrollable or blaming control are problems

          b.   Goal is to avoid guilt and self-blame while retaining self-efficacy

          c.   Ideas about control influenced by culture: primary control (modify situation) vs. secondary control (modify desires)

VI.   STRESS AND EMOTION

A.   Emotions and illness

    1.   Evidence that negative emotions affect the course of illness once a person has a medical condition; less clear whether negative emotions <u>cause</u> illness

    2.   Hostility and heart disease

          a.   Early research on the Type A pattern as risk factor for heart disease

          b.   Cynical or antagonistic hostility found to be related to heart disease

    3.   Depression may be a risk factor for heart disease and other diseases, but the evidence is somewhat contradictory

B.   Positive Emotions

    1.   Feeling happy, cheerful, and hopeful may protect a person from getting sick

C.   Managing Negative Emotions

    1.   Emotional inhibition

          a.   Trying to avoid bothersome thoughts has the opposite effect

          b.   Suppressors (those who deny feelings of anxiety, anger, or fear) may be at greater risk of becoming ill

    2.   "Confessing" worries and fears, as well as expressing long-held secrets, can reduce chance of illness if it produces insight and understanding

    3.   The benefits of forgiveness (letting grievances go) increase feelings of control, strengthens relationships, and promotes empathy

VII.   COPING WITH STRESS

A.   Mindfulness meditation – learning to accept negative emotions without judging them or attempting to get rid of them

B.   **Solving the problem**
1.   Emotion-focused coping – giving in to emotions right after tragedy
2.   Problem-focused coping – learning information about how to cope

C.   **Rethinking the problem**
1.   Reappraising the situation – thinking about a problem differently which changes a person's emotional response
2.   Learning from experience – finding benefit from a bad experience
3.   Making social comparisons – comparing self to others less fortunate

D.   **Drawing on social support**
1.   Studies show positive effects of friends on health and longevity
2.   Friends can be source of stress when there is arguing and hostility

PRACTICE TEST 1 – Multiple Choice

1.   Joni watches as a customer at another table yells at a waiter during lunch. Joni feels quite embarrassed for this waiter she has never met before. One possible reason for this is due to brain cells known as:
    A.   observational cells.
    B.   mirror neurons.
    C.   imitation pathways.
    D.   empathy synapses.

2.   Cultures can influence:
    A.   the way emotions are experienced.
    B.   the development of universal emotions.
    C.   whether or not you inherit certain emotions.
    D.   your ability to recognize basic facial expressions.

3.   Ekman's studies found that:
    A.   there are 15 universal facial expressions of emotion.
    B.   there are really no universal facial expressions of emotion because of the different meaning each culture attaches to the expressions.
    C.   there are seven basic facial expressions of emotion.
    D.   all facial expressions are learned.

4.   In some cultures it may be appropriate to slightly smile and nod when being criticized in order to show shame. In other cultures, it is more appropriate to not smile when feeling ashamed. Your culture's expectations for when and how to show shame is an example of:
    A.   social traps.
    B.   facial-emotive norms.
    C.   role work.
    D.   display rules.

5.   Which of the following statements about the brain and emotion is FALSE?
    A.   Damage to the amygdala can result in exaggerated fear responses.
    B.   Parts of the right prefrontal cortex are involved with withdrawal or escape.
    C.   Parts of the left prefrontal cortex are involved with approaching others.
    D.   Parts of the prefrontal cortex are involved in the regulation of emotion.

6. Ekman's cross-cultural studies on facial expressions suggest that:
   A. certain facial expressions are universal in their emotional meaning.
   B. people from different cultures can recognize the emotions in pictures of people who are entirely foreign to them.
   C. in the cultures they studied most people recognized the emotional expressions portrayed by people in other cultures.
   D. all of the above

7. Angela has been feeling quite depressed. However, she works as a greeter at a department store and knows that greeters aren't supposed to look sad. Therefore she puts on a happy face and enthusiastically greets all customers. Angela's public display of emotions that she actually isn't feeling is known as:
   A. contextual body language.
   B. emotion work.
   C. secondary emotional control.
   D. false facial feedback.

8. Which of the following is true?
   A. High levels of stress affect everyone equally.
   B. Low levels of stress affect everyone equally.
   C. How people are affected by stress depends upon their learning history.
   D. It appears that genetics play almost no role in our reaction to stress.

9. Which of the following is associated with good health?
   A. Primary emotional style
   B. Secondary emotional style
   C. Internal locus of control
   D. External locus of control

10. Clinical depression is correlated with:
    A. no increased risk of heart attacks.
    B. a doubled risk of heart attacks.
    C. 10 times increased risk of heart attacks.
    D. 20 times increased risk of heart attacks.

11. Mindfulness meditation works by:
    A. teaching people to get rid of undesired thoughts.
    B. distracting people from focusing on undesired thoughts.
    C. getting people to accept undesired thoughts without judgment.
    D. helping people to recognize and actively reduce undesired thoughts.

12. Which of the following is the best statement regarding confession and health?
    A. Divulging negative emotions only improves health when you confess to another person.
    B. Divulging negative emotions only improves health when you confess to yourself privately.
    C. Divulging negative emotions improves health when you confess to either yourself or another person.
    D. Divulging negative emotions appears to have no measurable impact upon one's health.

13. Jeffery lost his scholarship and now has to get a job to pay for his rent. Although he was originally highly stressed, he decides that this is a good opportunity to meet new people. Jeffery is using what stress reduction technique?
    A. Reappraisal
    B. Mindfulness
    C. Emotion-focusing
    D. Emotion work

14. Which of the following is one of the hormones that provides the energy of an emotion?
    A. Epinephrine
    B. Dopamine
    C. Insulin
    D. Serotonin

15. According to Selye, the body mobilizes to meet a threat during which stage?
    A. Alarm
    B. Resistance
    C. Activation
    D. Exhaustion

16. Which is (are) involved in the physiological experience of emotion?
    A. Amygdala
    B. Prefrontal cortex
    C. Autonomic nervous system
    D. All of the above

17. Ellen is in finals week and she has been getting by on very little sleep. She is managing to prepare for her tests, but she is more irritable than usual and feels like she might be getting the flu. This would be compatible with the _____ stage of Selye's model.
   A. alarm
   B. exhaustion
   C. resistance
   D. activation

18. Jonathan has been under stress for a long period of time. He is lonely at college, under pressure to do well, and in the middle of finals. Which of the following is true?
   A. He is at higher risk for getting sick.
   B. Persistent stress depletes the body of energy.
   C. How he responds will depend on his coping skills.
   D. All of the above are true.

19. My heart is beating, I'm hyperventilating, and my pupils are dilated. Which of the following is involved in this response?
   A. Epinephrine
   B. Adrenal glands
   C. Norepinephrine
   D. All of the above

20. In a series of experiments, students reported occasions in which they had succeeded or failed on an exam. Researchers found that the students' emotions were most closely associated with:
   A. whether they had passed or failed the exam.
   B. their explanations for their success or failure.
   C. other peoples' perceptions of their performance.
   D. past experiences with success or failure.

21. A study of Olympic athletes found that sometimes the third place winners were happier than the second place winners. Their emotional response depended on their:
   A. ability to rationalize.
   B. desire to win.
   C. thoughts about what might have been.
   D. country of origin.

22. Ramsey is stuck in a traffic jam and he is already late for his important appointment. This type of stressor:
    A. does not pose much threat to health.
    B. increases the risk of illness.
    C. is related to heart disease.
    D. decreases the risk of illness.

23. Scientists interested in exploring the links between psychological processes and the immune system created an interdisciplinary field called:
    A. health psychology.
    B. psychosomatic medicine.
    C. psychoneuroimmunology.
    D. behavioral medicine.

24. Who among the following men has a higher risk for coronary heart disease?
    A. John is intense, ambitious, hard-driving, and successful.
    B. Ron is complaining and irritable.
    C. Don is aggressive, confrontational, rude, cynical, and uncooperative.
    D. Lon is easy-going and calm.

25. Identifying a problem and learning as much as possible about it is part of:
    A. emotion-focused coping.
    B. rethinking the problem.
    C. problem-focused coping.
    D. cooling off.

26. _____ tends to increase self-efficacy, reduce anger, anxiety, and psychological stress.
    A. Problem-focused coping
    B. Avoidance
    C. External locus of control
    D. Looking outward

27. Which of the following statements is true?
    A. Women feel emotions more often and more intensely than men.
    B. Men are more likely than women to reveal negative emotions, such as sadness and fear.
    C. Men and women are fairly similar in how often they experience normal, everyday emotions.
    D. Powerful people are more sensitive to subordinates' nonverbal signals than vice versa.

28. Where are gender differences in emotion found?
    A.   There are some physiological differences in response to conflict.
    B.   There are differences in the perceptions and expectations that generate certain emotions.
    C.   There are different display rules.
    D.   All of the above

29. When is it best to use emotion-focused coping and when should one use problem-focused coping?
    A.   Problem-focused coping should be used at all times; it is never desirable to use emotion-focused coping.
    B.   Emotion-focused coping is useful following a trauma but a shift should be made to problem-focused coping.
    C.   Emotion-focused coping is called for when stressors are continuous or can be prepared for; problem-focused coping should be used when the stressor is sudden.
    D.   Emotion-focused coping should be used by people with Type A personalities, and problem-focused coping is appropriate for those with emotional inhibition.

30. Social support:
    A.   helps heart rate return to normal more quickly after a stressful episode.
    B.   can extend the survival time of people with serious illnesses, in some cases.
    C.   can contribute to longer life.
    D.   all of the above.

31. Which of the following is a psychological factor that is thought to be important to good health?
    A.   Social support
    B.   Ability to relax
    C.   Feelings of control
    D.   All of the above

PRACTICE TEST 2 – Short Answer

1. Friends and social supports can both _____ and _____ stress.

2. Regardless of culture, children recognize the prototypical emotions known as _____ emotions. As children develop, they recognize emotions that are less prototypical known as _____ emotions.

3. When it comes to uncontrollable negative events such as death and taxes, having an _____ locus of control may be harmful.

4. The seven universal facial expressions identified by Ekman are

    _____.

5. Depression itself might not directly lead to heart disease. The real culprits may be the _____ that depression can produce.

6. The _____ appears to be responsible for evaluating sensory information and quickly determining its emotional importance. The _____ subsequently provides a more accurate appraisal of incoming information.

7. When you are in a situation requiring the body to respond, the _____ nervous system sends out two hormones, _____ and _____ that produce a state of arousal.

8. Susan recently had breast cancer that required surgery on part of her breast. She was depressed, but then felt better by recalling other women have lost their entire breasts to mastectomy. Susan is using _____ to make herself feel better.

9. _____ are defined as the explanations that people make of their own and other people's behavior.

10. _____ introduced the modern era of stress research. He concluded that "stress" consists of a series of physiological reactions that occur in three phases: the _____ phase, the _____ phase, and the _____ phase.

11. An understanding of the reciprocal interaction between thoughts and feelings helps us to see that just as _____ affect emotions, so do _____ affect cognitions.

12. Some evidence for the existence of primary emotions comes from the fact that most languages have emotion _____, or agreed upon core examples of the concept emotion.

13. Whatever the emotion, every society has _____ governing how and when emotions may be expressed.

14. Acting out an emotion we don't really feel is called emotion _____.

15. When an _____ invades the body, the _____ system deploys white blood cells that produce chemicals that go to the brain.

16. The interdisciplinary specialty that investigates the exact mechanisms that link mind and body, and studies how stress causes problems is called _____.

17. If we define being "more emotional" in terms of physiological reactivity to _____, then men are more emotional than women. One possible explanation for this is that the male's autonomic nervous system is, on the average, more _____ than the female's.

18. Negative emotions such as worry can suppress the _____ system.

19. The factor that can be dangerous for health in the behavior of some Type A personalities is _____.

20. The one gender difference that undoubtedly contributes most to the stereotype that women are "more emotional" than men is women's greater willingness to _____ their feelings, nonverbally and verbally.

21. People can tolerate all kinds of stressors if they feel able to _____ them. For example, the crowd you choose to join at a football game is not as stressful as being trapped in a crowd on a busy street.

22. If you do not like a situation, you may try to change it or fight it. This represents _____ control. If you try to accommodate to reality by changing your own desires, you are demonstrating _____ control.

23. _____ coping, in which a person focuses on the anger, anxiety, or grief the problem has caused, is normal after a tragedy or trauma. However, over time _____ coping strategies are associated with better adjustment.

24. _____ a situation (taking a different perspective) can help a person to think about the problem differently.

PRACTICE TEST 3 – Essay

1.   A.   A nurse looks in on a patient shortly before surgery. The patient's heart rate and blood pressure are elevated, breathing is rapid, the pupils are dilated, and the patient appears flushed. The nurse concludes that the patient is fearfully anticipating the surgery. What physiological mechanism produces the pattern observed by the nurse?

        B.   The nurse tries to reassure the patient but he laughs and denies feeling nervous. In fact, the patient is not very cooperative and the nurse begins to feel irritated but continues to attempt to be comforting and pleasant. Explain the patient's and the nurse's behavior in terms of emotion work and display rules.

2.   Larry, Curly, and Moe all got a grade of 75 on a test, yet they each had different reactions to the grade. Larry felt disappointed and depressed. Curly felt relieved that he passed, though he didn't feel particularly happy or sad about the grade. Moe felt extremely happy. Using information about the influence of interpretations on feelings, identify expectations, surrounding events, and interpretations of each student's emotional responses.

3.   Apply Hans Selye's phases of stress response to people being held hostage. Describe what they would experience in the alarm, resistance, and exhaustion phases.

4.   Suppose that a group of hostages has been held by terrorists for several months. For each description, indicate whether stress has been reduced through attempts to solve, reappraise, or live with the problem, and identify the specific coping strategy being used.

        A.   Margaret has decided her captors have no bad intentions and are just trying to gain media attention to their cause.

        B.   Frank believes escape would be difficult but not impossible. He keeps formulating escape plans and explaining them to others.

        C.   Alberto believes this disaster has a bright side. Had another terrorist group taken them, there might have been torture as well as captivity.

        D.   Like Frank, Tony believes escape is possible, but only if the terrorists make an unexpected mistake. His goal is to remain as calm as possible and look for an opportunity. He refuses to waste energy and lose hope by developing or considering unrealistic escape plans.

        E.   Eleanor believes the group will remain in captivity virtually forever. Her goal is to eat as regularly as possible and combat inactivity through exercise.

CHAPTER 12

Motivation

LEARNING OBJECTIVES

The Hungry Animal: Motives to Eat

12.1 - The biological mechanisms that make it difficult for obese people to lose weight and keep it off.

12.2 - How notions of the ideal male and female body change over time and across cultures.

12.3 - Why people all over the world are getting fatter.

12.4 - The major forms of eating disorders, and why they are increasing among young men as well as women.

The Social Animal: Motives to Love

12.5 - How biology affects attachment and love.

12.6 - Some key psychological influences on whom and how you love.

12.7 - The three basic styles of attachment and how they affect your relationships.

The Erotic Animal: Motives for Sex

12.8 - Which part of the anatomy is the "sexiest sex organ."

12.9 - Why pleasure is only one of many motives for having sex.

12.10 - How culture affects sexual practices.

12.11 - The puzzling origins of sexual orientation.

The Competent Animal: Motives to Achieve

12.12 - The three kinds of goals most likely to improve the motivation to succeed.

12.13 - The important difference between mastery goals and performance goals.

12.14 - How the desire to achieve is affected by the opportunity to achieve.

12.15 - Which aspects of a job are more important than money in increasing satisfaction with work.

Motives, Values, and the Pursuit of Happiness

12.16 - Why people are poor at predicting what will make them happy or miserable.

12.17 - Three basic kinds of motivational conflicts.

Chapter 12 - Concept Map

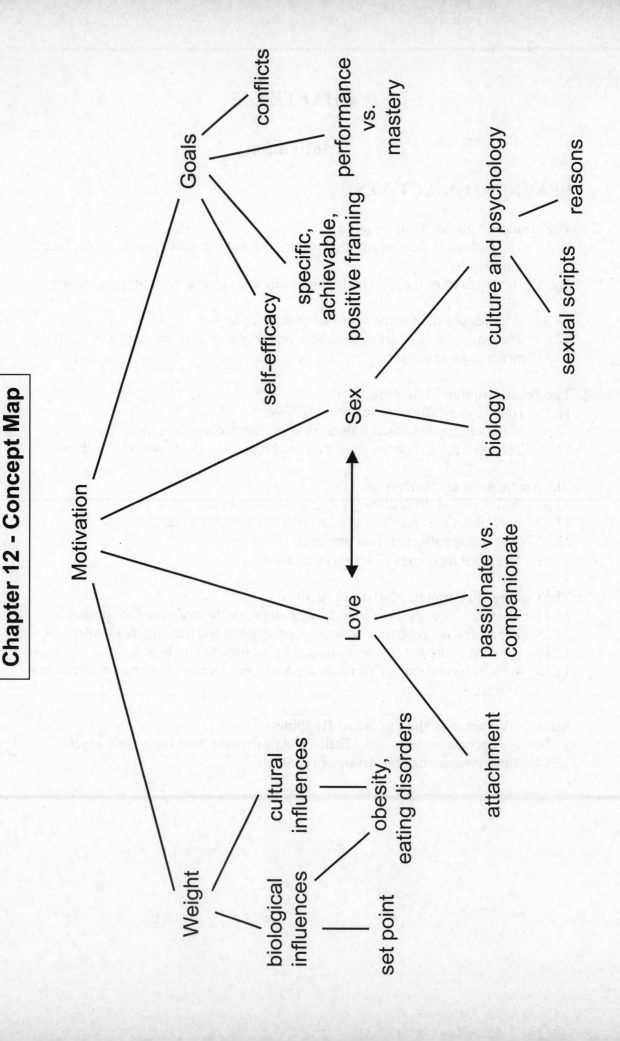

BRIEF CHAPTER SUMMARY

Chapter 12 describes four categories of motives: motives to eat, motives to love, motives for sex, and motives to achieve. Biological and cultural explanations for eating are discussed, as are the two types of eating disorders (anorexia and bulimia). Two approaches to studying love are described: passionate versus companionate love, and attachment theory. Biological, psychological, and cultural influences on the sexual motive are discussed. Kinsey introduced the scientific study of sex, which was continued by Masters and Johnson. Coercive sex, or rape, is considered an act of dominance or aggression rather than an act motivated by sexual desire. Different theories that attempt to explain sexual orientation are reviewed. These theories lead to the conclusion that sexual orientation is a result of the interaction of biology, culture, learning, and circumstances. The motive to achieve is influenced by internal factors, such as one's expectations, values, and needs for achievement, and by external factors, such as working conditions. Three types of motivational conflicts (e.g., approach-avoidance) are discussed, and Maslow's hierarchy of needs is described.

PREVIEW OUTLINE

Before you read the chapter, review the preview outline for each section of the text. After you have read the chapter, close this book and try to <u>recreate</u> the outlines on a blank piece of paper.

I.   **THE HUNGRY ANIMAL: MOTIVES TO EAT**
   A.   **The biology of weight**
      1.   We no longer think that being overweight is related only to emotional problems or overeating: biology plays a role
      2.   Set-point: biological mechanism that keeps a body at a genetically influenced set point; genetically programmed basal metabolism rate interacts with fat cells and hormones to keep people at their set point
      3.   The protein leptin plays a role in human obesity and the set-point, but that role is complicated
      4.   Debate over the source of the obesity "epidemic" in developed countries
   B.   **Culture, gender, and weight**
      1.   Obesity has increased greatly due to changes in diet and exercise, such as super-sized portions and varied food choices
      2.   Cultures' standards for ideal beauty influence eating and activity
   C.   **The body as battleground: Eating disorders**
      1.   Many women in cultures that value thinness become obsessed with weight
         a.   Bulimia involves binge eating and purges
         b.   Anorexia nervosa involves severely reduced eating and distorted body image

        c.   Ten times more common in women, begins in late adolescence

    2.   Genes interact with cultural rules, psychological needs, and personal habits to influence weight

II.   THE SOCIAL ANIMAL: MOTIVES TO LOVE

A.   The biology of love

    1.   Passionate (romantic) versus companionate (affectionate) love

    2.   Origins of passionate love start in infancy, with baby's attachment to mother

    3.   Role of endorphins in attachment

B.   The psychology of love

    1.   Basic predictors of love include proximity and similarity

    2.   Attachment theory of love (Shaver and Hazan)

        a.   Adult attachment styles originate in infant-parent relationship; people develop "working models" of relationships

        b.   Three styles are secure, avoidant, anxious-ambivalent

    3.   Ingredients of love: a mixture of passion, intimacy, and commitment

C.   Gender, culture, and love

    1.   No evidence that one sex is more loving than the other

    2.   Men and women tend to *express* love differently

III.   THE EROTIC ANIMAL: MOTIVES FOR SEX

A.   The biology of desire

    1.   The hormone testosterone promotes sexual desire in both sexes, but it doesn't "cause" sexual behavior in a direct way

    2.   First scientific sex research by Kinsey, furthered by Masters and Johnson, emphasized the similarities in arousal and orgasm by men and women

    3.   Researchers disagree about whether men and women have different biologically-based "sex-drives"

B.   The psychology of desire

    1.   Values, expectations, fantasies, beliefs affect sexual responsiveness

    2.   Motives for sex include enhancement, intimacy, coping, self-affirmation, partner approval, peer approval

    3.   Consenting to unwanted sex, sexual coercion, and rape

        a.   Anxiously attached more likely to consent to unwanted sex

        b.   Motives for rape vary – primarily an act of aggression

C.   The culture of desire

    1.   Sexual scripts – culture's rules for proper sexual behavior; they are based on gender roles, which result in different scripts

    2.   Sexual scripts can be powerful determinants of behavior

D.   Gender, culture, and sex

1.   Cultural psychologists look to gender roles, economic, and social arrangements to explain sexual scripts; evolutionary psychologists differ
2.   Sex ratios influence sexual norms and practices
3.   Biological explanations for sexual orientation are inconclusive; psychological theories have not been supported

IV.   **THE COMPETENT ANIMAL: MOTIVES TO ACHIEVE**
    A.   **The effects of motivation on work**
        1.   Level of need for achievement can be measured using Thematic Apperception Test (TAT)
        2.   Goals are likely to improve performance when the goal is specific, challenging but achievable, and is framed in terms of getting what you want (approach goals) versus avoiding what you don't want (avoidance goals)
        3.   Performance versus mastery goals
            a.   Performance goals – want to do well, failure is discouraging
            b.   Mastery (learning) goals – want to improve skills, failure is not as discouraging; feel greater intrinsic pleasure in the task
            c.   Children praised for ability and intelligence rather than effort are more likely to develop performance goals
        4.   Expectations and self-efficacy: Work harder if success expected; creates a self-fulfilling prophecy
    B.   **The effects of work on motivation**
        1.   Working conditions that influence work motivation and satisfaction: meaningfulness, ability to control aspects of work, varied tasks, clear and consistent rules, supportive relationships, useful feedback, opportunities for growth and development
        2.   Motivation is not increased by high pay but by how and when money is paid – incentive pay in particular
        3.   Motivation lower if a lack of opportunity to advance exists (glass ceiling, racism)

V.   **MOTIVES, VALUES, AND THE PURSUIT OF HAPPINESS**
    A.   **Kinds of motivational conflicts**
        1.   Approach-approach – equal attraction to two or more goals
        2.   Avoidance-avoidance – when you dislike two alternatives
        3.   Approach-avoidance – single activity has both positive and negative aspect
    B.   **Can motives be ranked?**
        1.   Maslow's Pyramid
            a.   Survival needs at the bottom, self-actualization needs at the top; lower need must be met before higher needs can be addressed

PRACTICE TEST 1 – Multiple Choice

1.   Set-point theory suggests that:
        A.   a genetically influenced weight range is maintained by a mechanism that regulates food intake, fat reserves, and metabolism.
        B.   in almost all cases, being overweight is caused by overeating.
        C.   obesity is an indicator of emotional disturbance.
        D.   weight is not influenced by genes but by learned behaviors.

2.   Set-point is to _____ as thermostat is to _____.
        A.   basal metabolic rate; furnace
        B.   fat cells; temperature
        C.   weight; furnace
        D.   genes; temperature

3.   The part of the brain that is involved in the regulation of appetite is the:
        A.   amygdala.
        B.   hippocampus.
        C.   prefrontal cortex.
        D.   hypothalamus.

4.   Extremely obese individuals who lack the protein _____ for genetic reasons benefit from injections of it.
        A.   leptin
        B.   endorphins
        C.   androgen
        D.   melatonin

5.   Adult love styles originate in a person's first and most important "love relationship," the infant-parent bond. Which approach to love does this describe?
        A.   Affiliation theory
        B.   Companionate theory
        C.   Attachment theory of love
        D.   Narrative theory of love

6.   Researchers have often called the brain the sexiest sex organ because:
        A.   it releases many neurotransmitters involved in sex such as adenosine.
        B.   during sex the amount of neuron pruning more than doubles.
        C.   roughly 80% of brain activity is directed towards sexual planning.
        D.   our perception of events alters our sexual desire and behavior.

7. Which of the following is true?
   A. Thinner women have consistently been rated as more attractive across time and cultures.
   B. Curvy women have consistently been rated as more attractive across time and cultures.
   C. Being both thin and curvy have consistently been rated as more attractive across time and cultures.
   D. Whether being thin or curvy is considered as attractive has changed across time and cultures.

8. Which of the following is true about gender and motives for sex?
   A. Motives for sex for men and women are generally quite similar.
   B. People rarely have sex when they don't want to.
   C. Women engage in sex when they don't want to but men do not.
   D. None of the above

9. Risky sexual behavior, such as not using birth control or having many partners, is associated with:
   A. extrinsic motives, such as intimacy or enhancement.
   B. intrinsic motives, such as intimacy or enhancement.
   C. extrinsic motives, such as gaining partner or peer approval.
   D. intrinsic motives, such as gaining partner or peer approval.

10. Which of the following has not contributed to the worldwide increases in body weight?
   A. A reduction in the variety of food types
   B. Increased availability of processed foods
   C. Consumption of high-calorie soft drinks
   D. Larger portion sizes of food and drinks

11. The development of mother-baby and adult lover attachments have which of the following in common?
   A. The corpus callosum develops more connections during attachment.
   B. Similar neurotransmitters and hormones are released during attachment.
   C. The thalamus begins to transmit messages at a much slower rate during attachment.
   D. Neurogenesis occurs at double the normal rate during attachment.

12. On average, which of the following statements are true?
   A. People who are the opposite of each other tend to be attracted.
   B. People who are similar to each other tend to be attracted.
   C. People who are the opposite of each other are always attracted.
   D. People who are similar to each other are always attracted.

13. Talking about sexual responses and motivations in a college class is embarrassing for Maia, who is from Morocco. She feels she should not be listening to this kind of information, particularly in a public place with males present. This is an example of:
   A. interpersonal scripts.
   B. intrapsychic scripts.
   C. cultural scripts.
   D. social scripts.

14. The eating disorder of bulimia is characterized by:
   A. episodes of bingeing followed by purging.
   B. a severely distorted body image.
   C. restricted eating and emaciation.
   D. extreme obesity.

15. The fact that boys are motivated to impress other males with their sexual experiences and girls are taught not to indulge in sexual pleasure demonstrates the effects of:
   A. hormones.
   B. sexual scripts.
   C. game-playing.
   D. sexual orientation.

16. Which of the following best describes current thinking about the origins of sexual orientation?
   A. Most research supports a genetic basis.
   B. Dominant mothers and absent/passive fathers contribute to male homosexuality.
   C. Brain differences between heterosexuals and homosexuals explain sexual orientation.
   D. Sexual identity and behavior involve an interaction of biology, culture, and experiences.

17. Which of the following explanations for homosexuality has been supported by research?
   A. Bad mothering
   B. Parental role models
   C. Same-sex sexual play in childhood
   D. None of the above

18. Which of the following represents an argument against a strict biological explanation of sexual orientation?
   A. The flexible sexual history of most lesbians.
   B. Most gay men and lesbians do not have a close gay relative.
   C. Studies on brain differences have not been reliable or replicated.
   D. All of the above

19. Which of the following motivations influences peoples' work habits?
    A. Their expectation and values
    B. How competent they feel
    C. The type of goals they have
    D. All of the above

20. Stacey is studying to be a master violin maker. When she makes a mistake she feels she has learned useful information about what to do next time. She knows that this process will take time and that she must be patient. She is motivated by:
    A. performance goals.
    B. learning and mastery goals.
    C. self-efficacy.
    D. all of the above.

21. The person who is more likely to work hard is
    A. someone who expects to succeed.
    B. someone with a high salary.
    C. someone who has performance goals.
    D. none of the above.

22. You want to have Chinese food for dinner but you also have a craving for Italian food. This represents a(n):
    A. approach-approach conflict.
    B. avoidance-avoidance conflict.
    C. approach-avoidance conflict.
    D. no lose situation.

23. Going to the dentist or having a tooth fall out is an example of a(n) _____ conflict; wanting to go out with Dan while continuing to date Stan is an example of a(n) _____ conflict; wanting to travel this summer but knowing that you would miss the summer with your friends is an example of a(n) _____ conflict.
    A. avoidance-avoidance; approach-approach; approach-avoidance
    B. approach-avoidance; approach-approach; avoidance-avoidance
    C. approach-approach; avoidance-avoidance; approach-avoidance
    D. approach-avoidance; approach-approach; approach-approach

24. It may not be fair to say that someone performs poorly at work and therefore deserves to be blamed because:
    A. research shows that a reduction in the quality of work in inevitable.
    B. one's motivation to succeed is primarily influenced by genetics and there is very little that can change that.
    C. motivation naturally increases and decreases in a fairly predictable pattern.
    D. systematic discrimination may have prevented the person from being given a chance.

25.   Which aspects of the work environment are likely to increase job satisfaction?
    A.   Reducing feedback to employees to prevent them from hearing bad news
    B.   Allowing the management to control most aspects of the work setting
    C.   Ensuring that works feels meaningful to employees
    D.   Creating tasks that are repetitive and therefore easy to predict

26.   Why are people typically poor at judging what will make them happy?
    A.   Most people have trouble distinguishing things they do and don't like.
    B.   They fail to account for how fast they will adapt to positive changes.
    C.   They do not recognize that positive events always bring stressful changes.
    D.   Many forget that material goods cannot be satisfying in the long run.

PRACTICE TEST 2 – Short Answer

1.   Achievement depends on having the _____ to achieve.

2.   In the past, a physically strong man was considered unattractive because _____. Now, it is considered attractive because it indicates _____.

3.   One approach to weight holds that a biological mechanism keeps a person's body weight at a genetically influenced _____, which is the weight you stay at when you are not consciously trying to gain or lose.

4.   Though there is considerable evidence that genes contribute to size and weight differences, it is also true that environmental influences such as _____ and _____ also play an important role.

5.   One contributor to the growing rise of obesity is the decline of _____.

6.   Three major attachment styles are _____, _____, and _____.

7.   One criticism of attachment theory is that the individual styles are not a result of how individuals are treated by their mother, but by _____.

8.   During the attachment process the brain releases chemicals called _____ that function as natural opiates.

9.   _____ theory of love says that the kind of relationships that people have as adults is strongly related to their reports of how their parents treated them.

10.   Men and women do differ, on average, in how they _____ love.

11.   Two major psychological predictors of attachment include _____ and _____.

12.   The hormone _____ seems to promote sexual desire in both sexes, though it does not "cause" sexual behavior, or any other behavior, in a simple, direct way.

13.   A study indicated that there were six factors underlying the many reasons that people give for having sex. The reasons are enhancement, intimacy, coping, self-affirmation, _____, and _____.

14.   In many species, infants release _____ after physical contact with the mother, which suggests a biological component to attachment.

15.   A person following a gender role needs a _____ script that teaches men and women how to behave in sexual matters.

PRACTICE TEST 3 – Essay

1. Donna is a college student. Her work and her household responsibilities are completed and she finds that she has free time. She decides to do the following: call her friend, visit her boyfriend, do an extra credit assignment, and work on an extra project for her job. Describe the influence of motives on her behaviors.

2. You are at a party and there is a debate about what "causes" homosexuality. Jose says it is a choice that people freely make. Amy says that it is clearly biological. Describe the information that supports and refutes each of their positions. What is the most accurate conclusion based on our current knowledge?

3. Identify the type of conflict associated with each example below.
    A. Krishneel promised the counselor that his third switch between chemistry and physics would be the last. He dreaded both courses but had to take one to fulfill requirements.
    B. When the networks put her favorite shows on at the same time, Mallory bought a DVR so she could watch one program and record the other for later viewing.
    C. Amitesh, an avid fisherman, just met new neighbors who made his day. The neighbors agreed to clean his fish and split the catch. Amitesh loved landing the fish but couldn't do the cleaning because it made him nauseous.

CHAPTER 13

Development Over the Life Span

LEARNING OBJECTIVES

From Conception Through the First Year
13.1 - The stages of prenatal development and some factors that can harm an embryo or fetus during pregnancy.
13.2 - How culture affects a baby's physical maturation.
13.3 - Why contact comfort and attachment are so important for infants (and adults).
13.4 - The varieties of infant attachment.

Cognitive Development
13.5 - The importance of "baby talk" in the development of language.
13.6 - Basic milestones in the development of language.
13.7 - Piaget's description of the major stages of cognitive development and their hallmarks.
13.8 - Modern approaches to children's mental development.

Moral Development
13.9 - How moral feelings and behavior develop.
13.10 - The importance of a child's ability to delay gratification.

Gender Development
13.11 - Why some people fail to identify themselves as either male or female.
13.12 - The biological explanation of why most little boys and girls are "sexist" in their choice of toys, at least for a while.
13.13 - When and how children learn that they are male or female.
13.14 - Learning explanations of some typical sex differences in childhood behavior.

Adolescence
13.15 - The physiological changes of adolescence.
13.16 - The psychological issues of adolescence.
13.17 - Findings on brain development and adolescence.

Adulthood
13.18 - Erik Erikson's theory of the stages of adult development.
13.19 - The typical attitudes and experiences of "emerging adulthood," the years from 18 to 25.
13.20 - Some common mid-life changes for women and men.
13.21 - Which mental abilities decline in old age and which ones do not.

The Wellsprings of Resilience
13.22 - Why terrible childhood experiences do not inevitably affect a person forever.
13.23 - What makes most children resilient in the face of adversity.

Chapter 13 - Concept Map

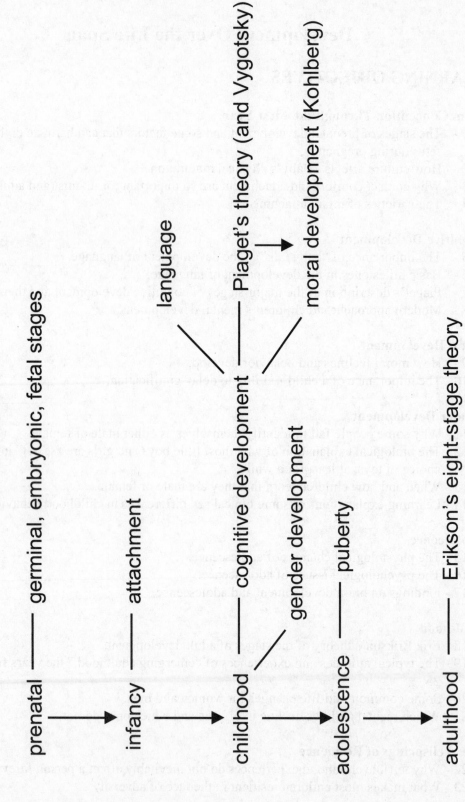

Development

prenatal —— germinal, embryonic, fetal stages

infancy —— attachment

childhood —— cognitive development

language

Piaget's theory (and Vygotsky) —→ moral development (Kohlberg)

gender development

adolescence —— puberty

adulthood —— Erikson's eight-stage theory

BRIEF CHAPTER SUMMARY

Chapter 13 describes the stages of prenatal development, which include the germinal stage, the embryonic stage, and the fetal stage. The newborn is capable of processing information, though there are many limitations to the newborn's abilities. According to Piaget's theory of cognitive development, thinking develops in four stages: the sensorimotor stage, the preoperational stage, the concrete operations stage, and the formal operations stage. Although elements of Piaget's theory have been refuted, other elements of it have been confirmed. Language, another aspect of cognitive development, is an evolutionary adaptation of the human species. Children are responsive to aspects of language in the first months of life, and by about two years of age, they are using two to three word combinations. Kohlberg's theory of moral reasoning, another stage theory, is described, as are more recent findings related to broad aspects of moral reasoning and moral behavior. The development of gender identity is discussed, along with the myths and realities of adolescent development. Erickson's theory, identifying eight stages of psychological development that occur across the lifespan, is presented. Aspects of adulthood are examined, including mid-life and aging.

PREVIEW OUTLINE

Before you read the chapter, review the preview outline for each section of the text. After you have read the chapter, close this book and try to <u>recreate</u> the outlines on a blank piece of paper.

I.   **FROM CONCEPTION THROUGH THE FIRST YEAR**
    A.   **Developmental psychologists** study universal aspects of life span development as well as cultural and individual variations; many study socialization
        Socialization – the process by which children learn rules and behavior expected of them by society
    B.   **Prenatal development** – maturation is the sequential unfolding of genetically influenced behavior and physical characteristics
        1.   Three stages: germinal stage (fertilized egg divides and attaches to the uterine wall); embryonic stage (embryo develops); fetal stage (organs and systems develop)
        2.   Harmful influences, like German measles, x-rays, sexually transmitted diseases, cigarette smoking, alcohol, drugs can cross the placental barrier
    C.   **The infant's world**
        1.   Physical and perceptual abilities – newborns have a series of reflexes and sense, not all of which are fully developed
        2.   Culture and maturation – infants all go through the same maturational sequence, but many aspects of development depend on culture

D.   **Attachment**
   1.   **Contact comfort** – Harlow studies show need for being touched and held
   2.   **Separation and security** – separation anxiety develops between six and eight months and lasts until middle of second year; experienced by all children
   3.   Ainsworth – studied attachment using the "strange situation" method
      a.   Secure – cry when mom leaves, happy upon return
      b.   Avoidant – don't care what mom does
      c.   Anxious/ambivalent – cry when mom leaves, resists upon return
E.   **Causes of insecure attachment**
   1.   Factors that may cause insecure attachment include
      a.   abandonment and separation in the first two years of life
      b.   abusive, neglectful, or erratic parenting style,
      c.   the child's genetic disposition
      d.   stressful family circumstances

II.   **COGNITIVE DEVELOPMENT**
A.   **Language** – An evolutionary adaptation of the human species
   1.   In first months, responsive to pitch, intensity, and sound of language
   2.   By 4 to 6 months, learn many basic sounds of own language
   3.   Between 6 months to one year, become more familiar with own language
   4.   At 11 months, babies develop symbolic gestures
   5.   Between 18 months and 2 years, use telegraphic communication
B.   **Thinking**
   1.   Piaget's theory – children make two mental adaptations to new experiences
      a.   Assimilation – fitting new information into existing schemas
      b.   Accommodation – changing schemas because of new information
   2.   Piaget proposed children go through four stages of cognitive development
      a.   Sensorimotor stage – birth to 2 years old, object permanence
      b.   Preoperational stage – ages 2 to 7, able to pretend, egocentric
      c.   Concrete operations stage – ages 7 to 12, conservation, identity
      d.   Formal operations stage – ages 12 to adulthood, abstract reasoning
   3.   Piaget underestimated children's abilities, overestimated adults' abilities

4. Vygotsky's theory – development depends on social/cultural context
5. Research has challenged many of Piaget's ideas (e.g., cognitive abilities develop more continuously, he underestimated children but overestimated many adults)

III. MORAL DEVELOPMENT
A. Moral reasoning
1. Kohlberg developed a theory with three levels of moral development
2. Moral reasoning is influenced by education and parent-child interaction styles
B. Moral behavior
1. Power assertion – parent uses punishment to correct child's misbehavior
2. Induction – parent appeals to child's sense of responsibility
C. Self-control and conscience
1. Self-regulation – ability to suppress initial wishes in favor of less rewarding activity

IV. GENDER DEVELOPMENT
A. Terms
1. Gender identity – sense of being male or female independent of behavior
2. Gender typing – process of learning what culture considers "appropriate"
3. Intersex – child born with ambiguous genitals or genitals that do not match chromosomes
B. Influences on gender development
1. Biological influences – toy and play preferences may be inborn
2. Cognitive influences – children, especially boys, develop gender schemas
3. Learning influences – gender socialization, adults' treatment of children

V. ADOLESCENCE
A. Adolescence – period of development between puberty and adulthood
B. The physiology of adolescence: Puberty and the onset of reproductive capacity
1. Capable of reproduction, emergence of secondary sex characteristics
2. Timing of puberty depends on genes and environment; is occurring earlier
3. Different adjustment issues related to early and late maturers

C. **The psychology of adolescence**
    1.   Teenagers have greater conflict with parents, mood swings, risky behavior
    2.   Conflict with parents can reflect teens' desire for more autonomy

VI.   **ADULTHOOD**
    A.   **Stages and ages** – Erikson identified eight stages from childhood to old age
        1.   Trust versus mistrust – first year
        2.   Autonomy versus shame and doubt – toddler
        3.   Initiative versus guilt – preschooler
        4.   Competence versus inferiority – school-age
        5.   Identity versus role confusion – adolescence
        6.   Intimacy versus isolation – young adulthood
        7.   Generativity versus stagnation – middle years
        8.   Ego integrity versus despair – old age
    B.   **The transitions of life**
        1.   Emerging adulthood – stage of life before career, marriage
        2.   The middle years – for most people, the prime of life
    C.   **Old age** – gerontologists have challenged stereotypes
        1.   Crystallized intelligence (knowledge/skills built over a lifetime) remains stable over the life span, but fluid intelligence (independent of education and experience) declines
        2.   Aging associated with improved well-being and increased happiness

VII. **THE WELLSPRINGS OF RESILIENCE**
    A.   **Events of childhood do not necessarily have permanent effects**
    B.   **Evidence** comes from studies of children who recovered from wars, from abusive or alcoholic parents, and sexual abuse; resilience is rather "ordinary"!

STAGES OF COGNITIVE DEVELOPMENT ACCORDING TO PIAGET

Complete the following chart by describing the characteristics, limitations, and achievements of each stage of Piaget's theory of cognitive development.

STAGE OF DEVELOPMENT	CHARACTERISTICS	LIMITATIONS	ACHIEVEMENTS
SENSORIMOTOR STAGE			
PREOPERATIONAL STAGE			
CONCRETE OPERATIONS STAGE			
FORMAL OPERATIONS STAGE			

PRACTICE TEST 1 – Multiple Choice

1.　The order of the three stages of prenatal development is:
A.　embryonic, germinal, fetal.
B.　germinal, fetal, embryonic.
C.　germinal, embryonic, fetal.
D.　fetal, germinal, embryonic.

2.　Which of the following could be a problem during pregnancy?
A.　Coffee
B.　Alcohol
C.　Cigarettes
D.　All of the above

3.　Many people in European countries believe that babies should sleep alone, whereas many people in African villages believe that babies should sleep with their parents. As such, infants in different parts of the world vary in their ability to fall asleep alone. This example illustrates the impact of:
A.　culture on maturation.
B.　maturation on culture.
C.　genetics on culture.
D.　culture on genetics.

4.　Jane has smoked heavily during her pregnancy. What are the risks?
A.　Increased chance of miscarriage
B.　Premature birth
C.　Her child may be hyperactive
D.　All of the above

5.　The ability of a child to suppress the desire to do something in favor of something else less fun predicts:
A.　their likelihood of developing assimilation skills.
B.　how quickly they will develop telegraphic speech.
C.　the pattern of attachment that will develop with their parents.
D.　their ability to control negative emotions later in life.

6.　"Hermaphroditism" is now usually referred to as:
A.　intersex conditions.
B.　emerging adulthood.
C.　identity crisis.
D.　gender schema activation.

7. The distress that babies experience when they are separated from their caregivers is called:
    A. separation anxiety.
    B. affiliation.
    C. contact comfort.
    D. security.

8. Harry and Margaret Harlow's studies, in which infant rhesus monkeys ran to soft, terry cloth "mothers" when they were frightened or startled, demonstrated the need for:
    A. affiliation.
    B. food.
    C. contact comfort.
    D. love.

9. Lucia's mom is not very comfortable with physical affection. Although she loves Lucia and takes good care of her, she does not hold or cuddle her. In contrast, her dad likes to hug and cuddle. Based on Harlow's experiments, to which parent would Lucia be most likely to go to when she is upset?
    A. Her mom
    B. Her dad
    C. Either
    D. Impossible to say

10. Baby Huey cries for his mother to pick him up, yet when she does, he wants to be put back down. According to Ainsworth's studies, Huey exhibits a(n):
    A. avoidant attachment style.
    B. ambivalent attachment style.
    C. secure attachment style.
    D. psychological problem.

11. Ainsworth identified mother's treatment of their babies as the primary determinant of attachment styles. What are other influences on attachment?
    A. Infant temperament
    B. Stressful events
    C. Family circumstances
    D. All of the above

12. The order of Piaget's stages of cognitive development is:
    A. preoperational, sensorimotor, concrete operations, formal operations.
    B. concrete operations, preoperational, sensorimotor, formal operations.
    C. sensorimotor, preoperational, formal operations, concrete operations.
    D. sensorimotor, preoperational, concrete operations, formal operations.

13. Fitting new information into your present system of knowledge and beliefs is called:
    A.   assimilation.
    B.   organization.
    C.   accommodation.
    D.   sensorimotor development.

14. According to Piaget, during the concrete operations stage, the child:
    A.   thinks egocentrically.
    B.   develops object permanence.
    C.   grasps conservation.
    D.   can reason abstractly.

15. While on a walk with his father, Lowell points to a cardinal and his father says, "Birdie." A little bit later, Lowell sees a blue jay and says, "Birdie." This is an example of:
    A.   assimilation.
    B.   conservation.
    C.   accommodation.
    D.   an operation.

16. During the first months, babies are highly responsive to:
    A.   normal adult talk.
    B.   the basic sounds of their native language.
    C.   the pitch, intensity, and sound of language.
    D.   all of the above.

17. Based on the stages of language development, which of the following would a four- to six-month-old baby be able to do?
    A.   Have a repertoire of symbolic gestures
    B.   Use telegraphic speech
    C.   Recognize "mommy" and "daddy"
    D.   All of the above

18. From a biological standpoint, boys and girls may be sexist in their selection of toys due to:
    A.   dopamine receptors being more inhibited in boys than girls.
    B.   the belief that certain toys are meant for one gender.
    C.   prenatal exposure to androgens.
    D.   different visual processing skills.

19. "Mama here," "go 'way bug," and "my toy" are examples of:
    A.   baby talk.
    B.   telegraphic speech.
    C.   babbling.
    D.   parentese.

20. A child's fundamental sense of maleness or femaleness that exists regardless of what one wears or does is called:
   A. gender schema.
   B. gender socialization.
   C. gender identity.
   D. sex-typing.

21. According to gender schema theory:
   A. gender-typed behavior increases once a gender schema is developed.
   B. gender schemas do not develop until a child is about four years old.
   C. gender schemas are formed early and basically do not change throughout life
   D. gender schemas disappear during adolescence.

22. After puberty:
   A. boys have more androgens and estrogens than girls.
   B. girls have more androgens and estrogens than boys.
   C. boys have more androgens and girls have more estrogens.
   D. boys have more estrogens and girls have more androgens.

23. The belief by children that bears, fire, anger, dogs, and the color black are "masculine" and butterflies, hearts, the color pink, and flowers are feminine indicates that:
   A. children have accurate gender identity.
   B. children have been reinforced for these types of distinctions.
   C. children are learning gender schemas.
   D. there is a biological basis for these distinctions.

24. Kohlberg's theory describes moral:
   A. emotions.
   B. behavior.
   C. reasoning.
   D. actions.

25. During adolescence, teenagers typically experience increased conflicts with parents, more mood swings and depression, and:
   A. the development of intense panic attacks.
   B. decreasing levels of crystallized intelligence.
   C. a desire to engage in generativity.
   D. higher rates of reckless and risky behavior.

26.	Full neurological and cognitive maturity often does not occur until about age:
	A.	16.
	B.	18.
	C.	25.
	D.	40.

27.	Noriko is going through menopause. If she is like most women, she will:
	A.	experience depression and other emotional reactions.
	B.	not experience unusually severe symptoms.
	C.	regret reaching menopause.
	D.	experience severe physical discomfort.

28.	When asked "Do you feel that you have reached adulthood?" which age range is most likely to respond with "yes and no"?
	A.	12-17 years old
	B.	18-25 years old
	C.	26-35 years old
	D.	36-55 years old

29.	Fluid intelligence:
	A.	tends to remain stable or even improve over the life span.
	B.	is influenced by an inherited predisposition, and it parallels other biological capacities in its growth and, in later years, decline.
	C.	is the knowledge and skills that are built up over a lifetime.
	D.	gives us the ability to solve math problems, define words, or summarize a president's policy.

30.	According to Erikson's theory, Hitomi, who is 16 years old, will be more likely to:
	A.	experience an identity crisis.
	B.	fight against stagnation.
	C.	learn to share herself with another person and make a commitment.
	D.	deal with her feelings of competence versus inferiority.

31.	Which of the following statements is FALSE regarding recent research on cognitive development?
	A.	Preschoolers are more egocentric than Piaget thought.
	B.	Cognitive development is greatly affected by a child's culture.
	C.	Piaget underestimated the understanding of children.
	D.	Cognitive development is more continuous than in discrete or stage form.

32. Studies of adults who were abused or molested as children demonstrate that:
    A. most overcome any harmful effects.
    B. most go on to develop a variety of severe mental disorders.
    C. they typically repress the experiences deep within their unconscious.
    D. they typically have trouble forming normal adult bonds and relationships.

33. One factor that helps children resist great adversity is that:
    A. adrenal glands have yet to begin full production.
    B. experiences can be interpreted in different ways.
    C. they lack the cognitive resources to understand trauma.
    D. their moral development is still incomplete.

PRACTICE TEST 2 – Short Answer

1. In the early 1990s, physicians advised parents to put babies on their backs. As a result, babies became much less likely to crawl. This is an example of how _____ can influence _____.

2. Prenatal development is divided into three stages: the _____ begins at conception, the _____ begins once the implantation of the _____ into the wall of the uterus is completed.

3. The _____, connected to the embryo by the umbilical cord, serves to screen out some, but not all, harmful substances. Some harmful influences, such as _____ and _____ can cross the barrier.

4. The ability to control an initial wish to do something fun in favor of something less fun is called _____.

5. In the Harlow experiments, the baby monkeys ran to the _____ "mother" when they were frightened or startled. This reaction demonstrated the need for _____.

6. During puberty, the brain's _____ begins to stimulate hormone production and the _____ and _____ glands.

7. The phase of life occurring between ages 18 and 25 is called _____.

8. Ainsworth believed that attachment styles were based on the way treated their babies in the first year. Subsequent research has found that other factors contribute to insecure attachment. These other factors include family circumstances, later stressful events in childhood, and the child's _____.

9. Jennifer is about _____ months old, and she has started to smack her lips when she is hungry, to blow on something to show that it is hot, and to shrug her shoulders to indicate that she doesn't know an answer to a question. Jennifer is demonstrating her developing repertoire of _____ gestures.

10. The Swiss psychologist, _____, proposed a theory of cognitive development.

11. When Bobby learns a _____ for birdies, he is able to identify robins, cardinals, and pet parakeets, as birdies. This demonstrates Piaget's concept of _____, or fitting new information into existing categories.

12. Jean-Paul is 12 months old. When his mother puts his favorite toy out of sight at meal time, he still cries for it and tries to move towards it. Jean-Paul has developed _____.

13. Cherie's dad asks her advice about a birthday present for her mom. Five-year-old Cherie suggests that they buy mom one of Cherie's favorite toys. Piaget's theory proposes that Cherie is demonstrating _____. Cherie is in Piaget's _____ stage of cognitive development.

14. Rich understands the principles of conservation and cause and effect, yet he cannot think in abstractions or use logical deductions. He is in the _____ stage of cognitive development.

15. _____ intelligence is relatively independent of education and experience and in later years it _____. _____ intelligence depends heavily on culture, education, and experience, and it tends to remain _____ over the life span.

16. Learning theorists point to the role of _____, or the reinforcers and societal messages children get about what "girls" and "boys" do.

17. The onset of menstruation is called _____. The cessation of menstruation is called _____.

18. When teenagers have conflicts with their parents over autonomy, they are usually trying to _____, to develop their own opinions, values, and style of dress and look.

19. Intersexed individuals often refer to themselves as _____.

20. Erik Erikson wrote that all individuals go through _____ stages in their lives, resolving an inevitable _____ at each one.

PRACTICE TEST 3 – Essay

1. Prenatal development is associated with several dangers. Identify the dangers associated with:
    A. X-rays
    B. cigarettes
    C. alcohol
    D. drugs

2. Many people think newborn attachment is instinctive. Discuss behaviors that contribute to attachment between the newborn and the caregiver.

3. A. A four-year-old girl insists small people must live in the TV because they are right there behind the glass. Identify her stage of cognitive development and the phenomenon being displayed by this child.
    B. A child adept at roller skating goes ice skating for the first time. She keeps trying to stand and move just as she would on roller skates but she falls again and again. According to Piaget, what is necessary for mastery of this new skill?
    C. A child threatened to tell his parents when his older brother gave him only one of the three candy bars they were supposed to share. The older child then broke his brother's bar in half and gave him two pieces. This satisfied both children because they each had two pieces. Identify the cognitive stages of these children and the disadvantage that allows the younger child to be cheated.
    D. Previously, whenever Shawn banged with a spoon, his mother would put it in a drawer and Shawn would quickly move on to something else. Now that he's eight months old, this isn't working. The child continues to demand the spoon even though he can't see it. Identify the cognitive stage of this child and the change that has taken place.

4. Harold has been babysitting for Azumi since she was an infant. She is now 23 months old. Harold has always tried to get Azumi to speak. He is now trying to get her to say, "The apple is on the table." Describe what Azumi's response might have been at 4 months old, 10 months old, 14 months old, and 23 months old.

CHAPTER 14

Theories of Personality

LEARNING OBJECTIVES

Psychodynamic Theories of Personality
14.1 - Freud's theory of the structure and development of personality.
14.2 - Carl Jung's theory of the collective unconscious.
14.3 - The nature of the "objects" in the object-relations approach to personality.
14.4 - Why many psychologists reject most psychodynamic ideas.

The Modern Study of Personality
14.5 - Whether you can trust tests that tell you what "personality type" you are.
14.6 - How psychologists can tell which personality traits are more central or important than others.
14.7 - The five dimensions of personality that describe people the world over.

Genetic Influences on Personality
14.8 - Whether animals have "personalities" just as people do.
14.9 - The extent to which temperamental and personality differences among people are influenced by genes.
14.10 - Why people who have highly heritable personality traits are not necessarily stuck with them forever.

Environmental Influences on Personality
14.11 - How social-cognitive theory accounts for personality change.
14.12 - The extent to which parents can—and can't—influence their children's personalities.
14.13 - How your peers shape certain of your personality traits, and suppress others.

Cultural Influences on Personality
14.14 - How culture influences your personality, and even whether you think you have a stable one.
14.15 - Why men in the South and West are more likely to get angry when insulted than other American men are.
14.16 - How to appreciate cultural influences on personality without stereotyping.

The Inner Experience
14.17 - How humanist approaches to personality differ from psychodynamic and genetic ones.
14.18 - The contributions of Abraham Maslow, Carl Rogers, and Rollo May to understanding our "inner lives."
14.19 - How your life story affects your personality—and vice versa.
14.20 - How psychological scientists evaluate humanist views of personality.

Chapter 14 - Concept Map

Theories of Personality

psychodynamic

- Freud
  - id, ego, superego
  - defense mechanisms
  - personality stages
- Freud's followers
  - Horney
  - Jung

trait

- Allport
- Cattell
- "Big Five"

genetic

- temperament
- heritability

environmental
culture

- situations
- parents
- peers

humanistic

- Maslow
  - hierarchy of needs
  - self-actualization
- Rogers
  - unconditional positive regard
- May
  - existentialism

BRIEF CHAPTER SUMMARY

Chapter 14 defines personality and reviews the major theoretical approaches that have been advanced to explain its development. The psychodynamic approach focuses on the role of unconscious processes, five developmental stages, and the development of the id, ego, and superego. Freud originally proposed this approach, and then other theorists such as Jung and Horney modified his work. Modern views of personality emphasize the trait approach of Cattell and the cross-cultural, empirical support for the "Big Five" personality traits. The biological approach focuses on the heritability of traits and the idea that there is a genetic basis for certain temperaments. Environmental influences also are important; theorists have emphasized the reciprocal interactions between specific situations and a person's cognitions and behaviors. Cognitions and behavior are also influenced by culture. The humanist and existential approaches reject the deterministic views of the psychoanalytic and behavioral approaches. Instead, they focus on the positive aspects of humanity and the idea that humans have free will to shape their own destinies.

PREVIEW OUTLINE

Before you read the chapter, review the preview outline for each section of the text. After you have read the chapter, close this book and try to <u>recreate</u> the outlines on a blank piece of paper.

I. **PSYCHODYNAMIC THEORIES OF PERSONALITY**
   A. **Personality** is a distinctive pattern of behavior, thoughts, motives, and emotions that characterizes an individual over time
   B. **Psychodynamic theories** emphasize unconscious dynamics and the importance of early childhood experiences
   C. **Freud and psychoanalysis**
      1. The structure of personality: id (source of sexual energy and aggressive instinct), ego (source of reason), superego (source of conscience)
      2. Defense mechanisms – reducing anxiety from conflict between id and society – include repression, projection, displacement, reaction formation, regression, denial
      3. The development of personality occurs in five psychosexual stages; if demands of a stage are too great, a child may get fixated, or stuck at a stage
         a. The oral stage – babies take the world in through their mouths
         b. The anal stage – may become over controlled (anal retentive) or under controlled (anal expulsive)
         c. The Oedipal stage – desire for opposite-sex parent, then identification with the same-sex parent
         d. The latency stage – supposedly nonsexual stage
         e. The genital stage – beginning of mature adult sexuality

209

4. Psychologists disagree strongly about the value of Freud's theory

D. Other psychodynamic approaches

1. Clara Thompson and Karen Horney – challenged the notion of penis envy and female inferiority
2. Jungian theory – biggest difference was the nature of the unconscious
   a. Collective unconscious contains the universal memory and history
   b. Concerned with archetypes – themes that appear in myths – such as shadow and hero
3. The object-relations school – emphasizes need for human relationships
   a. Emphasis on children's need for mother, which in early years is only a representation of her
   b. Males and females both identify first with mother, then boys must separate which can result in more rigid boundaries with others

E. Evaluating psychodynamic theories

1. Principle of falsifiability violated – can't confirm or disprove ideas
2. Theories based on fallible memories and retrospective accounts of atypical patients
3. In response to criticisms, some are using empirical methods and research

II. THE MODERN STUDY OF PERSONALITY

A. Popular personality tests

1. Extremely popular, but many such as the Myers-Briggs are useless from a scientific point of view
2. Objective tests or inventories – standardized questionnaires

B. Identifying core personality traits

1. Allport's trait theory – not all traits are equally important
   a. Central traits – characteristic ways of behaving
   b. Secondary traits – the more changeable aspects of personality
2. Cattell – studied traits using factor analysis; found 16 factors, later noting that only six have been confirmed
3. The "Big Five" traits: introversion/extroversion, neuroticism, agreeableness, conscientiousness, openness to experience
   a. Big Five have been replicated in many countries, but there are a few cultural differences
   b. Stable over a lifetime though some maturational changes exist

III. GENETIC INFLUENCES ON PERSONALITY
    A.   Heredity and temperament
        1.   Temperaments are physiological dispositions to respond to the environment in relatively stable ways (e.g., reactivity) that may later form the basis of personality traits
        2.   Highly reactive infants are excitable and nervous, whereas nonreactive infants lie quietly, don't cry, and are happy
    B.   Heredity and traits
        1.   Heritability estimates based on studies of adopted children and identical twins reared together and apart; for many traits, heritability is around .50
    C.   Evaluating Genetic Theories
        1.   Genetic *predisposition* does not imply genetic *inevitability*

IV. ENVIRONMENTAL INFLUENCES ON PERSONALITY
    A.   Situations and social learning
        1.   Behaviorists emphasize situations rather than traits; most personality researchers emphasize the interaction of personality and environment
        2.   According to social-cognitive learning theory, you choose your situations and your situations influence you (reciprocal determinism)
    B.   Parental influence and its limits
        1.   The shared environment of the home has little influence on personality
        2.   Few parents use a consistent child-rearing style
        3.   Even with consistency, parental behavior may not influence children
    C.   The power of peers
        1.   Once children are in school, peer influence becomes stronger than parental influence
        2.   Peer acceptance is often more important than parental approval

V. CULTURAL INFLUENCES ON PERSONALITY
    A.   Culture – program of shared rules that govern the behavior of people in a community or society – affects some traits such as risk-taking
    B.   Culture, values, and traits
        1.   Individualistic vs. collectivist cultures
        2.   Time seen as linear or organized on parallel lines
        3.   Culture of honor (American south/west) correlated with male aggression

C. **Evaluating cultural approaches**
    1.   Difficult to describe cultural influences without stereotyping or exaggerating
    2.   Key aspects of personality include the valued traits, sense of self versus community, and notions of the right way to behave

VI. **THE INNER EXPERIENCE**
   A.   **Humanist approaches** focus on a person's own view of the world and free will
       1.   Abraham Maslow – the traits of the self-actualized person are the most important – meaning, challenge, productivity
       2.   Carl Rogers – role of unconditional positive regard
       3.   Rollo May – free will accompanied by responsibility causes anxiety
   B.   **Narrative approaches** focus on the story a person develops over time to create meaning about their life experience
   C.   **Evaluating humanist and narrative approaches**
       1.   Many assumptions cannot be tested; concepts are hard to define operationally

PRACTICE TEST 1 – Multiple Choice

1. Research on the popular Myers-Briggs Type Indicator has found that it is:
    A. able to pinpoint approximately 48 different personality dimensions.
    B. most appropriate when applied to business settings.
    C. the most scientifically valid and useful personality test available.
    D. not a reliable measure of personality.

2. Which of the following is <u>NOT</u> one of the shared elements among psychodynamic theories?
    A. An emphasis on environmental influences
    B. The assumption that adult behavior is determined primarily by childhood experiences
    C. The emphasis on the unconscious mind
    D. The belief that psychological development occurs in fixed stages

3. Which part of the personality would be likely to want to go for a pizza rather than study for a test?
    A. Id
    B. Superego
    C. Ego
    D. Ego ideal

4. The function of defense mechanisms is to:
    A. make us look good in the eyes of other people.
    B. protect ourselves from negative environmental consequences.
    C. protect us from the conflict and stress of reality.
    D. all of the above.

5. When the MacDonalds brought home baby Cassie, four-year-old Ellie began acting like a baby herself by crawling around and wanting to drink out of a bottle. This is an example of:
    A. regression.
    B. identification.
    C. reaction formation.
    D. projection.

6. The psychosexual stages of personality development identified by Freud are (in order):
    A. oral, anal, latency, phallic, genital.
    B. oral, phallic, anal, genital, latency.
    C. oral, anal, phallic, latency, genital.
    D. anal, phallic, genital, oral, latency.

7.   According to Freud, the resolution of the _____ marks the emergence of the superego.
     A.   anal stage
     B.   unconscious conflict
     C.   Oedipus complex
     D.   latency stage

8.   Priscilla is having relationship problems. Which of the following approaches to her difficulties represents one of the shared elements of psychodynamic theories?
     A.   The problems are a result of her interpretation of what is going on.
     B.   The problems are a result of her previous relationship history.
     C.   The problems result from the lack of unconditional positive regard.
     D.   The problems are determined by experiences in her early childhood.

9.   Factor analysis can discover central traits by:
     A.   classifying traits along 16 different dimensions to find the most frequent traits.
     B.   pinpointing the secondary traits and assuming the remaining traits are central.
     C.   identifying related items that appear to measure some common variable.
     D.   having clients project their interpretations of ambiguous stimuli.

10. Vincent was sexually attracted to his step-sister, but never acknowledged it consciously. Around that time, Vincent began painting a lot of pictures of women. This is most likely an example of the defense mechanism of:
     A.   regression.
     B.   sublimation.
     C.   reaction formation.
     D.   projection.

11. Max has just had his sixth birthday. Freud would expect that:
     A.   he has resolved his Oedipal complex.
     B.   his personality pattern is basically formed.
     C.   his superego has emerged.
     D.   all of the above have occurred.

12. The fact that several basic archetypes appear in virtually every society supports which Jungian idea?
     A.   Penis envy
     B.   The strength of the ego
     C.   Psychosocial stages
     D.   The collective unconscious

13. Julia disagrees with Dr. Sigmund's interpretation that she is very angry at her mother. Dr. Sigmund says that Julia's disagreement is denial and, therefore, confirms that she is angry at her mother. This is an example of which criticism of psychodynamic theories?
    A. They draw universal principles from a few atypical patients.
    B. They base theories of development on retrospective accounts of patients.
    C. They violate the principle of falsifiability.
    D. They are based on the illusion of causality.

14. Studies have shown that the correlation between the personality traits of adopted children and adoptive parents is:
    A. weak to nonexistent.
    B. moderate to weak.
    C. strong to moderate.
    D. very strong to strong.

15. The idea that the human psyche contains the universal memories and history of humankind was contributed by:
    A. Freud.
    B. Jung.
    C. Erikson.
    D. Horney.

16. Which of the following is NOT one of the criticisms of psychodynamic theories?
    A. It violates the principle of falsifiability.
    B. It is based on retrospective memories.
    C. It is overly comprehensive; it tries to explain too much.
    D. It draws universal principles from studying selected patients.

17. Dr. West is studying depression. He has interviewed 50 subjects about their early lives and childhoods and he has identified common threads that fit an overall theory. This example represents which of the criticisms of psychodynamic theories?
    A. It violates the principle of falsifiability.
    B. It is a prospective study.
    C. It is based on the retrospective memories of subjects.
    D. People are seen as too malleable, like jellyfish.

18. The object-relations school predicts that adult males will have problems permitting close attachments because:
    A. their identities are based on not being like women, so they develop more rigid ego boundaries.
    B. their superegos are too strong.
    C. they have great difficulty resolving the anal stage.
    D. all of the above.

215

19. When compared to the influence of parents and peers on personality and behavior, researchers have found that:
   A.   peers typically exert more influence.
   B.   parents typically exert more influence.
   C.   peers and parents influence personality and behavior equally.
   D.   parents influence personality the most, but peers influence behavior the most.

20. The "Big Five" refers to:
   A.   the five main trait theories.
   B.   five types of traits, including cardinal, central, secondary, surface, and source.
   C.   robust factors that are thought to be able to describe personality.
   D.   five stages of personality development.

21. Woody is a complainer and a defeatist. He always sees the sour side of life. This demonstrates which of the following of the Big Five traits?
   A.   Introversion
   B.   Depressiveness
   C.   Neuroticism
   D.   Disagreeableness

22. Andre has a friend who grew up in Mexico. His friend is rarely on time and as such Andre considers him rude and inconsiderate. What important detail may Andre be neglecting when making such an attribution?
   A.   His friend is most likely genetically predisposed to be late.
   B.   Andre may be projecting his own insecurities about timeliness onto his friend.
   C.   Cultural norms may have caused his friend to view time differently.
   D.   Most people in America do not consider it important to be on time.

23. A study investigating personality in dogs found that dog owners, their friends, and neutral observers agreed strongly on the dogs' personalities for all of the following traits except:
   A.   neuroticism.
   B.   agreeableness.
   C.   extroversion.
   D.   conscientiousness.

24. Studies of twins have found that heritability for most traits is around .50. This means that:
    A.   if one twin has a trait, there is a 50 percent chance the other twin will have the same trait.
    B.   most people have a 50 percent chance of having a given trait.
    C.   within a group, about 50 percent of the variance in a trait is attributable to genes.
    D.   the differences between two groups of people can be explained.

25. Based on studies of twins, which of the following environmental factors would be expected to have the greatest influence on the personality of two siblings?
    A.   Having the same parents
    B.   Going to the same schools
    C.   Having different extracurricular activities
    D.   Having the same religious training

26. A study of Finnish twins, ages 18 to 59, found that the heritability of extroversion decreased from the late teens to the late twenties. What does this suggest?
    A.   Heritability of traits diminishes over time.
    B.   The influence of the environment increases over time.
    C.   For some traits, experiences at certain periods in life become more important.
    D.   All of the above

27. Which of the following suggests caution about the heritability of personality?
    A.   Not all traits are equally heritable or unaffected by shared environment.
    B.   Even highly heritable traits are not rigidly fixed.
    C.   The relative influence of genes versus environment can change over time.
    D.   All of the above

28. The social-cognitive theory can explain how a person can be friendly at work and hostile at home. The explanation is:
    A.   based on whether the person has internal or external locus of control.
    B.   the difference between a person's public and private personalities.
    C.   that personality traits can change depending on the situation and on how people perceive and interpret those situations.
    D.   an interaction of the id, ego, and superego.

29. Congruence and unconditional positive regard are part of:
    A.   Rogers' theory.
    B.   Maslow's theory.
    C.   May's theory.
    D.   existential philosophy.

30. The humanistic approach to personality focuses on:
    A. achieving one's full human potential.
    B. five universal and measurable traits.
    C. environmental influences such as peers.
    D. unconscious dynamics.

31. When researching why American Southerners tend to be more prone to quick violence, it was discovered that the current homicide rates could be predicted by:
    A. past concentrations of slave ownership.
    B. historical patterns of racial tensions.
    C. whether the land was used for herding in the past.
    D. poverty levels in the 1800s.

32. Which of the following is an important fact to remember about cultural influences on personality?
    A. While culture does influence personality, there is still a large amount of variability within cultures.
    B. People are typically unable to adapt their personality to new social norms when they move from one culture to another.
    C. Culture will only have a strong influence on the development of personality if a person is genetically predisposed towards that culture.
    D. Behavior is strongly affected by the local culture, but personality usually remains independent of cultural influence.

33. The story that people develop over time to explain their personalities and behavior is called:
    A. existentialism.
    B. peak experiences.
    C. historical perception theory.
    D. life narrative.

34. One of the major criticisms of humanistic theories of personality is that:
    A. the underlying assumption of optimism and personal growth is unrealistic.
    B. many of the humanist assumptions are untestable.
    C. its operational definitions cannot be generalized to everyday life.
    D. peak experiences occur too frequently to be indicators of self-actualization.

PRACTICE TEST 2 – Short Answer

1. _____ traits reflect characteristic ways of behaving, interacting with others, and adapting to new situations.

2. The saying "the squeaky wheel gets the grease" is more likely to be agreed with in a(n) _____ culture, whereas the saying "the quacking duck gets shot" is more likely to be agreed with in a(n) _____ culture.

3. _____ has identified two types of traits; _____ traits that reflect a characteristic way of behavior and reacting, and secondary traits, which are more _____ aspects of personality, such as music preferences.

4. The Big Five personality traits include introversion versus extroversion, neuroticism, _____, _____, and openness to experience.

5. The fact that Joey was excitable, nervous, and overreacted to every little thing suggests that he falls into Kagan's category of a _____ temperamental style.

6. In behavioral genetics, the _____ of personality traits is typically around .50.

7. In numerous behavioral genetic studies, the only environmental contribution to personality differences comes from having unique experiences that are _____ with other family members.

8. The process of _____ can account for why a person may be cheerful and friendly at work but hostile and obnoxious at home.

9. In comparison to children in other countries, American children tend to the _____ altruistic and the _____ egoistic.

10. In _____ cultures, group harmony takes precedence over the wishes of the individual.

11. List two examples of temperaments discussed in the text: _____.

12. _____ theories, which are based on the work of Freud, emphasize the movement of psychological energy within the person, in the form of attachments, conflicts, and motivations.

13. According to Freud, the _____ contains two competing basic instincts, the ego bows to the _____ of life, and the _____ represents morality.

14. In psychodynamic theory, the ego has tools, called _____, that deny or distort reality and operate unconsciously. These tools protect us from conflict and the stresses of reality.

15. Rashad was always aggressive as a child. Now that he is in high school, he has become the top football player. From the psychodynamic perspective, Rashad's athletic success might be attributable to the defense mechanism of _____.

16. The herding economy in the past required men to be alert and fast to retaliate. Even today these past cultural influences can be demonstrated by the fact that men in the South and West are more likely _____ to a perceived insult.

17. Jung introduced the idea of the _____ unconscious, which contains _____, universal memories, symbols, and images that are the legacy of human history.

18. Object-relations theory states that a child creates a(n) _____ of the mother and this unconsciously affects personality throughout life.

19. One of the criticisms of psychodynamic theories is that they violate the principle of _____.

20. Abraham Maslow said that people who strive for a life that is meaningful, challenging, and productive are _____. Carl Rogers believed that to become a fully _____ functioning person, you must receive _____ regard.

PRACTICE TEST 3 – Essay

1.   Lynne is having aggressive fantasies about her husband. Over a long period, he has gotten drunk on a regular basis. Lynne remembers her alcoholic father, who was never there when she needed him. She also remembers her mother, who suffered silently for years. Lynne swears this will not happen to her, but she can't seem to make anything change. She is hostile toward her children and her neighbors. Her husband is always repentant the next day, but his sorrow never lasts more than a week. Yet, Lynne doesn't take the final step of leaving. Identify which approach to personality each of the following set of comments represents.

      A.   Aggressiveness is Lynne's outstanding characteristic and it dominates her actions and relationships with most people.

      B.   Lynne's marriage to and anger with an alcoholic suggests many unresolved feelings toward her father. Her marriage to an alcoholic demonstrates her ongoing attachment to her father and the effort to resolve her issues with him. Her anger most likely is unresolved anger at her father. Her reluctance to leave reflects her desire to stay united with her father.

      C.   Lynne is struggling with her choices. While marriage is important to her, she realizes that her husband's alcoholism is a source of despair. She is struggling with her values, principles, desires for growth and fulfillment, and how they should influence her choices.

2.   Bernard had studied for his psychology test, but before he was finished studying, he agreed to go partying with his friends and stayed out late. The test was very difficult and he found he did not know many of the answers. The class was crowded and a good student was sitting very close to him. It would have been very easy to look over at her paper. He was worried because this test grade would make a big difference on his final grade. He struggled with whether or not he should cheat. He decided not to cheat because he felt that he would have let his parents down if he did. Instead, he decided that this grade really didn't matter so much. He felt guilty about not having studied enough and about having considered cheating.

Indicate whether the id, ego, or superego is involved in each of the following examples and explain the basis for your answer.

      A.   Bernard's studying for his test
      B.   Going out partying with his friends rather than studying
      C.   Wanting a good grade under any circumstance
      D.   Evaluating whether or not to cheat
      E.   Deciding not to cheat
      F.   Deciding that the grade did not matter so much
      G.   Feeling guilty about his behavior

3. Identify which defense mechanism each example represents.

    A. A mother shows exaggerated concern and love for her children, even though she unconsciously feels trapped and frustrated by motherhood.
    B. Bob, who tends to be negative and a gossip, often feels that other people don't like him and are talking behind his back.
    C. Jack is unconsciously attracted to his sister-in-law and, though he seems to have no awareness of it, his sister-in-law senses these feelings.
    D. Even after finding his lighter in the jacket worn the other day, Tony swears he never misplaces anything and someone must be playing a trick on him.
    E. Whenever he is frustrated, Jack has a tantrum and destroys anything he can get his hands on.
    F. The football coach loves to insult Willie and make him angry. Whenever he does this, the opposing team really suffers because then Willie begins to hit extra hard.

4. Below are criticisms of Freudian psychoanalysis. Identify which theorist would have been most likely to make each comment.

    A. Freud saw the importance of the individual's past but failed to see the contribution of humanity's past. People have universal memories owing to the ancestry they share.
    B. Freud misunderstood women. He believed they were motivated by envy for men when the true determining forces were social injustice and second-class treatment.
    C. Freud emphasized a child's fear of the powerful father, but ignored the child's need for a powerful mother, especially during the baby's early years. He emphasized the dynamics of inner drives and impulses, but paid little attention to the child's relationship with others.

5. Based on the three humanistic theorists, indicate how each thinker discussed in the text (Maslow, May, Rogers) might account for a person's failure to reach his or her full potential.

6. Using the "Big Five" trait approach, indicate which set of traits would be most useful for describing each of the individuals described below.

    A. Bob is stable, happy to meet people, and well liked. He has many friends and few worries.
    B. Mary is neat, timely, and dependable. She has relatively few interests or hobbies, but she is a good listener and is liked by her co-workers.
    C. John complains constantly and worries about his health and his life in general. He reads a lot and loves going to the movies and to museums, but he always goes alone.

CHAPTER 15

Psychological Disorders

LEARNING OBJECTIVES

Diagnosing Mental Disorders
15.1 - Why insanity is not the same thing as having a mental disorder.
15.2 - How mental disorders differ from normal problems.
15.3 - Why the standard professional guide to the diagnosis of mental disorders is controversial.
15.4 - Why popular "projective" tests like the Rorschach Inkblot Test are not reliable.

Anxiety Disorders
15.5 - The difference between ordinary anxiety and an anxiety disorder.
15.6 - Why the most disabling of all phobias is known as the "fear of fear".
15.7 - Why some people recover quickly after a trauma whereas others develop post-trauma stress disorder.

Mood Disorders
15.8 - The difference between major depression and the blues.
15.9 - Four contributing factors in depression.
15.10 - How some people can think themselves into depression.

Antisocial Personality Disorder
15.11 - Why some people are incapable of feeling guilt or any pangs of conscience.

Drug Abuse and Addiction
15.12 - How genes might contribute to alcoholism.
15.13 - Why alcoholism is more common in some cultures than others.
15.14 - Why policies of abstinence from alcohol do not reduce problem drinking.

Dissociative Identity Disorder
15.15 - Why most clinicians and researchers are skeptical about multiple personality disorder.
15.16 - Why the number of "multiple personality" cases jumped from a handful to many thousands in only a decade.

Schizophrenia
15.17 - The difference between schizophrenia and a "split personality".
15.18 - The five key signs of schizophrenia.
15.19 - Whether schizophrenia is partly heritable.
15.20 - Why schizophrenia might begin in the womb yet not emerge until adolescence.

Chapter 15 - Concept Map

Psychological Disorders

issues of definition, diagnosis (DSM), and measurement

theories of causes include biological, learning, cultural, and vulnerability-stress models

classes of disorders

anxiety disorders

OCD
PTSD
phobias
panic disorder
generalized anxiety disorder

drug abuse
and addiction

mood
disorders

major depression
bipolar disorder

dissociative
identity disorder

personality
disorders

narcissistic
antisocial

schizophrenia
(delusions,
hallucinations,
disorganized
speech,
inappropriate
behavior,
cognitive
impairments)

BRIEF CHAPTER SUMMARY

Chapter 15 discusses definitions of mental disorders. The issues and difficulties involved in developing a reliable and valid diagnostic system are also discussed. The *Diagnostic and Statistical Manual of Mental Disorders* (*DSM*), the manual that contains descriptions of all diagnostic categories of mental disorders, is described. Some of the advantages as well as problems of the *DSM* are described. There are numerous tools used to diagnose an individual, including projective tests (e.g., Rorschach Test) and objective tests (e.g., MMPI). Six general categories of disorders are reviewed. They consist of anxiety disorders (e.g., PTSD, phobias, OCD, panic disorder), mood disorders (e.g., depression, bipolar disorder), personality disorders (e.g., narcissistic personality disorder, antisocial personality disorder), addictions, dissociative identity disorder, and schizophrenia. The text describes symptoms, predisposing factors, and theories of causation for specific mental disorders under each broad disorder category.

PREVIEW OUTLINE

Before you read the chapter, review the preview outline for each section of the text. After you have read the chapter, close this book and try to <u>recreate</u> the outlines on a blank piece of paper.

I. **DEFINING AND DIAGNOSING DISORDERS**
   A. **Dilemmas of definition** – abnormal behavior is not the same as mental disorder
      1. Legal definition (insanity) – aware of the consequences of one's actions
      2. Harmful dysfunction – involves behavior or an emotional state that is:
         a. Harmful to oneself or others
         b. Dysfunctional because it is not performing its evolutionary function
   B. **Text's definition** – any condition that causes a person to suffer, is self-destructive, seriously impairs a person's ability to work or get along with others, or endangers others or the community.
   C. **Dilemmas of diagnosis**
      1. The *Diagnostic and Statistical Manual of Mental Disorders* (*DSM*) – standard reference used to diagnose disorders; primary aim is descriptive
         a. Lists symptoms and associated information for each disorder
         b. Classifies each disorder according to five axes or dimensions:
            (1) Primary clinical problem
            (2) Ingrained aspects of the individual
            (3) Medical conditions relevant to the disorder

(4)   Social and environmental problems

(5)   Global assessment of the patient's overall functioning

2.   Problems with the *DSM*: danger of over-diagnosis, power of diagnostic labels, confusion of serious mental disorders with normal problems, the illusion of objectivity and universality – beliefs about what is "normal" can change over time and across cultures

3.   Advantages of the *DSM*: new studies are improving empirical support for its categories, improves accuracy of diagnoses, biases in certain diagnoses can be corrected with awareness and better research

D.   Dilemmas of measurement

1.   Projective tests are used to infer a person's motives and conflicts based on interpretation of ambiguous stimuli (e.g., Rorschach Inkblot Test), but these tests have low reliability and validity

2.   Objective tests – standardized questionnaires requiring written responses (e.g., MMPI); are generally more reliable and valid but weaknesses include cultural and socioeconomic differences not taken into account

II.   ANXIETY DISORDERS

A.   Anxiety and panic

1.   Generalized anxiety disorder

a.   Characteristics: continuous and uncontrollable anxiety, feelings of dread, restlessness, difficulty concentrating, sleep disturbance

b.   May occur without specific anxiety-producing event, but may be related to physiological tendency to experience anxiety

2.   Posttraumatic stress disorder (PTSD) – anxiety results from uncontrollable and unpredictable danger such as rape, war, torture, or natural disasters

a.   Symptoms include reliving the trauma, "psychic numbing," increased arousal, inability to feel happy, detachment from others

b.   Associated with size of hippocampus

3.   Panic disorder – recurring attacks of intense fear or panic

a.   Symptoms include trembling, dizziness, heart palpitations, feelings of unreality, fear of dying, going crazy, or losing control

b.   Usually occurs in aftermath of stress or frightening experiences

c.   Interpretation of bodily reactions is part of the cause

B. **Fears and phobias – Exaggerated fear of a specific situation, activity, etc.**
   1. Some phobias may have an evolutionary basis (e.g., heights, snakes)
   2. Social phobia – fear of being observed and evaluated by others
   3. Agoraphobia – fear of being alone in a public place from which escape might be difficult or help unavailable
C. **Obsessions and compulsions**
   1. Obsessions – recurrent, persistent, unwished-for thoughts that are frightening or repugnant
   2. Compulsions – repetitive, ritualized behaviors over which people feel a lack of control (e.g., hand washing, counting, checking)
   3. Most sufferers know the behavior is senseless and don't enjoy it
   4. PET scans find parts of the brain are hyperactive in people with OCD

III. **MOOD DISORDERS**
A. **Major depression** – emotional, behavioral, cognitive, physical changes; more common in women than men
B. **Bipolar disorder** – depression alternates with mania, an abnormally high state of exhilaration, where person is full of energy, ambition, self-esteem, and often get into trouble with risky behavior (e.g., spending sprees, sexual escapades)
C. **Origins of depression** – "Vulnerability-stress" model emphasizes the interaction between individual vulnerability and environmental stress
   1. Genetic predispositions – heredity, chemical imbalances
   2. Violence, childhood physical abuse, and parental neglect – myth of depression being caused by sexual molestation
   3. Life experiences explanations emphasize stressful circumstances of people's lives such as interpersonal losses, rejection, and insecure attachments
   4. Cognitive explanations emphasize habits of thinking and interpreting events – depressed people have a pessimistic explanatory style and tend to ruminate or brood over the things that are wrong

IV. **PERSONALITY DISORDERS**
A. **Definition** – rigid, maladaptive traits that cause great distress or inability to get along with others
B. **Narcissistic personality disorder**
   1. Exaggerated sense of self-importance
C. **Antisocial personality disorder**
   1. Individuals who lack a connection to anyone so they can cheat, con, and kill without any problem; one type of psychopathy

2.	Symptoms include repeated law-breaking, deception, acting impulsively, fighting, disregarding safety, lacking remorse

3.	Often begin with problem behaviors in childhood; more common in males

4.	Causes of APD

a.	CNS abnormalities – inability to feel emotional arousal

b.	Impaired frontal-lobe functioning – reduced planning and impulse control

b.	Genetically influenced problems with impulse control

c.	Brain damage from physical abuse or neglect (prefrontal cortex)

V.	**DRUG ABUSE AND ADDICTION**

A.	**DSM definition of substance abuse** – maladaptive pattern of substance use leading to clinically significant impairment or distress

B.	**Biology and addiction** – addiction is a biochemical process influenced by genes

1.	Biological model: addiction due to biochemistry, metabolism, and genetics

2.	Genetic factors may affect impulsivity, protection against alcoholism

3.	Causal relationship also works the other way: heavy drinking reduces endorphin levels, shrinks cortex, damages liver

C.	**Learning, culture, and addiction** – challenges the biological model

1.	Addiction patterns vary with cultural practices and social environment

2.	Policies of total abstinence tend to increase rates of addiction

3.	Not all addicts go through withdrawal symptoms when they quit the drug

4.	Addiction depends on the drug AND the reason the person is taking it

D.	**Debating the causes of addiction**

1.	Biological and learning models contribute to our understanding

2.	Theoretical differences have treatment implications

3.	Most heated disagreement is about controlled drinking; research finds that some people can switch to moderate drinking under certain conditions

VI.	**DISSOCIATIVE IDENTITY DISORDER**

A.	**Definition** – the appearance of two or more distinct identities within one person

B.	**The MPD controversy** – two views among mental health professionals

1.	A real disorder, common but often under diagnosed; usually develops in childhood as a response to repeated trauma

2.	Creation of mental health clinicians – pressure and suggestive techniques

C. **The sociocognitive explanation** – an extreme form of a normal ability to present different aspects of our personalities to others

VII. **SCHIZOPHRENIA**
   A. **Schizophrenia** – a psychosis or condition involving distorted perceptions of reality and an inability to function in most aspects of life
   B. **Symptoms of schizophrenia**
      1. Symptoms
         a. Bizarre delusions – false beliefs
         b. Hallucinations – usually auditory – seem intensely real
         c. Disorganized, incoherent speech – illogical jumble of ideas
         d. Grossly disorganized and inappropriate behavior
         e. Impaired cognitive abilities
   C. **Origins of schizophrenia** – many variations and symptoms
      1. Genetic predispositions exist though no specific genes identified
      2. Prenatal problems possibly related to malnutrition or a virus
      3. Adolescent abnormalities in brain development – over-pruning synapses

VIII. **MENTAL DISORDER AND PERSONAL RESPONSIBILITY**
   A. **Dilemma regarding the relationship between mental disorder and personal responsibility**
      1. In some jurisdictions, a defendant may claim to have "diminished responsibility" for a crime

PSYCHOLOGICAL DISORDERS

Complete the following chart indicating the major symptoms, predisposing factors, and explanatory theories for each of the disorders described in the left-hand column.

TYPE OF DISORDER	MAJOR SYMPTOMS	PREDISPOSING FACTORS	EXPLANATORY THEORIES
ANXIETY DISORDERS Generalized Anxiety Disorder			
Social Phobia			
PTSD			
Panic Attack			
Obsessive-Compulsive Disorder			
MOOD DISORDERS Major Depression			
Bipolar Disorder			
PERSONALITY DISORDERS Borderline			
Narcissistic			
Antisocial			
DISSOCIATIVE IDENTITY DISORDER			
SUBSTANCE ABUSE			
SCHIZOPHRENIA			

PRACTICE TEST 1 – Multiple Choice

1. According to the _____ definition of mental disorder, a person living in North America who hears voices and sees images of a deceased loved one exhibits abnormal behavior.
    A. self-destructive behavior
    B. violation of cultural standards
    C. emotional distress
    D. impaired judgment

2. Which of the following is NOT one of the definitions of mental disorder?
    A. Statistical deviation
    B. Self-destructive behavior
    C. Violation of cultural standards
    D. Emotional distress

3. Whether a person is aware of the consequences of his or her actions and can control his or her behavior is at the heart of the legal term:
    A. mental disorder.
    B. insanity.
    C. neurotic.
    D. psychotic.

4. The primary aim of the *Diagnostic and Statistical Manual of Mental Disorders* (*DSM*) is to:
    A. provide clear criteria of diagnostic categories.
    B. describe the causes of particular disorders.
    C. describe the best course of treatment for a particular disorder.
    D. all of the above.

5. Which of the following statements about depression is true?
    A. Research has established that it is caused by low levels of serotonin.
    B. There is a genetic component and it is highly heritable disorder.
    C. Most instances of depression in women are caused by childhood sexual abuse.
    D. It is often preceded by the loss of an important relationship.

6. Which of the following is NOT one of the principal criticisms of the *DSM* discussed in the text?
    A. It may confound serious "mental disorders" with normal problems in living.
    B. Its heavy emphasis on theory may alienate clinicians from different perspectives.
    C. It gives the illusion of objectivity.
    D. It may foster over diagnosis and self-fulfilling prophecies.

7. The diagnoses of "Disorder of Written Expression" and "Caffeine-Induced Sleep Disorder" represent which criticism of the *DSM*?
   A. The idea that diagnosis can be made objectively scientific
   B. Misusing diagnoses for social and political purposes
   C. Confounding serious "mental disorders" with normal problems in living
   D. The fostering of over diagnosis and self-fulfilling prophecies

8. Generalized anxiety disorder is marked by:
   A. unrealistic fears of specific objects or situations.
   B. continuous, uncontrollable anxiety or worry.
   C. the sudden onset of intense fear or terror.
   D. unwished-for thoughts and repetitive behaviors.

9. The most disabling fear disorder that accounts for more than half of the phobia cases for which people seek treatment is called:
   A. panic disorder.
   B. social phobia.
   C. claustrophobia.
   D. agoraphobia.

10. The notion that a mental disorder involves behavior that hurts oneself or doesn't serve an evolutionary purpose is the definition of mental disorder based on:
    A. endangerment of others or the community.
    B. harmful dysfunction.
    C. violation of social norms.
    D. legal standards.

11. Unlike normal sadness or grief, major depression involves:
    A. panic attacks.
    B. fear of intimacy.
    C. a lack of interest in outside activities.
    D. feelings of worthlessness.

12. Recently Emily has had difficulty sleeping through the night, experienced a lack of energy and interest, and has had trouble concentrating. These physical changes can be signs of:
    A. a phobia.
    B. mania.
    C. depression.
    D. panic disorder.

13. The Rorschach Inkblot Test can reliably diagnose:
    A. depression.
    B. posttraumatic stress disorder.
    C. personality disorders.
    D. none of the above.

14. The tendency to brood about feeling hopeless predicts:
    A. depression.
    B. eating disorders.
    C. drug abuse.
    D. all of the above.

15. More women receive a diagnosis of depression than men. Which of the following is a possible explanation for this gender difference in depression?
    A. Women are more likely to have a history of sexual abuse.
    B. Women are more likely to lack fulfilling jobs.
    C. Mothers are vulnerable to depression.
    D. All of the above.

16. What cultural practice is most likely to reduce alcoholism?
    A. Teaching children to drink responsibly but approving of adult drunkenness
    B. Forbidding children from drinking but condemning adult drunkenness
    C. Teaching children to drink responsibly while condemning adult drunkenness
    D. Forbidding children from drinking but approving of adult drunkenness

17. The sociocognitive view of dissociate identity disorder suggests that:
    A. a history of sexual abuse and repression are the causes of multiple personalities.
    B. multiple personalities result from the suggestions of therapists.
    C. the disorder is caused by a genetic predisposition combined with stress.
    D. your identity may split if societal demands clash with your cultural upbringing.

18. Individuals suffering from antisocial personality disorder are often charming and can be highly successful:
    A. psychotherapists.
    B. con artists.
    C. teachers.
    D. advertisers.

19. Hypothesized causes of antisocial personality disorder include:
    A. problems in behavioral inhibition.
    B. neurological impairments.
    C. social deprivation.
    D. all of the above.

20. Which of the following statements about the Rorschach inkblot test is false?
    A. Evidence on the success of the Rorschach typically comes from workshop testimonials.
    B. While the Rorschach often detects psychological damage in adults, it typically fails to report harm in children.
    C. Efforts to confirm the reliability and validity of the Rorschach have repeatedly failed.
    D. The Rorschach does not reliably diagnose serious mental disorders.

21. A local university is considering implementing a "no alcohol" policy for all of its students. Based on the previous research findings, what is the most likely outcome?
    A. The rate of alcoholism will increase when given the chance to drink.
    B. Alcohol is likely to become less valued to the students.
    C. A steady and gradual decrease in consumption of alcohol.
    D. A sharp initial decrease in alcoholism followed by no more decreases.

22. The disease model of addiction:
    A. requires abstinence.
    B. maintains that people have an inherited predisposition for alcoholism.
    C. holds that addiction is related to biochemistry, metabolism, and genetics.
    D. incorporates all of the above.

23. At the heart of the debate between the disease and learning models of addiction is the question of whether:
    A. moderate drinking is possible for former alcoholics.
    B. alcoholics should be blamed for their alcoholism.
    C. there is an alcoholic personality.
    D. alcoholics are "bad" or "sick."

24. An "alter" is:
    A. an emerging personality in dissociative identity disorder.
    B. someone with bipolar disorder.
    C. someone co-dependent with an individual with borderline personality disorder.
    D. a principal symptom of post-traumatic stress disorder.

25. The controversy among mental health professionals about dissociative identity disorder has to do with whether:
   A. it is a common and under-diagnosed disorder or whether it is concocted by mental health professionals and suggestible patients.
   B. it should be treated with traditional techniques or whether special treatments should be utilized.
   C. it is a biologically-based disorder or whether it results from psychosocial factors.
   D. the alternate personalities should be "seen" in treatment or whether they should be ignored by the therapist.

26. Amanda thinks she is the singer Madonna. When she speaks she often does not make any sense at all and at times she appears to be talking to herself. She is most likely experiencing:
   A. schizophrenia.
   B. antisocial personality disorder.
   C. dissociative identity disorder.
   D. mania.

27. Lisa has bizarre delusions, hallucinations, incoherent speech, and disorganized and inappropriate behavior. Lisa is exhibiting _____ symptoms of schizophrenia.
   A. positive or active
   B. negative
   C. catatonic
   D. maladaptive

28. Negative symptoms of schizophrenia:
   A. may begin before and continue after positive symptoms.
   B. include loss of motivation.
   C. include diminished thought and emotional flatness.
   D. include all of the above.

29. Support for the idea of an infectious virus during prenatal development as a cause of schizophrenia comes from the fact that:
   A. there is a significant association between a mother's exposure to a virus during prenatal development.
   B. most schizophrenics have very low immune functioning.
   C. most schizophrenics show abnormalities on chromosome 5.
   D. most schizophrenics have extra dopamine receptors.

30. The idea that genetic or brain abnormalities combine with family or other pressures to trigger schizophrenia reflects the:
   A.   interactionist model.
   B.   learning theory model.
   C.   vulnerability-stress model.
   D.   biology-pressure model.

31. A recent approach to understanding the causes of schizophrenia has focused on adolescence, when:
   A.   a shortage of intimate friends may predispose someone to schizophrenia.
   B.   an over-pruning of synapses may occur.
   C.   punitive parental treatment may predispose someone to schizophrenia.
   D.   viruses may damage the hippocampus.

PRACTICE TEST 2 – Short Answer

1. One perspective defines mental disorders as a violation of _____ standards.

2. Depressed people often _____, which results in them focusing on what is wrong with their lives and why they should feel hopeless.

3. The definition of a mental disorder as a _____ helps rule out behavior that simply deviates from what people consider healthy or normal.

4. _____ anxiety disorder is continuous, uncontrollable anxiety or worry.

5. Typical anxiety symptoms of _____ include reliving the trauma in recurrent, intrusive thoughts or dreams.

6. The essential difference between people who develop panic disorder and those who do not may reside in how they _____ their bodily reactions.

7. Veronica will not take a class if a class presentation is one of the requirements. She is terrified of speaking in class because she worries that she will do or say something embarrassing. The most likely diagnosis for Veronica is _____.

8. The most disabling fear disorder which accounts for more than half of the phobia cases for which people seek treatment is _____.

9. Factors that contribute to depression include _____, _____, _____, and _____.

10. People who suffer from major depression experience emotional, _____, and _____ changes severe enough to disrupt their ordinary functioning.

11. There is good evidence for the existence of a _____ contribution to schizophrenia.

12. An infectious _____ during prenatal development may affect the likelihood of schizophrenia developing

13. The _____ model of antisocial personality disorder says that disorder is more likely to develop when biological predispositions are combined with physical abuse, parental neglect, lack of love, or other environmental _____.

14. The _____ test requires respondents to interpret abstract, symmetrical inkblots.

15. On one side of the MPD controversy, some think that MPD is _____, but often misdiagnosed. On the other side are those who believe that most cases of MPD are actually generated by _____, either knowingly or unknowingly.

16. The _____ explanation of MPD holds that it is simply an extreme form of the ability we all possess to present different aspects of our personalities to others.

17. The _____ model holds that addiction, whether to alcohol or any other drug, is due primarily to a person's biochemistry, metabolism, and genetic predisposition.

18. The _____ model of addiction argues that a problem drinker can become a social drinker and acquire other ways of coping with stress.

19. Schizophrenia is an example of a _____, a mental condition that involves distorted perceptions of reality and an inability to function in most aspects of life.

20. Two active or positive symptoms of schizophrenia include _____ or false beliefs, and _____, or the perception of stimuli that are not actually present.

PRACTICE TEST 3 – Essay

1.   Jason spends all day at the shopping mall. Every day he stops people who look in his direction and literally begs for their forgiveness. Jason's boldly colored sweatshirts make Jason quite noticeable. These are worn every day, over his coat when it's cold, and each one has exactly the same inscription: "Jason is not a thief." Discuss the aspect of Jason's behavior that conforms to each of the following definitions of mental disorder.

      A.   Violation of cultural standards
      B.   Self-destructive or harmful behavior
      C.   Emotional distress

2.   For each description below, indicate whether the anxiety that is present is normal or abnormal. When it is abnormal, suggest the most likely diagnostic category.

      A.   Karl loves the racetrack but he will not go there again. The last time he was there he suddenly felt his heart racing, he was gasping for breath, his hands began to tremble and he broke out into a cold sweat.

      B.   Mayumi is very clean! She feels contaminated unless she bathes and changes her clothes at least four times a day, and she is meticulous about the house as well. Every room is scrubbed at least twice a week and the bathroom is cleaned daily.

      C.   Tes, a college student, becomes anxious whenever assigned a project that requires speaking in front of class. The anxiety motivates meticulous preparation and the student rehearses material again and again.

      D.   Angela was stranded in a building for over two hours. The stairway was blocked by men moving large cartons, and the only way down was the elevators. Elevators cause Angela to sweat, tremble, and suffer from images of being crushed. She decided to wait rather than take the elevator.

      E.   Craig has had problems since returning from Iraq. He is listless and quarrelsome, and has fitful sleeps, reliving his past in nightmarish dreams.

3. Josephine is highly mistrustful of airline personnel. She believes that airplanes dirty the streets and sidewalks by dripping oil and that pilots have a power called "telectic penetration." On hearing a plane, Josephine becomes introspective and claims she is being used as radar. She feels the pilots are tuning in to her latitude and longitude and asking her questions about her location. She is unable to speak until the plane has left.

A. Does Josephine have delusions? If so, what type?
B. Is Josephine hallucinating? If so, describe her hallucinations.
C. Is Josephine having any disorganized or incoherent speech? If so, describe.
D. Is Josephine demonstrating any disorganized or inappropriate behavior? If so, describe it.
E. Is Josephine demonstrating emotional flatness? If so, describe it.

CHAPTER 16

Approaches to Treatment and Therapy

LEARNING OBJECTIVES

Biological Treatments for Mental Disorders

16.1 - What types of medications are used to treat psychological disorders.

16.2 - Six important cautions about medications for emotional problems.

16.3 - Ways of electrically stimulating the brain—and whether they work.

Major Schools of Psychotherapy

16.4 - The major approaches to psychotherapy.

16.5 - How behavior therapists can help you change bad habits and cognitive therapists can help you get rid of self-defeating thoughts.

16.6 - Why humanist and existential therapists focus on the "here and now" instead of the "why and how."

16.7 - The benefits of treating a whole family instead of only one of its members.

Evaluating Psychotherapy

16.8 - The meaning of the "scientist–practitioner gap" and why it has been widening.

16.9 - Which form of psychotherapy is most likely to help if you are anxious or depressed.

16.10 - Why psychotherapy can sometimes be harmful.

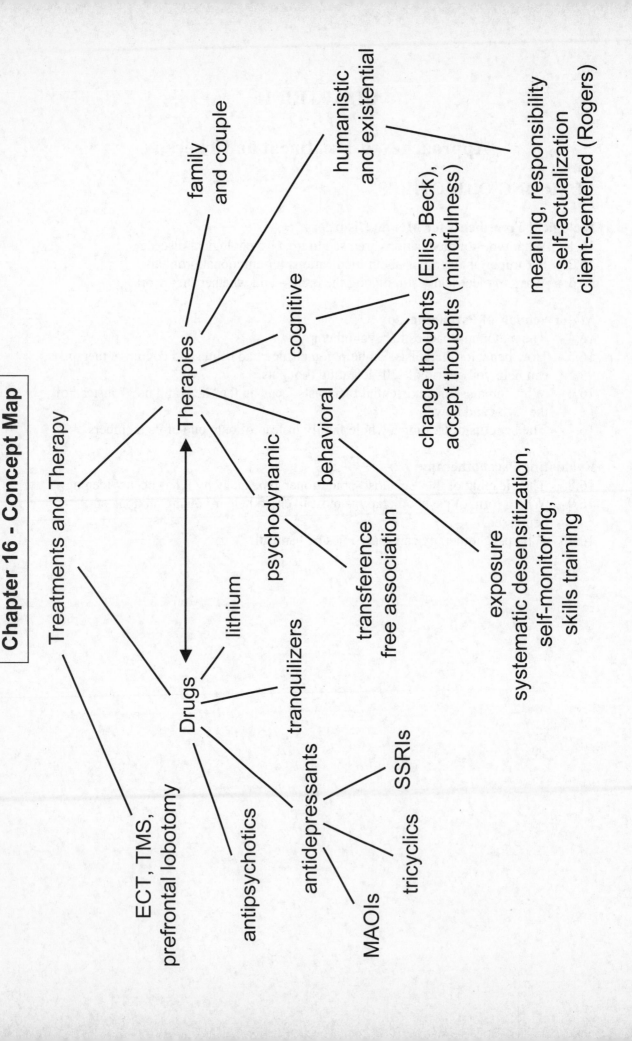

Chapter 16 - Concept Map

Treatments and Therapy

Therapies

Drugs

ECT, TMS, prefrontal lobotomy

family and couple

humanistic and existential

meaning, responsibility
self-actualization
client-centered (Rogers)

cognitive

change thoughts (Ellis, Beck),
accept thoughts (mindfulness)

behavioral

exposure
systematic desensitization,
self-monitoring,
skills training

psychodynamic

transference
free association

lithium

tranquilizers

antipsychotics

antidepressants

SSRIs

MAOIs

tricyclics

BRIEF CHAPTER SUMMARY

Chapter 16 describes various approaches to the treatment of mental disorders. Three general types of approaches are reviewed. Medical approaches include drug treatments, psychosurgery, and electroconvulsive therapy. Drug treatments include antidepressant, anti-anxiety, and antipsychotic medications. Although drug therapies have produced significant advances in the treatment of mental disorders, they require great caution in their use. Psychosurgery, which was used more commonly in the 1950s, is rarely used today because of its serious and irreversible side effects. Electroconvulsive therapy is still used for serious cases of depression that do not respond to other treatments. Types of psychotherapy are based on many of the major perspectives in psychology (e.g., psychodynamic, behavioral, cognitive, humanistic). The general principles and techniques of each of these approaches are reviewed, along with research on their effectiveness. Although there are certain commonalities among all the different types of psychotherapy, research indicates that some approaches are more effective for particular problems. Cognitive and behavioral approaches, for example, are successful in treating depression, phobias, and other anxiety disorders, and childhood behavior problems.

PREVIEW OUTLINE

Before you read the chapter, review the preview outline for each section of the text. After you have read the chapter, close this book and try to <u>recreate</u> the outlines on a blank piece of paper.

I.   **BIOLOGICAL TREATMENTS FOR MENTAL DISORDERS**
    A.   **The question of drugs**
        1.   Biological treatments are enjoying a resurgence because of evidence that some disorders have a biological component
        2.   Drugs commonly prescribed for mental disorders
            a.   Antipsychotic drugs (neuroleptics) for schizophrenia and other psychoses; more effective on positive than negative symptoms
            b.   Antidepressant drugs – include (MAO) inhibitors, tricyclics, and SSRIs – nonaddictive, but can have unpleasant side effects
            c.   Tranquilizers such as Valium – increase activity of GABA
            d.   Lithium carbonate – prescribed for bipolar disorder; must be administered in the correct dose or can be dangerous
        3.   Cautions about drugs include overprescription, relapse and drop-out rates, dosage problems, long-term risks, and placebo effect (to what extent is the effectiveness of a drug due simply to belief in the drug's effectiveness?)

B.   Direct brain intervention
      1.   Prefrontal lobotomy – surgery to destroy selected areas of the brain
      2.   Electrically stimulating the brain: Electroconvulsive therapy or ECT (works for severely depressed people, though it is unclear why it works) and transcranial magnetic stimulation or TMS (involves magnetic coil)

II.   MAJOR SCHOOLS OF PSYCHOTHERAPY

A.   Psychodynamic therapy
      1.   Probes the past and the unconscious with techniques such as free association and transference
      2.   Traditional psychoanalysis evolved into psychodynamic therapies
      3.   They do not aim to solve an individual's immediate problem – symptoms are seen as the tip of the iceberg

B.   Behavior and cognitive therapy – focus is behavior change not insight
      1.   Behavioral techniques – derived from classical and operant conditioning
            a.   Exposure (graduated exposure or flooding) – imagined or actual
            b.   Systematic desensitization – step-by-step process of "desensitizing" a client to a feared object or experience; uses counterconditioning
            c.   Behavioral self-monitoring
            d.   Skills training – practice in behaviors necessary for achieving goals
      2.   Cognitive techniques
            a.   Aim is to identify thoughts, beliefs, and expectations that might be prolonging a person's problems
            b.   Albert Ellis and rational emotive behavior therapy – therapist challenges unrealistic beliefs directly with rational arguments
            c.   Beck's approach uses less direct techniques
            d.   Mindfulness and acceptance – awareness of thoughts and emotions without judgment or attempt to control

C.   Humanistic and existential therapy
      1.   Humanistic therapies – assume that people seek self-actualization
      2.   Do not delve into the past; help people to develop will and confidence to change and achieve goals
      3.   Client-centered or nondirective therapy by Carl Rogers – unconditional positive regard and empathy by therapist
      4.   Existential therapy – helps client explore meaning of existence, choose a destiny, and accept self-responsibility

D.   Family and couples therapy
      1.   Family therapy – believes that the problem developed and is maintained in the social context, and that is where change must occur

2.   The family as a changing pattern in which all parts affect each other and efforts to treat a single member are doomed to fail; observing the family together reveals family tensions and imbalances

3.   Couples therapy involves both parties; integrative approach popular

III. EVALUATING PSYCHOTHERAPY

A. The therapeutic alliance

1.   Some participants will do better than others in therapy (e.g., those motivated to improve or who have family support)

2.   Understanding role of the client's culture is also important

B. The scientist-practitioner gap

1.   Conflict between scientists and practitioners about the relevance of research findings to clinical practice

2.   Breach between scientists and therapists has widened, partly due to professional schools that are unconnected to academic departments

C. When therapy helps

1.   Randomized controlled trials reveal empirically validated treatments

2.   Which therapy for which problem?

     a.   Behavior and cognitive therapies are the method of choice for depression, anxiety disorders, anger and impulsive violence, health problems, and childhood behavior problems

     b.   Family intervention therapies help schizophrenics by teaching their families skills for dealing with the schizophrenic children

     c.   No single type of therapy can help everyone

D. When therapy harms

1.   Use of empirically unsupported, potentially dangerous techniques

2.   Prejudice or cultural ignorance on the part of a therapist

3.   Inappropriate or coercive influence

4.   Sexual intimacies or other unethical behavior

IV. THE VALUE AND VALUES OF PSYCHOTHERAPY

A. Does psychotherapy promise too much or foster a preoccupation with the self?

B. Make wise decisions when choosing a therapist, choosing a therapy, and deciding when to leave.

APPROACHES TO PSYCHOTHERAPY

Complete the following chart by listing specific techniques and general goals of therapy for each of the approaches in the left-hand column.

THERAPY APPROACH	SPECIFIC TECHNIQUES	GENERAL GOALS OF THERAPY
PSYCHODYNAMIC APPROACHES		
BEHAVIORAL APPROACH		
COGNITIVE APPROACHES		
HUMANISTIC APPROACHES		
FAMILY AND COUPLES THERAPY		

PRACTICE TEST 1 – Multiple Choice

1.   The most widespread biological treatment for mental disorders is:
      A.   medication.
      B.   psychosurgery.
      C.   ECT.
      D.   psychotherapy.

2.   Antipsychotic drugs do NOT:
      A.   restore normal thought patterns.
      B.   lessen hallucinations.
      C.   reduce dramatic symptoms.
      D.   have side effects.

3.   Vladimir is taking antipsychotic medication. Which of the following should
      concern him?
      A.   The possibility of tardive dyskinesia
      B.   The fact that while the more dramatic symptoms may be helped, normal
            thinking may not
      C.   Though he may be well enough to be released from a hospital, he may not
            be able to care for himself
      D.   All of the above

4.   Lithium carbonate is often effective in treating people who:
      A.   have schizophrenia.
      B.   have tardive dyskinesia.
      C.   complain of unhappiness or anxiety.
      D.   have bipolar disorder.

5.   Due to unpleasant side effects, approximately how many people stop taking the
      drugs they were prescribed for a psychological disorder?
      A.   10-15%
      B.   30-45%
      C.   50-65%
      D.   80-95%

6.   Felicia has been prescribed an antidepressant. Based on the cautions about drug
      treatment, Felicia should probably have concerns about all of the following
      EXCEPT whether:
      A.   the drug is more effective than a placebo.
      B.   the drug has been tested for long-term use.
      C.   she will become addicted to the drug.
      D.   the right dosage has been identified.

7.   All of the following are potential problems with using drugs in treating psychological disorders EXCEPT:
A.   there are high drop-out rates.
B.   clinical psychologists are more likely to prescribe them than psychiatrists.
C.   there is a strong placebo effect in evaluating the effectiveness of such drugs.
D.   tests of drug effects in long-term usage are often nonexistent.

8.   Systematic desensitization is based on the behavioral principle of:
A.   reinforcement.
B.   punishment.
C.   stimulus generalization.
D.   counterconditioning.

9.   Among the following patients, who would be a likely candidate for electroconvulsive therapy (ECT)?
A.   Fran is suicidally depressed.
B.   Dan is anxious.
C.   Stan is moderately depressed.
D.   ECT should not be used on any of them, since it is outdated and dangerous.

10.   Critics of ECT say that it:
A.   only helps people with minor psychological problems.
B.   is too often used improperly, and it can damage the brain.
C.   requires high voltages, which could be fatal.
D.   causes epileptic seizures.

11.   In psychodynamic therapies, the patient's displacement of emotional elements in his or her inner life onto the therapist is called:
A.   free association.
B.   transference.
C.   insight.
D.   dynamic focus.

12.   A type of therapy that takes the individual right into the most feared situation is called:
A.   systematic desensitization.
B.   aversive conditioning.
C.   flooding.
D.   brief psychodynamic therapy.

13.   Systematic desensitization, aversive conditioning, flooding, and skills training are all:
A.   techniques used in cognitive therapies.
B.   psychodynamic techniques.
C.   methods employed by humanists.
D.   behavioral techniques.

14.   To help Yuta with his fear of flying, Dr. Chappell teaches Yuta to relax while they proceed through a series of steps that go from reading a story about an airplane, to visiting an airport, to boarding a plane, to taking a short flight. This _____ technique is called _____.
A.   cognitive; systematic desensitization
B.   cognitive; flooding
C.   behavioral; systematic desensitization
D.   behavioral; flooding

15.   Cognitive therapies focus on changing _____, whereas humanistic therapies focus on _____.
A.   beliefs; self-acceptance
B.   behaviors; changing families
C.   behaviors; insight into the past
D.   thoughts; skills

16.   Which two therapies often borrow each other's methods, so that a combination of the two is more common than either method alone?
A.   Psychoanalysis and behavior therapy
B.   Family therapy and group therapy
C.   Cognitive therapy and behavior therapy
D.   Support groups and group therapy

17.   In which approach does the therapist challenge the client's illogical beliefs?
A.   Cognitive therapy
B.   Humanistic therapy
C.   Psychodynamic therapy
D.   Existential therapy

18.   What type of therapy emphasizes unconditional positive regard?
A.   Cognitive
B.   Humanistic
C.   Psychodynamic
D.   Existential

19.   Which type of therapist is most likely to make use of insight, transference, and free association?
A.   A humanistic therapist
B.   A behaviorist therapist
C.   A psychodynamic therapist
D.   A cognitive therapist

20. Sam's therapist notes that his problems extend beyond himself, but also involve the significant others around him. As such, his therapist wants Sam to start bringing his parents and siblings with him to therapy. Which therapeutic technique is mostly likely involved in this situation?
    A.   Interlocking contingencies approach
    B.   Family-systems perspective
    C.   Applied significant connections treatment
    D.   Wholeness-centered therapy

21. David is a psychotherapist who argues that therapy is an art, and as such, it is inappropriate to try to measure outcomes. His attitude has also led him ignore psychological research and, as such, David is ignorant of the latest empirical findings. David's approach is contributing to the:
    A.   scientist-practitioner gap.
    B.   loss of therapeutic alliance.
    C.   nonempirical therapist syndrome.
    D.   problem of finding representative samples.

22. Robin has been suffering from depression for many months. What therapeutic approach is most likely to be beneficial for her?
    A.   Cognitive-behavioral
    B.   Psychodynamic
    C.   Humanist
    D.   Medication

23. Justin frequently has uncontrollable anxiety. What therapeutic approach is most likely to be beneficial for him?
    A.   Cognitive-behavioral
    B.   Psychodynamic
    C.   Humanist
    D.   Medication

24. In which of the following cases is Elaina most likely to find the therapeutic experience harmful?
    A.   Her therapist firmly believes that Elaina was sexually abused in childhood, though she has no memories of this and does not believe it is so.
    B.   Her therapist disagrees with her about several issues.
    C.   Her therapist does not always give her an immediate appointment when she calls.
    D.   All of the above may be harmful.

25. Which factors can cause psychotherapy to be harmful?
    A.   Coercion
    B.   Bias
    C.   Therapist-induced disorders
    D.   All of the above

PRACTICE TEST 2 – Short Answer

1. Neuroleptics, or antipsychotic drugs, are used in the treatment of _____ and other _____.

2. One of the side effects of the antipsychotic drugs is a neurological disorder called _____, which is characterized by hand tremors and other involuntary muscle movements.

3. Monoamine oxidase inhibitors, tricyclics, and selective serotonin reuptake inhibitors are all examples of _____ drugs.

4. _____ is a special category of drug which often helps people who suffer from bipolar disorder.

5. People who take antidepressant drugs without also learning how to cope with their problems are more likely to _____ in the future.

6. _____ and _____ therapies are ones in which the client is taught to identify and accept whatever unpleasant thoughts and feelings occur, without any attempt to eliminate or control them.

7. _____ is used as a treatment for severe depression, for patients who are at risk of committing suicide who cannot wait for antidepressants or psychotherapy to take effect.

8. To bring unconscious conflicts to awareness, Dr. MacLeod, a _____ therapist, often asks her clients to say whatever comes to mind. This technique is called _____.

9. Derek has been seeing Dr. Merod. Derek has always felt that his mother rejected him and now he finds that he is furious at Dr. Merod for planning a vacation. According to the psychodynamic approach, this reaction is called _____.

10. _____ is one of the _____ techniques that involves a step-by-step process of desensitizing a client to a feared object or experience.

11. The technique of _____ involves having clients who are suffering from specific anxieties confront the feared situation or memory directly.

12. Cognitive therapists require clients to examine the _____ for their beliefs and to consider other _____ of events that might result in less disturbing emotions.

13. One of the best-known schools of cognitive therapy was developed by Albert Ellis and is now called rational _____ behavior therapy.

14. _____ therapy, developed by Carl Rogers, the therapist listens to the client in an accepting, nonjudgmental way and offers _____ positive regard.

15. _____ therapists maintain that problems develop in a social context, and that any changes a person makes in therapy will affect that context.

16. The scientist-practitioner gap refers to the breach between scientists and therapists about the importance of _____ methods and findings on the practice of psychotherapy.

17. In some cases, psychotherapy has been found to be harmful because the therapist may be _____, inducing the client to produce the symptoms the therapist is looking for.

18. _____ is an approach to therapy that emphasizes how people interact with their families and that many problems require treatment of all the individuals involved, not just a single client.

19. A task force from the American Psychological Association found that _____ therapy is particularly effective for depression and _____ disorders.

20. The lack of communication between those who research therapy and those who conduct it is called the _____.

21. _____ influence, sexual intimacies, or other unethical behavior can result in harm to the client.

PRACTICE TEST 3 – Essay

1.   Describe the biological treatments for psychological disorders.

2.   Identify the drugs typically prescribed for each of the disorders listed below and then briefly explain some drawbacks to drug therapy.

        A.   Anxiety disorders
        B.   Mood disorders
        C.   Psychotic disorders

3.   Summarize the major features of each of the major approaches to psychotherapy: psychodynamic, cognitive, behavioral, humanistic, and family. Specify the goals and common techniques of each.

4.   Identify and briefly describe the factors that can contribute to therapeutic harm.

APPENDIX A

Statistical Methods

LEARNING OBJECTIVES

A.1 - What is a frequency distribution?

A.2 - What are measures of central tendency and why are they important descriptive statistics?

A.3 - What are measures of variability and why are they important descriptive statistics?

A.4 - How do percentile scores and Z-scores work?

A.5 - What are the basic properties of a normal distribution?

A.6 - What is the distinction between a null hypothesis and an alternative hypothesis?

A.7 - How do scientists undertake the process of hypothesis testing?

A.8 - What does it mean to say an experimental result is "statistically significant"?

PREVIEW OUTLINE

Before you read the appendix, review the preview outline for each section. After you have read the appendix, close this book and try to <u>recreate</u> the outlines on a blank piece of paper.

I. **ORGANIZING DATA**
    A.   **Constructing a frequency distribution** – often the first step in organizing data
        1.   Shows how often each possible score actually occurred
        2.   Grouped frequency distributions (groups adjacent scores into equal-sized classes or intervals) are sometimes used when there are many possible scores
    B.   **Graphing the data**
        1.   A graph is a picture that depicts numerical relationships
        2.   Types of graphs
            a.   Histogram or bar graph – draw rectangles or bars above each score indicating the number of times it occurred from the bar's height
            b.   Frequency polygon, or line graph – each score is indicated by a dot placed directly over the score on the horizontal axis
        3.   Caution about graphs – they can mask or exaggerate differences

II. **DESCRIBING DATA**
    A.   **Measuring central tendency** – single representative number for a set of data
        1.   The mean or "average"
            a.   Add up a set of scores and divide by the total number of scores
            b.   Means can be misleading because very high or very low scores can dramatically raise or lower the mean
        2.   The median
            a.   The median is the midpoint in a set of scores ordered
            b.   A more representative measure when extreme scores occur
        3.   The mode
            a.   The score that occurs most often
            b.   Used less often than other measures of central tendency
    B.   **Measuring variability** – tells whether the scores are clustered closely around the mean or widely scattered
        1.   The mode – simplest measure of variability – found by subtracting the lowest score from the highest one
        2.   The standard deviation – tells how much, on the average, scores in a distribution differ from the mean

a. To compute the standard deviation: Subtract the mean from each score yielding deviation scores, square deviation scores, average the squared deviation scores, then take the square root of the result

b. Large standard deviations signify that scores are widely scattered and the mean is probably not very representative

C. **Transforming scores** – used when researchers don't want to work directly with raw scores

1. Percentile scores – percentage of people scoring at or below a given raw score

2. Z-scores or standard scores

a. Tell how far a given raw score is above or below the mean, using the standard deviation as the unit of measurement

b. They preserve the relative spacing of the original raw scores

c. Z-scores comparisons must be done with caution

D. **Curves**, or the pattern of the distribution

1. A normal distribution has a symmetrical, bell-shaped form when plotted in a frequency polygon – called a normal curve

2. Characteristics of a normal curve: symmetrical, all measures of central tendency (mean, median, mode) have the same value

3. Not all types of observations are distributed normally; some are lopsided or skewed

a. When the tail goes to the left, it is a negative skew

b. When the tail goes to the right, it is a positive skew

III. DRAWING INFERENCES

A. **The null versus the alternative hypothesis**

1. The null hypothesis states the possibility that the experimental manipulations will have no effect on the subjects' behavior

2. The alternative hypothesis states that the average experimental group score will differ from the average control group score

3. The goal is to reject the null hypothesis

B. **Testing hypotheses**

1. Goal – to be reasonably certain the difference did not occur by chance

2. Sampling distribution is used – the theoretical distribution of differences between means

3. When the null hypothesis is true, there is no difference between groups

4. If there is a difference, how likely is it to occur by chance?

5. If it is highly improbable that a result occurs by chance, it is said to be statistically significant

6. Characteristics of statistical significance

a. Finding accepted as statistically significant if the likelihood of its occurring by chance is five percent or less ($p < .05$)

b. Statistically significant results are not always psychologically interesting or important
c. Statistical significance is related to sample size – results from a large sample are likely to be found statistically significant

PRACTICE TEST 1 – Multiple Choice

1. The first step in organizing raw data is to:
    A. get a measure of the central tendency.
    B. establish the range.
    C. construct a frequency distribution.
    D. identify standard deviation.

2. Dr. Starr gives 10-question quizzes in her psychology class. When she returns quizzes, she puts on the board how many people scored a 10, 9, 8, 7, 6, 5, 4, 3, 2, and 1. This is called a:
    A. normal curve.
    B. frequency distribution.
    C. frequency polygon.
    D. histogram.

3. A "histogram" is the technical term that describes a:
    A. bar graph.
    B. polygon.
    C. mean.
    D. line graph.

4. A histogram is to a polygon as:
    A. a line is to a bar.
    B. null is to alternative.
    C. a bar is to a line.
    D. normal is to skewed.

5. The most frequently occurring score in a distribution is called the:
    A. mean.
    B. median.
    C. standard deviation.
    D. mode.

6. The mean, median, and mode are:
    A. measures of central tendency.
    B. measures of variability.
    C. characteristics of a normal distribution, but not a skewed distribution.
    D. characteristics of a skewed distribution, but not a normal distribution.

7. A measure of variability that indicates the average difference between scores in a distribution and their mean is called the:
    A. range.
    B. standard deviation.
    C. mode.
    D. z-score.

8.	A score that indicates how far a given score is from the mean is called a:
   A.	range.
   B.	mode.
   C.	standard deviation.
   D.	z-score.

9.	Students in Dr. Friedlander's class got the following scores on their first test: 75, 77, 87, 63, 93, 77, 72, 80, 57, 68, 76. What is the mode?
   A.	77
   B.	75
   C.	36
   D.	76

10.	What is the median in the distribution of scores in question 9?
   A.	77
   B.	75
   C.	36
   D.	76

11.	What is the range in the distribution of scores in question 9?
   A.	77
   B.	36
   C.	30
   D.	76

12.	If the mean is 10, and the standard deviation is 2, a person with a raw score of 8 has a z-score of:
   A.	8.
   B.	-1.
   C.	1.
   D.	2.

13.	A lopsided distribution in which scores cluster at the high or low end of the distribution is referred to as:
   A.	normal.
   B.	bimodal.
   C.	skewed.
   D.	standard.

14.	What asserts that experimental manipulations have no effect?
   A.	Null hypothesis
   B.	Sampling distribution
   C.	Alternative hypothesis
   D.	Statistical significance

15. If the null hypothesis is true, differences between experimental and control groups are due to:
    A. standard deviations.
    B. skew.
    C. chance fluctuations.
    D. true differences.

16. Results that are not attributable to chance are referred to as:
    A. non chance fluctuations.
    B. skewed.
    C. statistically significant.
    D. all of the above.

17. The theoretical distribution of the results of the entire population is called the:
    A. null hypothesis.
    B. sampling distribution.
    C. statistical significance.
    D. random error.

18. Statistical significance:_____
    A. suggests that a result would be highly improbable by chance alone.
    B. does not necessarily have anything to do with psychological importance.
    C. is a likely outcome with a large sample.
    D. incorporates all of the above.

PRACTICE TEST 2 – Short Answer

1. A _____ distribution shows how often each possible score occurs.

2. In a frequency _____, each score is indicated by a dot placed on a horizontal axis at the appropriate height on the vertical axis.

3. The _____ is calculated by adding up a set of scores and dividing by the number of scores in the set. The _____ is the score that occurs most often.

4. The above terms are ways of characterizing an entire set of data in terms of a representative number. They are measures of _____ tendency.

5. The _____ is the simplest measure of variability, whereas the standard tells how much, on average, scores in a distribution differ from the _____.

6. When researchers don't want to work directly with raw scores, they can convert the scores to either _____ or to _____.

7. A _____ distribution has a symmetrical, bell-shaped form when plotted on a frequency polygon.

8. When a distribution of scores is lopsided and the longer tail goes to the left, it is characterized as _____ skewed.

9. The _____ hypothesis states the possibility that the experimental manipulations will have no effect on the behavior of the participants.

10. If it is highly improbable that a result occurs by chance, it is said to be _____ significant.

PRACTICE TEST 3 – Essay

1.   Researchers organize and describe data in a variety of ways. Below, different statistical devices have been grouped together. Examine each grouping and describe the common purpose of the statistics within each.

      A.   Mean, median, mode
      B.   Range and standard deviation
      C.   Frequency distributions, bar graphs (histograms), and line graphs (frequency polygons)
      D.   Percentile scores and z-scores

2.   Assume that the height of the male population is normally distributed with a mean of 70 inches and a standard deviation of 3 inches. Given such information, examine each of the statements below and decide whether it is justified or unjustified. Explain the basis for your answer.

      A.   The most frequently occurring male height is 70 inches.
      B.   The percentage of men above 70 inches is much higher than the percentage below this height.
      C.   If the height requirement for entering the police academy were set at 73 inches, less than half the male population would qualify.
      D.   A curve depicting the height of players in professional basketball would also be normally distributed.

3.   Below are two inaccurate statements about hypothesis testing and statistical significance. Revise each statement so that it is accurate.

      A.   The null hypothesis is accepted whenever results are statistically significant.
      B.   Statistical significance is a measure of the relative strengths of experimental and control treatments.

ANSWER KEYS FOR ALL CHAPTERS

Each answer in the key references the relevant learning objective, in parentheses.

ANSWER KEYS FOR CHAPTER 1

ANSWER KEY – PRACTICE TEST 1 – MULTIPLE CHOICE

1. B (1.1)	2. B (1.1)	3. D (1.2)	4. A (1.3)
5. A (1.3, 1.4)	6. D (1.7)	7. A (1.8)	8. C (1.8)
9. D (1.8)	10. D (1.9)	11. D (1.6)	12. A (1.9)
13. D (1.9)	14. A (1.9)	15. A (1.6)	16. B (1.10)
17. C (1.9)	18. B (1.9)	19. D (1.11)	20. D (1.11)
21. B (1.13)	22. D (1.12)	23. A (1.12)	24. C (1.12)
25. C (1.12)	26. A (1.12)	27. B (1.12)	28. C (1.14)
29. C (1.9, 1.14)			

ANSWER KEY – PRACTICE TEST 2 – SHORT ANSWER

1. behavior and mental processes (1.1)
2. empirical (1.1)
3. Critical thinking (1.3)
4. any two of the following: ask questions, define your terms, examine the evidence, analyze assumptions and biases, avoid emotional reasoning, don't oversimplify, consider other interpretations, tolerate uncertainty (1.5)
5. empirical (1.6)
6. first psychological laboratory (1.7)
7. structuralism (1.8)
8. conflicts and traumas from early childhood (1.9)
9. psychodynamic (1.9)
10. biological, learning, cognitive, sociocultural, psychodynamic (1.9)
11. learning (1.9)
12. free will (1.11)
13. cognitive perspective (1.9)
14. social and cultural forces (1.9)
15. sociocultural psychologists (1.9)
16. feminist (1.11)
17. based on empirical evidence (1.4)
18. Industrial/occupational; educational (1.12)
19. clinical psychology, counseling psychology, school psychology (1.12)
20. it is vague (1.2)
21. license; doctorate (1.12)
22. psychotherapist, psychoanalyst, psychiatrist (1.14)
23. Psychiatrists; psychotherapists (1.12, 1.14)
24. language, methods, and standards of acceptable evidence (1.10)

25. Evolutionary (1.12)
26. teaching and doing research in academic settings; providing health or mental health services; research and applications in nonacademic settings (1.13)

ANSWER KEY – PRACTICE TEST 3 – ESSAY

1. A.   This activity is an area of basic psychology because this research is not applying the measurement of intelligence for a particular use. This falls in the area of psychometrics, which is a nonclinical specialty. (1.12, 1.13, 1.14)

    B.   The study of vision falls in the area of basic research, since the findings are not concerned with the practical uses of its findings. This research is conducted by experimental psychologists because they conduct laboratory studies of sensation as well as other areas. Experimental psychology is a nonclinical specialty. (1.12, 1.13, 1.14)

    C.   Piaget's work is an example of basic psychology because the theory does not address practical uses of the knowledge. This activity falls in the area of developmental psychology because Piaget studied how people change and grow over time. It is a nonclinical area. (1.12, 1.13, 1.14)

    D.   Studying work motivations falls in the basic psychology area because this project does not involve direct use or application of the findings. This type of research falls into the specialty area of industrial or organizational psychology, which studies behavior in the workplace. It is a nonclinical specialty. (1.12, 1.13, 1.14)

    E.   Milgram's study represents basic psychology because there is no direct application of the findings. It falls under the nonclinical specialty area, social psychology. The study examines how the social context influences individuals. (1.12, 1.13, 1.14)

    F.   Strupp's study is basic research because direct application for these findings is not part of the purpose of the study. It falls under the specialty of clinical psychology, which is interested in treating mental or emotional problems and is a clinical specialty area. (1.12, 1.13, 1.14)

    G.   The study of children's self-esteem is applied research, since it was used to make changes in the school systems. This type of research falls under the specialty area of developmental psychology, since it deals with how people change and grow over time. Developmental psychology is a nonclinical specialty. (1.12, 1.13, 1.14)

    H.   Using findings from career development research to assist students is an example of applied psychology. This activity falls into the specialty of counseling psychology, a clinical area, because it is dealing with problems of everyday life rather than with mental disorders. (1.12, 1.13, 1.14)

2. Learning theory or behaviorism would explore how Harold learned his behavior and how his environmental conditions encouraged his drug abuse. Specifically, behaviorists would be interested in the payoffs or rewards that result from the

drug use. Social learning theorists might wonder if Harold had learned this behavior from observing or imitating others, such as peers or parents.

Psychologists from a psychodynamic perspective would understand Harold's drug abuse as a result of unconscious conflicts that remain unresolved from his early childhood. Harold is unaware of his true motivations because they are unconscious.

The biological perspective understands Harold's drug abuse as a direct result of addictive processes by which the body comes to crave and depend on drugs. If Harold were to attempt to discontinue his drug use, he would experience unpleasant bodily sensations related to withdrawal. Therefore, to avoid bodily withdrawal symptoms, his drug use is continued. Biological predispositions may be operating that may have made Harold more sensitive to drug exposure.

Cognitive psychologists would be interested in Harold's perception and reasoning about drug use. Are his ideas about drugs irrational or unreasonable? What does he tell himself about drug use or nonuse? For example, does he believe that he must use drugs to be accepted by his peers? Cognitive psychologists would be interested in whether Harold believes he has control of himself or whether he sees his drug use as a problem.

Sociocultural psychologists would look to the attitude in the culture toward alcohol use. They would understand the role alcohol plays for people and how it is expected to be used. For example, attitudes and expectations for alcohol use are different in other countries where alcohol is used as a beverage at meals and is consumed at meal times by adolescents and sometimes children.

According to humanists, Harold's drug abuse represents a choice. He is freely choosing to use drugs and is equally free to choose not to do so. Humanists may inquire whether he believes it assists him in dealing with questions about reaching his full potential.

Feminist psychologists would be interested in gender differences in drug abuse. They would see Harold's drug use as a way of dealing with emotions that are compatible with the male gender role in this society. Since the expression of certain emotions is not considered masculine, they might speculate that drug use would be a way of dealing with "unmasculine" emotions. (1.9, 1.11)

3.   A psychologist would use psychotherapy based on psychological theories to treat Juanita's depression. The psychologist would have formal training and would hold either a Ph.D., an Ed.D., or a Psy.D. A psychiatrist would be likely to prescribe medication for Juanita's depression. A psychiatrist is a medical doctor (M.D.) with a residency in psychiatry. A psychoanalyst would use psychoanalysis, which is a type of psychotherapy based on the work of Sigmund Freud. To practice psychoanalysis, specialized training at a recognized

psychoanalytic institute is required. A psychotherapist may or may not have formal education in psychology or a related field. Because the term is not regulated, psychotherapy can describe almost any type of traditional or non traditional therapy (e.g., hypnotherapy, rebirthing therapy). (1.12)

4.   Zainab's experience is obviously a very emotional one, but she should not let her emotions dominate her thinking. She should examine the evidence more closely, and she should define her terms: what does she mean by "psychic" anyway? Has she had experiences like this before? Even better, how could she gather additional evidence to investigate her supposed powers? She could write down her dreams for two weeks and see how many come true and how many do not. In addition, Zainab should not rely only on her personal experience but other sources of evidence. One important source is whether or not psychologists have found evidence in controlled research for psychic phenomena.

Zainab should try not to oversimplify, and she should consider other explanations. For example, is it possible that the dream coming true was a coincidence? One coincidence by itself is (by definition) very rare, but coincidences in general always happen sooner or later! Is it possible that Zainab dreamed about her hero because he was planning to come to her campus soon? In other words, we might dream about events that are likely to come true anyway (how many people dream about tests?). Is it possible that her dreaming about this issue actually influenced her behavior (going to listen to a speech by her hero), such that she had a role in the dream being fulfilled that does not involve any supernatural process? Zainab should analyze any assumptions or biases she might have, even including a tendency to provide supernatural explanations for events. (1.3, 1.4, 1.5)

ANSWER KEYS FOR CHAPTER 2

ANSWER KEY – PRACTICE TEST 1 – MULTIPLE CHOICE

1. B (2.1)	2. A (2.1)	3. C (2.2)	4. A (2.5)
5. A (2.3)	6. C (2.3)	7. A (2.4)	8. B (2.8)
9. D (2.7)	10. D (2.8)	11. C (2.7)	12. A (2.8)
13. B (2.8)	14. B (2.8)	15. C (2.8)	16. D (2.8)
17. C (2.8)	18. B (2.10)	19. B (2.9)	20. D (2.6)
21. C (2.10)	22. B (2.12)	23. A (2.12)	24. D (2.12)
25. B (2.12)	26. B (2.14)	27. D (2.15)	28. A (2.15)
29. A (2.13)	30. B (2.16)	31. D (2.17)	32. A (2.17)
33. D (2.18)			

ANSWER KEY – PRACTICE TEST 2 – SHORT ANSWER

1. unfounded belief (2.7)
2. hypothesis (2.9)
3. operational (2.3)
4. principle of falsifiability (2.4)
5. replicated (2.5)
6. descriptive (2.7)
7. verify (2.5)
8. naturalistic observational studies (2.8)
9. Objective; projective (2.8)
10. representative (2.6)
11. reliability (2.8)
12. validity (2.8)
13. criterion validity (2.8)
14. representative (2.6)
15. cause and effect (2.11)
16. correlation; variables (2.9)
17. variability (2.14)
18. experimental method (2.11)
19. independent; dependent (2.12)
20. experimental; control (2.12)
21. descriptive (2.15)
22. significant (2.15)

1. A. Survey. Adolescents constitute a large population and the information sought should be accessible through questionnaires or interviews. Care is needed to construct a sample that is representative of the population under consideration. (2.7)

    B. Psychological tests. The goal is to measure psychological qualities within an individual. Other methods (e.g., case history, naturalistic observation) might be employed, but they are more time consuming and do not offer the degree of standardization, reliability and validity found in a well-constructed test. (2.7)

    C. Experiment. Cause-and-effect information is being sought. In science this information is obtained through experiments in which the proposed causal variable is manipulated under controlled conditions. (2.7)

    D. Correlation. This technique is used to determine if and how strongly two variables are related. Establishing that a correlation exists, however, does not address the problem of why two things are related. Note that an experiment cannot be conducted on this question. (2.7)

    E. Naturalistic observation. A description of behavior as it occurs in a real-life situation is being sought. Making the observations without arousing suspicion in subjects could be problematic. (2.7)

    F. Case study. Making this determination requires in-depth information about the way a variety of psychological factors – expectation, values, motives, past experiences, and so forth – blend together within the person. This kind of information is unique to the person under consideration and could not be assessed through standardized tests. (2.7)

    G. Laboratory observation. The goal is to identify what the parents are doing that may be contributing to the child's problems and help them to parent differently. To ascertain what is currently going on in the family, observing them interact in the laboratory would be the best way to actually see what is occurring. Information could be collected with an interview or questionnaire, but parents may not be aware of what they are doing. (2.7)

2. A. Hypothesis: Caffeine improves studying
        Independent variable and its operational definition: caffeine; ounces
        Dependent variable and its operational definition: studying; test score
        Experimental condition: group receiving caffeine
        Control group: group receiving decaffeinated beverage (2.12)

B. Hypothesis: Heavy metal music increases aggression
Independent variable and its operational definition: music; jazz, classical, heavy metal
Dependent variable and its operational definition: aggression; amount of time spent punching bag
Experimental condition: groups exposed to jazz, classical, and heavy metal music
Control group: group exposed to white noise machine (2.12)

C. Hypothesis: Exercise increases relaxation
Independent variable and its operational definition: exercise; aerobics, number of sit-ups and push-ups
Dependent variable and its operational definition: relaxation; heart rate, muscle tension, respiration, blood pressure
Experimental condition: groups engaging in aerobics, sit-ups, and push-ups
Control group: group having supervised study session (2.12)

3. A. Positive   B. Negative
    C. Negative   D. Positive
    E. Zero   F. Negative
    G. Negative   H. Positive
    I. Negative   J. Zero (2.9)

4. A. Unethical. Requiring research participation for a course, without providing an alternate way of satisfying the course requirement, violates the principle of voluntary consent. (2.17)
    B. Unethical. Not only should subjects be free to withdraw at any time, but they should also be informed of this right before they begin to participate. (2.17)
    C. Ethical if the experimenter believes that subjects will act differently if they know the hypothesis. (2.17)
    D. Ethical. Under the American Psychological Association's guidelines, the use of animals is acceptable in research that reduces human suffering and promotes human welfare. (2.17)
    E. Ethical. The investigator is obligated to protect subjects from physical and mental discomfort by using both voluntary and informed consent. (2.17)

5. The key elements of an experiment are the manipulation of an independent variable and random assignment to groups. There must be at least two levels of the independent variable. Your experiment should label the variable you manipulated as the independent variable, and the variable affected by the IV as the dependent variable. Subjects must be randomly assigned to the different levels of the IV. (2.12)

ANSWER KEYS FOR CHAPTER 3

ANSWER KEY – PRACTICE TEST 1 – MULTIPLE CHOICE

1. C (3.2)	2. A (3.2)	3. B (3.9)	4. D (3.1)
5. A (3.1)	6. C (3.1)	7. C (3.1)	8. A (3.1)
9. D (3.9)	10. B (3.3)	11. A (3.3, 3.4)	12. D (3.3, 3.4)
13. C (3.11)	14. A (3.5)	15. C (3.7)	16. D (3.7)
17. C (3.8)	18. D (3.8)	19. D (3.8)	20. B (3.10)
21. C (3.10)	22. D (3.12)	23. A (3.13)	24. B (3.13)
25. A (3.15)	26. C (3.14)	27. D (3.16)	28. B (3.16)
29. B (3.17)	30. D (3.18)	31. D (3.18)	

ANSWER KEY – PRACTICE TEST 2 – SHORT ANSWER

1. Genes; chromosomes (3.1)
2. genome (3.2)
3. social experience (3.9)
4. survival (3.4, 3.10)
5. evolution (3.3)
6. mutate (3.3)
7. natural selection (3.4)
8. modules (3.5)
9. language; mating (3.6)
10. rules; elements (3.7)
11. deep; surface (3.7)
12. promiscuous (3.10)
13. Chomsky; acquisition (3.8)
14. similar stages (3.8)
15. relative power of biology and culture (3.12)
16. stereotypes (3.11)
17. heritability (3.13)
18. individuals (3.14)
19. identical (monozygotic); fraternal (dizygotic) (3.15)
20. .50; .60 -.80 (3.16)
21. group (3.17)
22. prenatal care; malnutrition or exposure to toxins or large family size or stressful family circumstances (3.18)

ANSWER KEY – PRACTICE TEST 3 – ESSAY

1. A.   The basic elements of DNA within the genes influence protein synthesis in the body by specifying the sequence of amino acids, which are the building blocks of the proteins. The sequence of amino acids is affected by the arrangement of the basic elements, which comprises a chemical code. Proteins then go on to affect virtually all structural and biochemical characteristics of the organism. Genes for alcoholism might influence the basic elements of DNA or their arrangement, which then go on to influence the amino acids, the proteins and the structures or biochemistry of the body. (3.13, 3.14)

    B.   This statement misinterprets heritability estimates. Heritability estimates do <u>NOT</u> apply to individuals, only to variations within a group. No one can determine the impact of heredity on any particular individual's trait. For one person, genes may make a tremendous difference; for another, the environment may be more important. This statement ignores the fact that even highly heritable traits can be modified by the environment. This statement ignores environmental influences. (3.13, 3.14)

    C.   One might use a linkage study, which would examine large families in which alcoholism is common. (3.13, 3.14)

2. A.   The feeling of disgust may have been useful in warding off contamination from disease and contagion. (3.4)
    B.   Intuition may have allowed people to anticipate others' behaviors based on their beliefs and desires and thereby prepare for problems. (3.4)
    C.   Self-concept may have been useful in knowing one's value to others. (3.4)
    D.   Male promiscuity has the effect of increasing the offspring of any individual male, thereby continuing his genes. (3.4)
    E.   Female selectivity increases the chances of conceiving with the best genes. (3.4)

3.   Until the middle of this century, views about language acquisition suggested that language is learned (not inborn) bit by bit and that children learn to speak by imitating adults and paying attention when adults correct their mistakes. Chomsky stated that language was too complex to learn in this way. He said that children learn not only which sounds form words, but can apply the rules of syntax and discern underlying meaning. He said that the capacity for language is inborn and that the brain has a language acquisition device, or a "mental module" that allows children to develop language if they are exposed to an adequate sampling of speech. According to Chomsky, human beings are designed to use language. The following support his position:
    1.   Children everywhere seem to go through similar stages of linguistic development.

2. Children combine words in ways that adults never would, and so could not simply be imitating.
3. Adults do not consistently correct their children's syntax.
4. Even children who are profoundly retarded acquire language. (3.8)

4. A. The study would use pairs of identical twins reared apart. IQ tests would be given to both members of the pairs and the following comparisons would be made:
   1. Scores of both members of the pairs of identical twins
   2. Scores of identical twins reared together
   3. Scores of siblings reared apart
   4. Scores of siblings reared together
   5. Scores of unrelated people

   The conclusions would depend on the results of these comparisons. Similarity of IQ scores based on genetic similarity, regardless of shared environment, would be supportive evidence for heritability estimates. Cautionary statements would include:
   1. Heritable does not mean the same thing as genetic.
   2. Heritability applies only to a particular group living in a particular environment, and estimates may differ for different groups.
   3. Heritability estimates do not apply to individuals, only to variations within a group.
   4. Even highly heritable traits can be modified by the environment. (3.16, 3.18)

   B. The following recommendations would be made:
   1. Develop a prenatal care program for mothers-to-be that involves education about drug use, nutrition, health, environmental pollutants
   2. Nutrition program for young children
   3. Assistance related to exposure to toxins
   4. Information on the importance of mental stimulation
   5. Family therapy and support to reduce stressful family circumstances
   6. Training in parent-child interactions (3.16, 3.18)

ANSWER KEYS FOR CHAPTER 4

ANSWER KEY – PRACTICE TEST 1 – MULTIPLE CHOICE

1. D (4.1)	2. B (4.1)	3. A (4.1)	4. D (4.1)
5. A (4.1)	6. C (4.1)	7. C (4.1)	8. D (4.2)
9. A (4.2)	10. B (4.2)	11. A (4.2)	12. A (4.2)
13. B (4.2)	14. A (4.3)	15. B (4.2)	16. D (4.2)
17. B (4.2)	18. B (4.4)	19. D (4.6)	20. A (4.7)
21. B (4.8)	22. D (4.10)	23. D (4.10)	24. B (4.11)
25. A (4.10)	26. A (4.10)	27. D (4.7)	28. C (4.13)
29. D (4.17)	30. B (4.5)	31. A (4.9)	32. C (4.12)
33. D (4.14)	34. A (4.15)	35. D (4.16)	

ANSWER KEY – PRACTICE TEST 2 – SHORT ANSWER

1. central; peripheral (4.1)
2. somatic; autonomic (4.1)
3. sympathetic; parasympathetic (4.1)
4. cell body (4.2)
5. dendrites; axon (4.2)
6. myelin sheath (4.3)
7. synapse (4.2)
8. axon terminal; neurotransmitters (4.2)
9. all or none (4.2)
10. Endorphins; neurotransmitters (4.2)
11. endocrine (4.7)
12. norepinephrine and serotonin; acetylcholine (4.6)
13. androgens; estrogen; progesterone (4.7)
14. electroencephalogram (4.8)
15. magnetic resonance imaging (4.8)
16. reticular activating (4.10)
17. pons; medulla; cerebellum (4.10)
18. thalamus (4.10)
19. hypothalamus (4.10)
20. limbic (4.10)
21. hippocampus (4.10)
22. occipital; parietal; temporal; frontal (4.10)
23. corpus callosum (4.13)
24. Wernicke's; temporal; Broca's; frontal (4.10)
25. behavior (4.17)
26. Glial cells (4.3)
27. neurogenesis; stem cells (4.4)
28. melatonin; oxytocin; adrenal hormones; sex hormones (4.7)
29. where; why or how (4.9)
30. prefrontal cortex (4.12)
31. The left hemisphere (4.14)

1.   A.   The dendrites of neurons in the ear are stimulated and the message is sent to the cell body, which causes an inflow of sodium ions and an outflow of potassium ions that result in a wave of electrical voltage travelling down the axon. At the end of the axon, synaptic vesicles release neurotransmitters, which cross the synaptic cleft and lock into receptor sites on the next neuron. (4.1)

        B.   The sound causes neurons in the ear to fire, going via sensory neurons to the thalamus, which directs the message to the auditory cortex in the temporal lobes, to the prefrontal lobes to figure out what to do and make a plan, to the motor cortex in the frontal lobe, out of the brain via motor neurons to the skeletal muscles to get up and move. (4.2)

        C.   Information from the ears goes to the brain via the somatic nervous system of the peripheral nervous system. Once at the thalamus, it is in the central nervous system. As information exits the brain from the motor cortex, the somatic nervous system gets involved again as messages go to the muscles that allow you to cross the room. Your feeling nervous involves the autonomic nervous system, which carries messages from the central nervous system about your preparedness for the test to the glands and organs. (4.10)

2.   A.   Hypothalamus (4.10)
        B.   Thalamus (4.10)
        C.   Prefrontal lobe (4.10)
        D.   Broca's area (4.10)
        E.   Hippocampus (4.10)
        F.   Cerebellum (4.10)

3.   It is hard to say exactly, but the cerebrum, which is responsible for higher functioning, has been damaged. Parts of the brain stem, specifically the medulla, which is responsible for heart rate and respiration, are still intact, but because Helen is not conscious, it is possible that the pons, which is responsible for sleeping and waking, may be damaged. (4.10)

4.   A.   Frontal lobes; personality, planning, initiative (4.10)
        B.   Parietal lobes; body senses and location (4.10)
        C.   Occipital lobes; vision (4.10)

5.   A.   Right (4.10)
        B.   Left (4.10)
        C.   Right (4.10)
        D.   Left (4.10)
        E.   There are problems with functions controlled by the left hemisphere, but not with the right hemisphere. (4.10)

ANSWER KEYS FOR CHAPTER 5

ANSWER KEY – PRACTICE TEST 1 – MULTIPLE CHOICE

1. A (5.1)	2. C (5.2)	3. C (5.1)	4. C (5.1)
5. D (5.3)	6. D (5.6)	7. B (5.2)	8. D (5.4)
9. D (5.4)	10. D (5.6, 5.7)	11. A (5.5)	12. C (5.5)
13. B (5.5)	14. C (5.5)	15. B (5.5)	16. B (5.6)
17. B (5.8)	18. C (5.11)	19. C (5.12)	20. D (5.12)
21. A (5.14)	22. C (5.14)	23. C (5.14)	24. B (5.6)
25. C (5.16)	26. D (5.15)	27. D (5.9)	28. B (5.15)
29. C (5.16)	30. D (5.17)	31. A (5.9)	32. B (5.10)
33. D (5.13)	34. B (5.16)		

ANSWER KEY – PRACTICE TEST 2 – SHORT ANSWER

1.   circadian rhythms; melatonin (5.3)
2.   circadian (5.1)
3.   suprachiasmatic nucleus (5.1)
4.   biological rhythm (5.1)
5.   desynchronization (5.2)
6.   hormones (5.4)
7.   REM sleep (5.5)
8.   spindles (5.5)
9.   inactive; active (5.5)
10.   Sleep apnea (5.6)
11.   manifest; latent (5.8)
12.   problem-focused (5.9)
13.   activation-synthesis (5.11)
14.   hidden observer (5.14)
15.   pseudomemories (or false) (5.12)
16.   dissociation (5.14)
17.   medical and psychological (5.13)
18.   sociocognitive (5.14)
19.   Psychoactive (5.15)
20.   central nervous system (or neurotransmitters) (5.16)
21.   stimulants (5.15)
22.   tolerance (5.15)
23.   neurotransmitter (5.15)
24.   physical factors, experience with drug, environmental setting, or mental set (5.17)
25.   narcolepsy (5.6)

ANSWER KEY – PRACTICE TEST 3 – ESSAY

1.   A.   The definition of PMS is important because physical and emotional symptoms often appear on the same questionnaire. Because many women may experience physical symptoms, they are likely to have a higher score than if these two categories of symptoms were presented separately. (5.4)

      B.   Negative moods are likely to be attributed to PMS when they occur just prior to the onset of menstruation, whereas negative moods that occur at different stages of the menstrual cycle are likely to be attributed to other factors. Another problem related to the self-reporting of PMS symptoms is the tendency to notice negative moods that occur before menstruation, and to ignore the absence of negative moods before menstruation. (5.4)

      C.   Expectations can influence perceptions. The very title of a widely used questionnaire, the Menstrual Distress Questionnaire, can bias responders to look for and find certain symptoms, while ignoring other, more positive, symptoms. (5.4)

      D.   Research findings include:
          1.   Women and men do not differ in the emotional symptoms or number of mood swings they experience over the course of a month.
          2.   For most women, the relationship between cycle stage and symptoms is weak or nonexistent.
          3.   There is no reliable relationship between cycle stage and behaviors that matter in real life.
          4.   Women do not consistently report negative psychological changes from one cycle to the next. (5.4)

2.   A.   Sleep consists of REM and four distinct non-REM periods. (5.5)

      B.   The extra alertness results from the fact that the body is synchronized to wake itself up as the morning approaches. Loss of sleep is not invigorating. (5.5)

      C.   Although theorists do not agree on the exact functions of sleep, rest is one of its presumed functions. (5.5)

      D.   Though people can function pretty well after losing a single night's sleep, mental flexibility, originality, and other aspects of creative thinking may suffer. Problem-solving ability can be affected by the loss of sleep. (5.5)

      E.   We display four to five REM periods each night, and laboratory research indicates that we dream every night. (5.5)

3.   A.   Activation-synthesis theory or dreams as interpreted brain activity (5.11)
      B.   Dreams as thinking (5.10)
      C.   Dreams as unconscious wishes or psychoanalytic theory (5.8)
      D.   Dreams as problem-solvers (5.9)

4.   Hypnosis is associated with changes in sensations, perceptions, thoughts, feelings, and behavior. Although people can perform uninhibited or even embarrassing acts

while under hypnosis, they are turning over responsibility to the hypnotist. There is no evidence that individuals will actually violate their morals or put themselves into danger.

Hypnosis occasionally improves recall for forgotten experiences. However, it also tends to boost the number of errors someone makes. This is particularly problematic because hypnotized people are often convinced that their memories are completely true. There is little evidence that regression to childhood under hypnosis can help individuals re-experience long-ago events.

Hypnosis is used for many medical and psychological purposes. It can be useful for eliminating nail biting or smoking. It can boost the confidence of athletes and help reduce nausea for those undergoing chemotherapy. It has been used as an anesthetic for people undergoing dental procedures or even surgery. Hypnotic suggestions also have been used to reduce stress or extreme pain. (5.12)

5. A1. Depressant
   A2. Disinhibition, anxiety reduction, slower reaction times, memory loss, poor coordination
   A3. Death, psychosis, organic damage, blackouts

   B1. Depressant
   B2. Sedation, anxiety and guilt reduction, release of tension
   B3. Tolerance and addiction, sensory and motor impairment, coma, death

   C1. Opiate
   C2. Pain reduction, euphoria
   C3. Addiction, convulsions, nausea, death

   D1. Stimulant
   D2. Elevated metabolism and mood, increased wakefulness
   D3. Nervousness, delusions, psychosis, death

   E1. Stimulant
   E2. Appetite suppression, excitability, euphoria
   E3. Sleeplessness, sweating, paranoia, depression

   F1. Psychedelic
   F2. Hallucinations and visions, feelings of insight, exhilaration
   F3. Psychosis, panic, paranoia

   G1. Classification unclear, some say mild psychedelic
   G2. Relaxation, increased appetite, culturally determined effects
   G3. Controversial abusive effects (5.5)

ANSWER KEYS FOR CHAPTER 6

ANSWER KEY – PRACTICE TEST 1 – MULTIPLE CHOICE

1. C (6.1)	2. C (6.1)	3. A (6.4)	4. C (6.1)
5. B (6.2)	6. C (6.6)	7. A (6.2)	8. A (6.3)
9. C (6.3)	10. D (6.5)	11. A (6.4)	12. B (6.4)
13. A (6.7)	14. B (6.8)	15. C (6.8)	16. D (6.8)
17. D (6.8)	18. C (6.9)	19. B (6.9)	20. B (6.12)
21. C (6.10)	22. A (6.11)	23. A (6.14)	24. C (6.13)
25. A (6.13)	26. B (6.13)	27. A (6.15)	28. B (6.15)
29. B (6.23)	30. C (6.17)	31. A (6.18)	32. B (6.18)
33. D (6.19)	34. A (6.21)	35. D (6.16)	36. B (6.20)
37. A (6.22)			

ANSWER KEY – PRACTICE TEST 2 – SHORT ANSWER.

1. Perception (6.1)
2. anatomical; functional (6.2)
3. inattentional blindness (6.6)
4. absolute (6.3)
5. just noticeable difference (jnd) (6.3)
6. sensory; decision (6.3)
7. adaptation (6.4)
8. perceptual illusion (6.12)
9. retina (6.8)
10. rods; cones (6.8)
11. Feature-detector (6.8)
12. different times (6.14)
13. our sense of smell is impaired (6.16)
14. constancies (6.11)
15. off (6.9)
16. basilar membrane; cochlea (6.13)
17. disorienting (6.2)
18. salty, sour, bitter, and sweet; umami (6.15)
19. culture (6.15)
20. touch (or pressure), warmth, cold, pain (6.15)
21. gate-control (6.17)
22. Kinesthesis; equilibrium (6.18)
23. visual cliff (6.19)
24. emotions, expectations (6.21)
25. the placebo effect (or expectations) (6.23)
26. glial (6.17)
27. Inattentional blindness (6.8)

ANSWER KEY – PRACTICE TEST 3 – ESSAY

1.   A.   Signal detection theory indicates that active decision making is involved in determining an absolute threshold. The fatigue, as well as attention, of subjects may be interfering with decision making. (6.3, 6.4)

      B.   A reduction in sensitivity results from unchanging, repetitious stimulation or sensory adaptation. John may be having trouble feeling the glasses on his head,because they have been there for a long time. (6.3, 6.4)

      C.   When people find themselves in a state of sensory overload, they often cope by blocking out unimportant sights and sounds and focusing only on those they find useful. Unimportant sounds are not fully processed by the brain. This capacity for selective attention protects us from being overwhelmed by all the sensory signals impinging on our receptors. (6.3, 6.4)

2.   Light, the stimulus for vision, travels in the form of waves. Waves have certain physical properties: length, which corresponds to hue or color; amplitude, which corresponds to brightness; and complexity, which corresponds to saturation or colorfulness. The light enters the cornea and is bent by the lens to focus. The amount of light that enters the eye is controlled by muscles in the iris, which surrounds the pupil. The pupil widens or dilates to influence the amount of light let in. The light goes to the retina located in the back of the eye. The retina contains rods and cones, which are the visual receptors. The cones are responsible for color vision; the rods for black-and-white vision and seeing things in dim light. The fovea, where vision is sharpest, is in the center of the retina and contains only cones. Rods and cones are connected to bipolar neurons that communicate with ganglion cells. The axons of the ganglion cells converge to form the optic nerve, which carries information out through the back of the eye and on to the brain. (6.8)

3.   A.   Three colors will be needed – blue, red, and green – corresponding to three types of cones. Combining such colors produces the human color spectrum. (6.9)

      B.   Four colors will be needed – blue, yellow, red, and green. They must be paired in a way that allows them to function as opposites. (6.9)

4.   Infants were placed on the middle of a table. One side of the table appeared to have sharp drop and the other side appeared to have no drop. In truth, there was no drop because [ED/AU: MISSING COPY?] covered the entire surface of the table. The mothers coaxed their infants to approach them from both sides of the table. Researchers observed whether infants were willing to cross the side of the table that appeared to have a deep drop to get to their mothers. The researchers were interested in studying depth perception. (6.10)

5. A. Your expectation could influence your interpretation of what you saw and what happened. (6.21)
    B. Your belief about your neighbor's character could influence your perception that he was sneaking around. (6.21)
    C. Your emotions could influence your perception that someone was at the door. (6.21)

ANSWER KEYS FOR CHAPTER 7

ANSWER KEY – PRACTICE TEST 1 – MULTIPLE CHOICE

1. C	2. A	3. B	4. C
5. A	6. B	7. D	8. A
9. D	10. A	11. D	12. B
13. C	14. C	15. B	16. A
17. B	18. C	19. B	20. A
21. B	22. B	23. B	24. A
25. C	26. A	27. B	28. D
29. C	30. A	31. B	

ANSWER KEY – PRACTICE TEST 2 – SHORT ANSWER

1. conditioned response
2. conditioned stimulus
3. extinction
4. higher-order
5. generalization
6. discrimination
7. predicts
8. conditioned stimulus; conditioned response
9. operant; consequences
10. reinforcement
11. classical
12. smell
13. positive; negative
14. negative; punishment
15. expectations
16. intermittent (or partial)
17. shaping
18. extinction; reinforcement
19. not to do; what should be done instead
20. biological
21. latent
22. observational
23. increase
24. restaurant phenomenon

1.   A.   CS = first and middle name; US = father's anger; UR = anxiety; CR = anxiety (7.1)

         B.   CS = sight of flowers; US = pollen; UR = sneezing; CR = sneezing (7.1)

         C.   CS = perfume; US = true love; UR = happy; CR = happy (7.1)

         D.   CS = Park Place and Main Street; US = accident; UR = fear; CR = fear (7.1)

2.   A.   Dogs are often disciplined by being swatted (US) with rolled-up newspapers (CS). Fear is a natural response (UR) to being hit and a learned response to such objects (CR). Furthermore, stimulus generalization is demonstrated in that the dog gives the CR to other types of rolled-up papers. (7.1)

         B.   When attacked (US) by a Doberman (CS) in the past, Sara experienced fear (US). Since that time, she has been nervous about all Dobermans (stimulus generalization), though not around other dogs (stimulus discrimination). Her reduction of fear toward Dobermans represents extinction. (7.1)

         C.   The sudden noise of screeching tires (CS) often causes people to tense up and flinch (CR). The lack of response during a car race is stimulus discrimination. (7.1)

         D.   Getting sick (UR) from spoiled chicken (US) caused Masato to experience stimulus generalization to turkey (CS), which is similar to the chicken on which he originally became ill, and to experience a CR to the turkey. (7.1)

3.   A.   The tendency to buckle-up is strengthened through negative reinforcement (the desire to eliminate the sound of the buzzer). (7.9)

         B.   Punishment is weakening the tendency to smoke around the roommate. This becomes more complicated because of the addictive process, which negatively reinforces smoking by removing uncomfortable withdrawal symptoms. (7.9)

         C.   Reinforcement is strengthening Nobu's dishwashing behavior. (7.9)

         D.   Punishment is weakening Fred's tendency to go down the most difficult slopes. (7.9)

4.   A.   Eliza Jane is on a partial reinforcement schedule. This may be enough to maintain a behavior once it is well established. However, when a response is weak initially, it should be reinforced each time it occurs (continuous reinforcement). (7.9)

         B.   By picking him up sometimes in response to his cries, Ari's parents have put him on a partial reinforcement schedule, which causes behaviors to be very persistent and difficult to extinguish. To change this pattern, they must consistently respond by not picking him up when he cries and eventually the behavior will extinguish. It will take longer to do so now that he is on this intermittent schedule. (7.9)

C. It appears that all the things the teacher is trying to use as punishment are reinforcing Sue's behavior. They all involve extra attention. Therefore, by finding a consequence that is unpleasant and does not involve attention, this behavior might be decreased by using punishment. She might also try teaching her and then reinforcing her for other types of attention. (7.9)

5. The initial punishment occurs long after the marks are made and therefore may not be associated with the behavior that is being punished. The parent is also scolding the child when he or she is feeling angry and therefore he or she may be harsher than usual. The child may also be aroused because of the punishment. Ideally, the behavior should be directed to an appropriate medium, such as paper or coloring books, and then that behavior should be reinforced. (7.14)

ANSWER KEYS FOR CHAPTER 8

ANSWER KEY – PRACTICE TEST 1 – MULTIPLE CHOICE

1. A (8.1)	2. B (8.3)	3. B (8.3)	4. B (8.3)
5. B (8.3)	6. B (8.3)	7. D (8.3)	8. A (8.5)
9. A (8.4)	10. D (8.4)	11. C (8.5)	12. B (8.5)
13. A (8.5)	14. C (8.5)	15. A (8.2)	16. C (8.7)
17. B (8.12)	18. C (8.6)	19. C (8.16)	20. D (8.8)
21. D (8.9)	22. A (8.9)	23. C (8.10)	24. C (8.11)
25. A (8.11)	26. D (8.13)	27. C (8.6)	28. C (8.14)
29. A (8.15)	30. D (8.14)	31. B (8.15)	32. A (8.18)
33. D (8.7)	34. C (8.9)	35. B (8.11)	36. B (8.17)
37. D (8.17)	38. A (8.19)		

ANSWER KEY – PRACTICE TEST 2 – SHORT ANSWER

1. Roles (8.1)
2. two-thirds (8.3)
3. roles (8.3)
4. manners; entrapment (8.3)
5. entrapment (8.2)
6. situational (8.4)
7. dispositional; situational; fundamental (8.5)
8. self-serving bias (8.5)
9. just-world hypothesis (8.5)
10. affiliation; conservatism (8.7)
11. validity (8.6)
12. ethnic identity (8.12)
13. Obedience; conformity (8.3)
14. groupthink (8.9)
15. diffusion of responsibility (8.10)
16. uninteresting (8.10)
17. deindividuation (8.10)
18. social distance; what people do when stressed or angry; brain activity; implicit attitudes (8.16)
19. social (8.12)
20. ethnocentrism (8.13)
21. emphasize; underestimate (8.14)
22. openness to experience (8.7)
23. acculturation (8.12)

ANSWER KEY – PRACTICE TEST 3 – ESSAY

1.   The prison study: The students were either playing the roles of prison guards or prisoners. These roles were governed by norms of how prisoners and guards should behave. The students knew the roles and the norms that governed them and played the parts.

      The obedience study: The roles of the research subject and authority figure were known to the study participants, who then played the role of obedient subject. Knowing the norms for both sets of roles made it difficult for subjects to violate their roles and defy the authority figure. (8.3)

2.   A.   Dispositional attribution (8.4)
      B.   Just-world hypothesis (8.4)
      C.   Situational attribution – self-serving bias (8.4)
      D.   Situational attribution (8.4)

3.   To reduce social loafing, Dr. Wong should make sure each student is responsible for a different part of the project that is essential to the whole project. She might make part of the grade an individual grade and part of the grade a group grade. To reduce groupthink, she might want to make grades dependent on the presentation of multiple points of view and different positions and approaches. She will want to structure the project so that success depends on the cooperation and interdependence of all students. Finally, to promote altruism and independent action, she might want students to volunteer at a homeless shelter to get to know some homeless people personally. (8.9, 8.10)

4.   A.   Underestimating differences within other groups (8.14)
      B.   Accentuating differences between groups (8.14)
      C.   Producing selective perceptions (8.14)

5.   Factors that contribute to the persistence of prejudice include:
      1.   Socialization – children learn prejudices from their parents.
      2.   Social benefits – prejudices bring support from others who share them and the threat of losing support when one abandons the prejudice.
      3.   Economic benefits and justification of discrimination – when economic or social times are difficult, prejudice increases.

      A program to reduce prejudice should include: multiple efforts, the cooperation of both sides, equal status and economic standing of both sides, comprehensive support from authorities, and the opportunity to work and socialize together, both formally and informally. (8.15)

ANSWER KEYS FOR CHAPTER 9

ANSWER KEY – PRACTICE TEST 1 – MULTIPLE CHOICE

1. C (9.1)	2. A (9.1)	3. C (9.1)	4. C (9.1)
5. D (9.3)	6. C (9.3)	7. A (9.5)	8. D (9.5)
9. A (9.5)	10. D (9.7)	11. B (9.7)	12. B (9.8)
13. C (9.8)	14. C (9.2)	15. B (9.9)	16. B (9.12)
17. A (9.13)	18. A (9.4)	19. D (9.6)	20. C (9.16)
21. C (9.16)	22. B (9.16)	23. D (9.18)	24. C (9.6)
25. D (9.19)	26. B (9.20)	27. C (9.20)	28. A (9.10)
29. D (9.11)	30. B (9.14)	31. A (9.14)	32. C (9.15)
33. D (9.17)			

ANSWER KEY – PRACTICE TEST 2 – SHORT ANSWER

1.   mental (9.1)
2.   concept (9.1)
3.   basic (9.1)
4.   new evidence (9.4)
5.   subconscious (9.3)
6.   nonconscious (9.3)
7.   must; is probably (9.5)
8.   formal; algorithm (9.5)
9.   dialectical reasoning (9.6)
10.   reflective (9.7)
11.   quasi-reflective (9.7)
12.   mental sets (9.8)
13.   availability heuristic (9.9)
14.   heuristics (9.6)
15.   Whorf (9.2)
16.   dialectical (9.6)
17.   biased (9.5)
18.   general; multiple (9.3)
19.   triarchic; contextual (9.16)
20.   componential, experiential, contextual (9.16)
21.   metacognition (9.16)
22.   gains; losses (9.10)
23.   lower (9.18)
24.   displacement; productivity (9.20)
25.   anthropomorphism (9.20)
26.   20-30 (9.11)

ANSWER KEY – PRACTICE TEST 3 – ESSAY

1.   A.   Coat (9.1)   B.   Horse (9.1)
      C.   Dog (9.1)   D.   Uncle (9.1)

2.   A.   The ship's position must be deduced. The position of the North Star and the formula are two premises that, once known, will allow the conclusion to be determined with certainty. (9.5)
      B.   Scientists of all types rely on inductive reasoning. Enough cases must be collected before a conclusion can be drawn. (9.5)
      C.   The overall process is dialectical reasoning, which is likely to incorporate inductive and deductive reasoning. It will be necessary to assess potential outcomes, risks, losses, and appropriate considerations. (9.5)
      D.   Again, the overall process is dialectical reasoning, which will probably incorporate inductive and deductive reasoning. (9.5)

3.   A.   Availability heuristic (9.8)   B.   Cognitive dissonance (9.8)
      C.   Confirmation bias (9.8)

4.   A.   Componential intelligence (9.16)   B.   Contextual intelligence (9.16)
      C.   Experiential intelligence (9.16)

5.   A.   Evidence supporting cognitive abilities in nonhumans:
           1.   Evidence on herons, sea otters and assassin bugs related to their food gathering habits reflect behaviors that appear intelligent.
           2.   Some chimpanzees use objects as rudimentary tools, and there is evidence for some summing abilities and the use of numerals to label quantities.
           3.   Some primates demonstrate the ability to use some aspects of language such as: learning sign language, understanding words and some sentences, using signs to converse with each other, ability to manipulate keyboard symbols to request food without formal training, use of some simple grammatical rules.
           4.   Other evidence exists from dolphins and parrots.

      B.   Evidence against cognitive abilities in nonhumans:
           1.   The meaning of these abilities is questioned; human meaning may be attributed to these actions.
           2.   Early studies were overinterpreted and biased.
           3.   It's unclear whether the use of signs and symbols were strung together without any particular order or syntax.
           4.   While an animal may be "conscious," in the sense of being aware of its environment, it does not know that it knows and is unable to think about its own thoughts in the way that human beings do. (9.19)

ANSWER KEYS FOR CHAPTER 10

ANSWER KEY – PRACTICE TEST 1- MULTIPLE CHOICE

1. A (10.1)	2. D (10.2)	3. D (10.2)	4. C (10.3)
5. B (10.4)	6. C (10.5)	7. D (10.6)	8. D (10.6)
9. A (10.8)	10. B (10.11)	11. B (10.6)	12. C (10.7)
13. A (10.6)	14. C (10.6)	15. D (10.13)	16. D (10.13)
17. D (10.6)	18. A (10.9)	19. C (10.9)	20. A (10.9)
21. B (10.11)	22. A (10.12)	23. A (10.10)	24. D (10.14)
25. C (10.16)	26. B (10.16)	27. C (10.16)	28. D (10.18)
29. D (10.18)	30. D (10.19)	31. A (10.15)	32. B (10.17)

ANSWER KEY – PRACTICE TEST 2 – SHORT ANSWER

1. reconstructive (10.1)
2. source (10.2)
3. stable (10.2)
4. suggestive (10.3)
5. the; a (10.3)
6. adrenal glands (10.12)
7. information-processing (10.5)
8. information-processing (10.6)
9. chunks (10.6)
10. semantic (10.6)
11. Semantic; episodic; declarative (10.9)
12. Maintenance; elaborative (10.13)
13. epinephrine (10.12)
14. decay (10.6)
15. retroactive; proactive (10.16)
16. retrieval; cue-dependent (10.16)
17. state-dependent (10.16)
18. amnesia (10.18)
19. mood-congruent recall (10.16)

ANSWER KEY – PRACTICE TEST 3 – ESSAY

1. To be remembered, material first must be encoded into the form in which it is to be retained. Storage takes place in various areas of the brain, which appears to correspond to structural changes in the brain. Retrieval is the process by which stored material is located for current use. (10.6)

2. Information entering through the senses is briefly held in sensory memory, where preliminary sorting and encoding take place. It is then transferred to short-term storage, where it is rehearsed. Finally, as a result of deep processing or elaborative rehearsal, it is forwarded to long-term storage, where it is indexed and organized to become part of the network of more permanent material. (10.6)

3. A. Procedural memory (10.9)
    B. Episodic memory (10.9)
    C. Semantic memory (10.9)

4. A. According to decay theory, virtually all the details should be forgotten because of the long time interval involved. The only memories remaining should be those used from time to time as the person grew older. (10.16)
    B. The absence of retrieval cues is often a source of forgetting. The example suggests that the mental image created by the description of the homeroom was a cue that released a set of associated memories. (10.16)
    C. Some emotionally unpleasant situations may be forgotten more rapidly and may be harder to recall than other situations. For the sake of emotional comfort, Henry may be motivated to forget situations associated with personal distress. (10.16)

5. Interference arises as memory incorporates similar material in succession. Assuming there is greatest similarity between Italian and Spanish, these should be kept as separate as possible, as well as over-learned and frequently reviewed. Breaks would also help as you go from one topic of study to another. A sequence like Italian, math, English, history and Spanish (with breaks in between) would be better than Spanish, Italian, English, math and history. (10.16)

ANSWER KEYS FOR CHAPTER 11

ANSWER KEY – PRACTICE TEST 1 – MULTIPLE CHOICE

1. B (11.3)	2. A (11.6)	3. C (11.1)	4. D (11.8)
5. A (11.2)	6. D (11.1)	7. B (11.9)	8. C (11.12)
9. C (11.14)	10. B (11.16)	11. C (11.18)	12. C (11.17)
13. A (11.20)	14. A (11.4)	15. A (11.11)	16. D (11.2)
17. C (11.11)	18. D (11.13)	19. D (11.4)	20. B (11.5)
21. C (11.5)	22. A (11.15)	23. C (11.13)	24. C (11.15)
25. C (11.19)	26. A (11.19)	27. C (11.10)	28. D (11.10)
29. B (11.19)	30. D (11.21)	31. D (11.14, 11.18, 11.21)	

ANSWER KEY – PRACTICE TEST 2 – SHORT ANSWER

1. reduce; cause (11.21)
2. primary; secondary (11.7)
3. internal (11.14)
4. sadness, happiness, contempt, disgust, surprise, anger, fear (11.1)
5. lethargy and overeating (11.16)
6. amygdala; cerebral cortex (11.2)
7. sympathetic (or autonomic); epinephrine; norepinephrine (11.4)
8. social comparison (11.20)
9. Attributions (11.5)
10. Selye; alarm; resistance; exhaustion (11.11)
11. cognitions; emotions (11.5)
12. prototypes (11.7)
13. display rules (11.8)
14. work (11.9)
15. antigen; immune (11.13)
16. psychoneuroimmunology (11.13)
17. provocation; sensitive (11.10)
18. immune (11.13)
19. hostility (11.13)
20. express(11.10)
21. control (11.14)
22. primary; secondary (11.14)
23. Emotion-focused; problem-focused (11.19)
24. Reappraising (11.20)

ANSWER KEY – PRACTICE TEST 3 – ESSAY

1.   A.   An increase in epinephrine and norepinephrine is brought about by the adrenal glands and under the control of the autonomic nervous system. Involvement of the amygdala, limbic system, and cortex contribute to this arousal response. (11.4, 11.8, 11.9)

        B.   The patient is functioning according to the display rules for men, which dictate that men should not feel fear or anxiety. The nurse is doing the emotion work associated with the role of a nurse. Nurses are supposed to be comforting and pleasant to patients. (11.4, 11.8, 11.9)

2.   These results are consistent with the idea that it is our interpretation of events that is instrumental in the experiencing of emotion rather than the event itself. The students' reactions are based on their explanations and interpretations of why they got those grades. Larry studied hard and expected a better grade. His depressive reaction may have to do with the fact that since he studied and did not do better, he may see himself as stupid, which is an internal and stable interpretation. Curly studied a little bit for the test so he felt relieved that he received a C. The grade has no bearing on his view of himself. He did not expect to fail, but did not really expect a better grade. Moe did not study at all so he interpreted the grade as very lucky. The grade did not influence his view of himself, but rather he interpreted it as due to external luck. (11.5)

3.   A.   The alarm phase will be the most prominent as the person is being captured. Bodily resources will be mobilized as the person attempts to fight or flee. (11.11)

        B.   Resistance will coincide with early captivity. Its duration is related to the victim's capacity to manage potentially overwhelming events. Signs of arousal will be prominent and bodily preparedness will be the rule. Biologically, use of energy resources will be above normal. Psychologically, the victim is actively fighting the situation. (11.11)

        C.   The timing of exhaustion depends on individual characteristics, such as coping styles. Biologically, it is signaled by bodily fatigue and susceptibility to illness. Psychologically, the person shows signs of giving up and wearing down. (11.11)

4.   A.   Margaret is rethinking the problem and using some denial. (11.19, 11.20)

        B.   The situation is being directly attacked with a problem-focused strategy. (11.19, 11.20)

        C.   Alberto is reappraising the problem using social comparisons. (11.19, 11.20)

        D.   Tony is using more of an emotion-focused strategy than a problem-focused one. (11.19, 11.20)

        E.   Eleanor is trying to live with the problem (an example of secondary control). (11.19, 11.20)

ANSWER KEYS FOR CHAPTER 12

ANSWER KEY – PRACTICE TEST 1 – MULTIPLE CHOICE

1. A (12.1)	2. A (12.1)	3. D (12.1)	4. A (12.1)
5. C (12.7)	6. D (12.8)	7. D (12.2)	8. A (12.9)
9. C (12.9)	10. A (12.3)	11. B (12.5)	12. B (12.6)
13. C (12.10)	14. A (12.4)	15. B (12.10)	16. D (12.11)
17. D (12.11)	18. D (12.11)	19. D (12.12, 12.14)	20. B (12.13)
21. A (12.13)	22. A (12.17)	23. A (12.17)	24. D (12.14)
25. C (12.15)	26. B (12.16)		

ANSWER KEY – PRACTICE TEST 2 – SHORT ANSWER

1. opportunity (12.14)
2. indicated he was poor; wealth (12.2)
3. set-point (12.1)
4. diet; exercise (12.3)
5. exercise (12.3)
6. secure, anxious, and avoidant (12.7)
7. temperament (12.7)
8. endorphins (12.5)
9. Attachment (12.7)
10. express (12.8)
11. proximity; similarity (12.6)
12. testosterone (12.5)
13. partner approval; peer approval (12.9)
14. endorphins (12.5)
15. sexual (12.10)

ANSWER KEY – PRACTICE TEST 3 – ESSAY

1. We cannot be certain what motivates any given behavior. Each behavior described may be activated by a variety of different motives. Below are some possible explanations.
    a.   Calling her friend shows a need for affiliation or intimacy.
    b.   Visiting her boyfriend demonstrates the motivation for love.
    c.   Doing extra credit assignments and an extra work project could reflect need for achievement, performance goals, or learning goals. (12.12, 12.13, 12.14)

2. <u>Information that supports homosexuality as a choice and refutes the biological argument</u>:
    a.   The fluidity of women's experiences
    b.   There are flaws in the biological evidence
             *Methodological problems in the findings on brain differences
             *The majority of homosexuals do not have a close gay relative
    c.   Psychological theories have not been well-supported

    <u>Information that supports the biological information and refutes the choice position</u>:
    a.   Research findings that women with a history of prenatal exposure to estrogen are more likely to become bisexual or lesbian
    b.   Research findings on differences in brain structures of homosexual and heterosexual men
    c.   Studies that show a moderate heritability

    The bottom line is that we still do not know very well what the causes of homosexuality are. It is probably safest to say that there are a variety of causes, both biological and psychological. Genetics and biology alone cannot account for the variety of experiences among homosexuals. It is even possible that the routes to homosexual orientation differ for males and females and differ for individuals. (12.11)

3. A.   Avoidance-avoidance conflict (12.17)
    B.   Approach-approach conflict (12.17)
    C.   Approach-avoidance conflict (12.17)

ANSWER KEYS FOR CHAPTER 13

ANSWER KEY – PRACTICE TEST 1 – MULTIPLE CHOICE

1. C (13.1)	2. D (13.1)	3. A (13.2)	4. D (13.1)
5. D (13.10)	6. A (13.11)	7. A (13.3)	8. C (13.3)
9. B (13.3)	10. B (13.4)	11. D (13.4)	12. D (13.7)
13. A (13.7)	14. C (13.7)	15. A (13.7)	16. D (13.5)
17. C (13.6)	18. C (13.12)	19. B (13.6)	20. C (13.13)
21. B (13.13)	22. C (13.16)	23. C (13.14)	24. C (13.9)
25. D (13.16)	26. C (13.17)	27. B (13.20)	28. B (13.19)
29. B (13.21)	30. A (13.18)	31. A (13.8)	32. A (13.22)
33. B (13.23)			

ANSWER KEY – PRACTICE TEST 2 – SHORT ANSWER

1.   culture; maturation (13.2)
2.   germinal; embryonic; embryo (13.1)
3.   placenta; x-rays; drugs (13.1)
4.   self-regulation (13.10)
5.   terry cloth; contact comfort (13.3)
6.   pituitary gland; adrenal; reproductive (13.15)
7.   emerging adulthood (13.19)
8.   mothers; temperament (13.4)
9.   eleven; symbolic (13.6)
10.   Piaget (13.7)
11.   schema; assimilation (13.7)
12.   object permanence (13.7)
13.   egocentrism; preoperational (13.7)
14.   concrete operations (13.7)
15.   Fluid; declines; Crystallized; stable (13.21)
16.   socialization (13.14)
17.   menarche; menopause (13.15, 13.20)
18.   individuate (13.16)
19.   transgender (13.11)
20.   eight; crisis (13.18)

ANSWER KEY – PRACTICE TEST 3 – ESSAY

1. A. Fetal abnormalities and deformities (13.1)
    B. There is an increased likelihood of miscarriage, premature birth, abnormal fetal heartbeat, and underweight babies; after the child's birth, there are increased rates of sickness and Sudden Infant Death Syndrome; in later childhood, hyperactivity and difficulties in school. (13.1)
    C. Fetal alcohol syndrome (13.1)
    D. Effects vary with specific drugs; extreme caution must be exercised, even with prescribed and over-the-counter drugs. (13.1)

2. Newborns are sociable from birth and show a preference for the human face. They can distinguish their primary caregiver by smell, sight, or sound almost immediately. (13.3, 13.4)

3. A. The child is in the preoperational stage and is demonstrating egocentric thinking. (13.7)
    B. The child is incorrectly trying to use assimilation; she should use accommodation. (13.7)
    C. The younger child is in the preoperational stage and lacks the ability to conserve; the older child is in the concrete operations stage. (13.7)
    D. Shawn is in the sensory-motor stage and has developed object permanence. (13.7)

4. At 4 months old: Azumi would cry and coo and respond to high-pitched and more varied verbalizations in which the intonation is exaggerated. She can recognize her own name.
    At 10 months old: She would be increasingly familiar with the sound structure of her native language. She might be making babbling sounds such as "ba-ba" or "goo-goo."
    At 14 months old: She could begin using gestures.
    At 23 months old: She would use telegraphic speech because she is not yet able to use article and auxiliary words. She would probably say, "Apple table." (13.6)

ANSWER KEYS FOR CHAPTER 14

ANSWER KEY – PRACTICE TEST 1 – MULTIPLE CHOICE

1. D (14.5)	2. A (14.1)	3. A (14.1)	4. C (14.1)
5. A (14.1)	6. C (14.1)	7. C (14.1)	8. D (14.1)
9. C (14.6)	10. B (14.1)	11. D (14.1)	12. D (14.2)
13. C (14.4)	14. A (14.12)	15. B (14.2)	16. C (14.4)
17. C (14.4)	18. A (14.3)	19. A (14.13)	20. C (14.7)
21. C (14.7)	22. C (14.14)	23. D (14.8)	24. C (14.9)
25. C (14.9)	26. D (14.10)	27. D (14.10)	28. A (14.11)
29. A (14.18)	30. A (14.17)	31. C (14.15)	32. A (14.16)
33. D (14.19)	34. B (14.20)		

ANSWER KEY – PRACTICE TEST 2 – SHORT ANSWER

1.   Central (14.6)
2.   individualistic; collectivistic (14.14)
3.   Allport; central; secondary (14.6)
4.   agreeableness; conscientiousness (14.7)
5.   reactive (14.9)
6.   heritability (14.9)
7.   nonshared (14.10)
8.   reciprocal determinism (14.11)
9.   less; more (14.14)
10. collectivist (14.14)
11. Any two of the following: reactivity, soothability, positive emotionality, negative emotionality (14.9)
12. Psychodynamic (14.1)
13. id; realities; superego (14.1)
14. defense mechanisms (14.1)
15. sublimation (14.1)
16. respond with violence (14.15)
17. collective; archetypes (14.2)
18. representation (14.3)
19. falsifiability (14.4)
20. self-actualized; unconditional positive (14.18)

ANSWER KEY – PRACTICE TEST 3 – ESSAY

1.　A.　Trait approach (14.1, 14.6, 14.17)
　　B.　Psychodynamic approach (14.1, 14.6, 14.17)
　　C.　Humanistic approach (14.1, 14.6, 14.17)

2.　A.　According to the reality principle, the ego would seek to prepare for the test. (14.1)
　　B.　The id seeks pleasure and immediate gratification, according to the pleasure principle. (14.1)
　　C.　The id seeks pleasure and is not concerned with the consequences of reality. (14.1)
　　D.　The ego is appraising reality. (14.1)
　　E.　The internalized parental values of the superego are discouraging him from cheating. (14.1)
　　F.　The ego is defending against threats from the superego. (14.1)
　　G.　Violations of the superego produce guilt. (14.1)

3.　A.　Reaction formation (14.1)　　D.　Denial (14.1)
　　B.　Projection (14.1)　　　　　　E.　Regression (14.1)
　　C.　Repression (14.1)　　　　　　F.　Displacement (14.1)

4.　A.　Phallic stage (14.4)　　　　　C.　Phallic stage (14.4)
　　B.　Oral stage (14.4)　　　　　　D.　Anal stage (14.4)

5.　Self-actualization was a basic need for Maslow. However, its achievement depended on gratifying even more fundamental needs, such as physiological drives and social needs.

　　May believes that alienation, loneliness, and helplessness are basic components of human existence. The person strives to overcome these through effective choices.

　　According to Rogers, self-actualization and full functioning are related to the presence of unconditional positive regard. However, most children and adults live in situations in which they experience conditional positive regard. (14.18)

6.　A.　Low levels of neuroticism, high levels of extroversion and agreeableness (14.7)
　　B.　High levels of conscientiousness, and probably agreeableness, and a low level of openness to experience (14.7)
　　C.　High levels of neuroticism and openness to experience, but a low level of extroversion (14.7)

ANSWER KEYS FOR CHAPTER 15

ANSWER KEY – PRACTICE TEST 1 – MULTIPLE CHOICE

1. B (15.1)	2. A (15.1)	3. B (15.1)	4. A (15.3)
5. D (15.9)	6. B (15.3)	7. C (15.3)	8. B (15.5)
9. D (15.6)	10. B (15.2)	11. D (15.8)	12. C (15.8)
13. D (15.4)	14. D (15.10)	15. D (15.8)	16. C (15.13)
17. B (15.16)	18. B (15.11)	19. D (15.11)	20. B (15.4)
21. A (15.14)	22. D (15.12)	23. A (15.12)	24. A (15.15)
25. A (15.15)	26. A (15.17)	27. A (15.18)	28. D (15.18)
29. A (15.19)	30. C (15.20)	31. B (15.20)	

ANWER KEY – PRACTICE TEST 2 – SHORT ANSWER

1. cultural (15.2)
2. ruminate (15.10)
3. harmful dysfunction (15.2)
4. Generalized (15.5)
5. post-traumatic stress disorder (15.7)
6. interpret (15.6)
7. social phobia (15.5)
8. agoraphobia (15.6)
9. genetics; violence, abuse, and neglect; loss of importance relationships, cognitive habits (15.9)
10. behavioral, cognitive (15.8)
11. genetic (15.19)
12. virus (15.19)
13. vulnerability-stress; stresses (15.11)
14. Rorschach Inkblot (15.4)
15. common; clinicians (15.15)
16. sociocognitive (15.15)
17. biological or disease (15.12)
18. learning (15.13)
19. psychosis (15.17)
20. delusions; hallucinations (15.18)

ANSWER KEY – PRACTICE TEST 3 – ESSAY

1. A.   This definition considers the violation of norms and standards to be abnormal. Jason violates norms governing social interaction, appearance, and good taste. (15.2)

    B.   Maladaptive behavior is behavior that results in disharmony and distress to oneself or others. Jason is behaving disruptively toward others. (15.2)

    C.   This definition emphasizes signs of subjective distress. Jason is apparently seeking forgiveness based on some internal experience of guilt or anxiety. (15.2)

2. A.   Abnormal: panic attack (15.2)
    B.   Abnormal: obsessive-compulsive disorder (15.2)
    C.   Normal (15.2)
    D.   Abnormal: phobia (15.2)
    E.   Abnormal: post-traumatic stress disorder (15.2)

3. A.   Josephine has delusions. The fact that she believes that airplanes dirty the streets and sidewalks by dripping oil, that pilots have a power called "telectic penetration," and that she is being used as a radar are all examples of delusions. (17.18)

    B.   Josephine is experiencing hallucinations. She hears the pilots talking to her about her location. (17.18)

    C.   Josephine is demonstrating incoherent associations, including "telectic penetration," her latitude and longitude, and airplanes. (17.18)

    D.   Josephine's behavior is inappropriate in that she withdraws and is unable to speak. (17.18)

    E.   From the description, it is unclear if Josephine is exhibiting emotional flatness. (17.18)

ANSWER KEYS FOR CHAPTER 16

ANSWER KEY – PRACTICE TEST 1 – MULTIPLE CHOICE

1. A (16.1)	2. A (16.1)	3. D (16.2)	4. D (16.1)
5. B (16.2)	6. C (16.2)	7. B (16.2)	8. D (16.4)
9. A (16.3)	10. B (16.3)	11. B (16.4)	12. C (16.4)
13. D (16.4)	14. C (16.4)	15. A (16.5, 16.6)	16. C (16.5)
17. A (16.4)	18. B (16.6)	19. C (16.4)	20. B (16.7)
21. A (16.8)	22. A (16.9)	23. A (16.9)	24. A (16.10)
25. D (16.10)			

ANSWER KEY – PRACTICE TEST 2 – SHORT ANSWER

1. schizophrenia; psychoses (16.1)
2. tardive dyskinesia (16.2)
3. antidepressant (16.1)
4. Lithium carbonate (16.1)
5. relapse (16.2)
6. Mindfulness; acceptance (16.4)
7. Electroconvulsive therapy (16.3)
8. psychodynamic; free association (16.4)
9. transference (16.4)
10. Systematic desensitization; behavioral (16.4)
11. flooding (16.4)
12. evidence; interpretations (16.4)
13. emotive (16.5)
14. Client-centered; unconditional (16.6)
15. Family (16.7)
16. research (16.8)
17. coercive (16.10)
18. Family-systems perspective (16.7)
19. cognitive; anxiety (16.9)
20. scientist-practitioner gap (16.8)
21. Coercive and/or Inappropriate (16.10)

ANSWER KEY – PRACTICE TEST 3 – ESSAY

1.   Medical treatments feature drugs and other forms of organic intervention. Drugs are very useful for psychotic disorders, and, sometimes in combination with psychotherapy, are effective against other disorders, including major depression, bipolar disorder, and some anxiety disorders. Others approaches include psychosurgery techniques. (16.1, 16.3)

2.   A.   Anxiety disorders: minor tranquilizers
          B.   Mood disorders: antidepressants
          C.   Psychotic disorders: antipsychotics

Drug treatments are limited by the complications of side effects and finding the right dosage. They may not be effective for everyone or may work effectively only in the short term. Often there is little research on the effects of long-term usage. Moreover, drugs relieve symptoms and do not help people learn new coping skills. (16.1, 16.2)

3.   Psychodynamic therapies strive for insight into the unconscious processes that produce a problem. With insight and emotional release, symptoms should disappear. The goal of treatment is not to solve an individual's immediate problem, since it is only the tip of the iceberg. Techniques include free association and transference. Psychoanalysis was the original model proposed by Freud in which a patient was seen several times a week for many years.

Cognitive therapy aims to correct distorted, irrational, and unrealistic thoughts, beliefs, and expectations. Techniques vary but revolve around examining negative thoughts, formulating reasonable responses, and using realistic perspectives. Clients are challenged to examine the evidence for their claims. The approach assumes that more rational thinking should reduce or eliminate emotional problems.

Behavior therapy attempts to eliminate maladaptive responses and behavior patterns. Techniques are based on learning principles and include systematic desensitization, aversive conditioning, flooding, and operant strategies. Often, the technique is designed to unlearn a maladaptive response (counterconditioning).

Humanistic therapies are designed to increase self-esteem, positive feelings, taking responsibility, and self-actualization. Approaches include client-centered therapy and existential therapy. Client-centered therapists utilize unconditional positive regard, empathy, and genuineness.

Family therapy aims to correct the forces in the family that are contributing to the expression of a problem. The family systems approach emphasizes that each member of a family influences every other member.

The shared features include: support factors, which allow the client to feel secure and safe; learning factors, which allow the client to see and experience his or her problems in a new light and think about how to solve them; and action factors, which allow the client to reduce fears, take risks, and make necessary changes. (16.4)

4.   Coercion by the therapist to accept the therapist's advice, sexual intimacies, or other unethical behavior by the therapist can cause harm. Bias on the part of a therapist who doesn't understand the client because of the client's gender, race, religion, sexual orientation, or ethnic group is another problem. Therapist-induced disorders can be harmful, such as when therapists so zealously believe in the prevalence of certain problems that they induce the client to produce the symptoms they are looking for. (16.10)

ANSWER KEYS FOR APPENDIX A

ANSWER KEY – PRACTICE TEST 1 – MULTIPLE CHOICE

1. C (A.1)	2. B (A.1)	3. A (A.1)	4. C (A.1)
5. D (A.2)	6. A (A.2)	7. B (A.3)	8. D (A.3)
9. A (A.2)	10. D (A.2)	11. B (A.3)	12. B (A.4)
13. C (A.5)	14. A (A.6)	15. C (A.7)	16. C (A.8)
17. B (A.8)	18. D (A.8)		

ANSWER KEY – PRACTICE TEST 2 – SHORT ANSWER

1. frequency (A.1)
2. polygon (A.1)
3. mean; mode (A.2)
4. central (A.2)
5. range; deviation; mean (A.3)
6. percentages; z-scores (A.4)
7. normal (A.5)
8. negatively (A.5)
9. null (A.6)
10. statistically (A.8)

ANSWER KEY – PRACTICE TEST 3 – ESSAY

1. A. These descriptive statistics are measures of central tendency and describe data by a single, representative number. (A.2, A.3, A.4)
    B. These descriptive statistics measure variability and reflect the spread of obtained scores. (A.2, A.3, A.4)
    C. These statistical pictures are used to organize data in terms of an overall visual summary. (A.2, A.3, A.4)
    D. These transformations are used when scores are put in a standardized format for easier comparisons. (A.2, A.3, A.4)

2. A. This statement is justified because the mean and mode are equal in a normal distribution. (A.3, A.5)
    B. This statement is unjustified because the normal distribution is symmetrical, with either side of the mean mirror-imaging the other. (A.3, A.5)
    C. This statement is justified because less than 16 percent of the population receives a score about one standard deviation from the mean. (A.3, A.5)
    D. This statement is unjustified because this curve is likely to be skewed to the right given that basketball players are chosen for their height. (A.3, A.5)

3. A. The null hypothesis is rejected whenever results are statistically significant. (A.7, A.8)
   B. Statistical significance occurs when differences between the experimental and control groups are very unlikely to be caused by chance or random errors. (A.7, A.8)

Notes

Notes